Watercolor for Relaxation

25 Meditative Projects to Help You Unwind

Angelica Torres
Creator of Love Letters to Milo

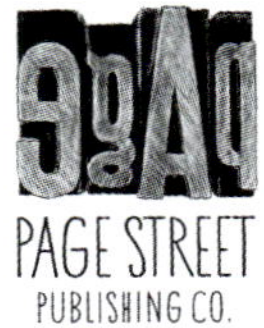

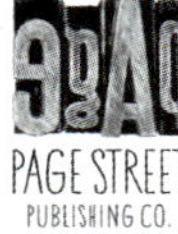

First published in 2021 by
Page Street Publishing Co.
27 Congress Street, Suite 105
Salem, MA 01970
www.pagestreetpublishing.com

Distributed by Macmillan, sales in Canada by The Canadian Manda Group.

25 24 23 22 21 1 2 3 4 5

ISBN-13: 978-1-64567-400-9
ISBN-10: 1-64567-400-2

Library of Congress Control Number: 2021931397

Cover and book design by Molly Kate Young for Page Street Publishing Co.
Photography by Angelica Torres

Printed and bound in the United States

Page Street Publishing protects our planet by donating to nonprofits like The Trustees, which focuses on local land conservation.

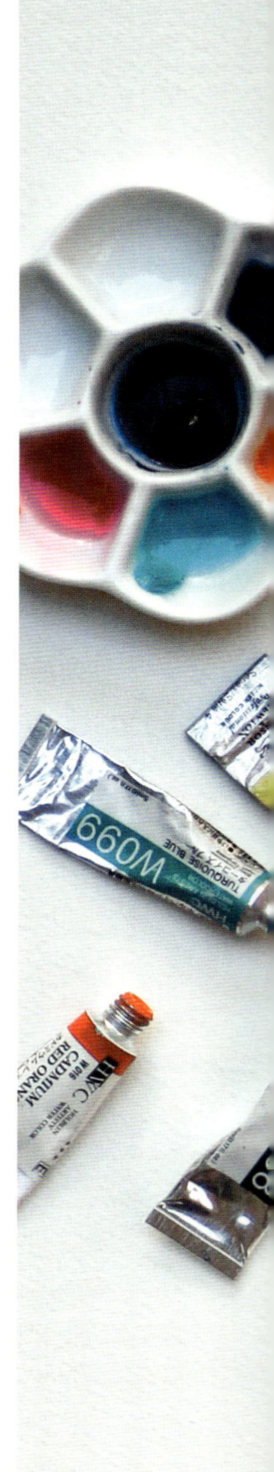

For Milo

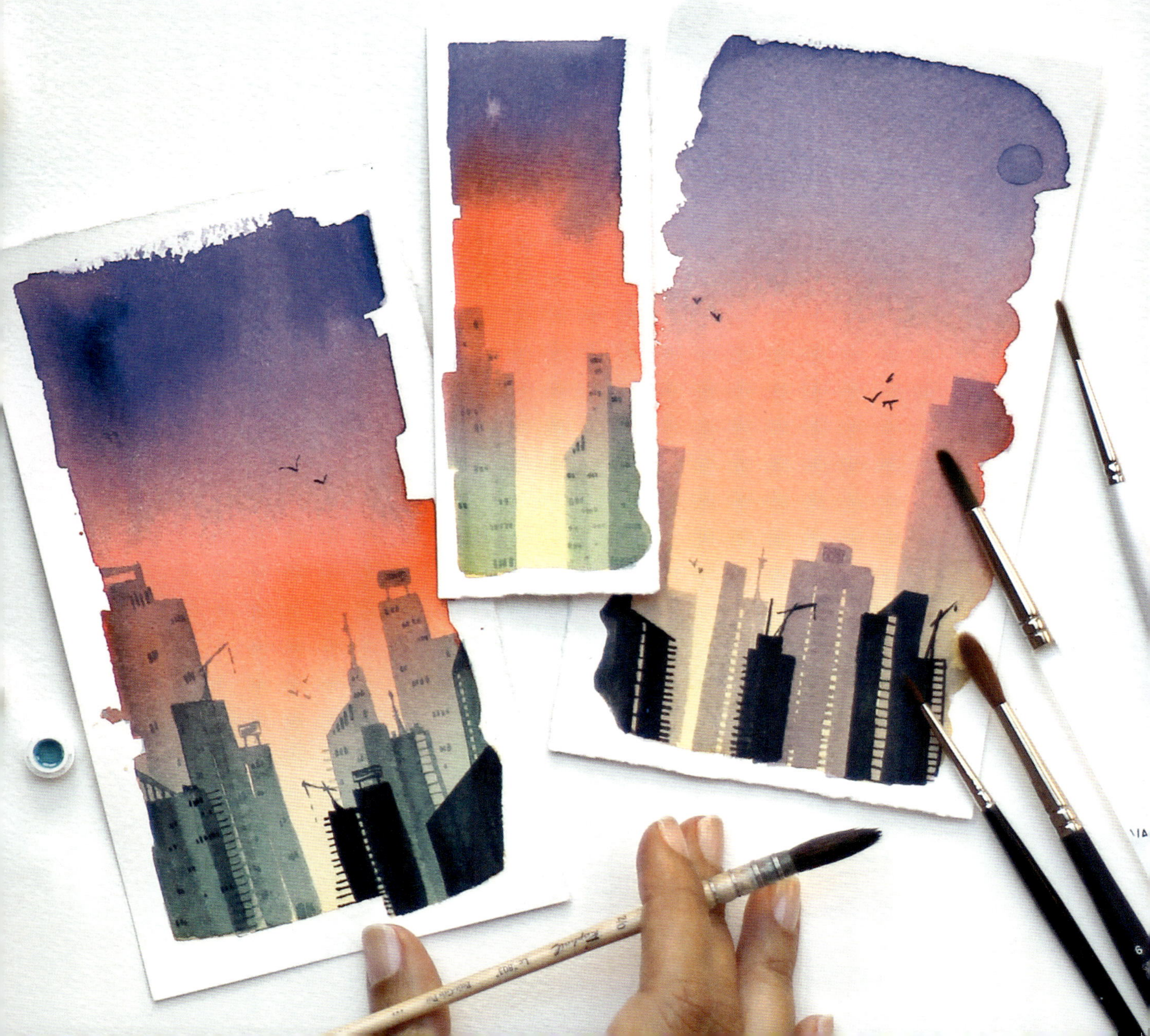

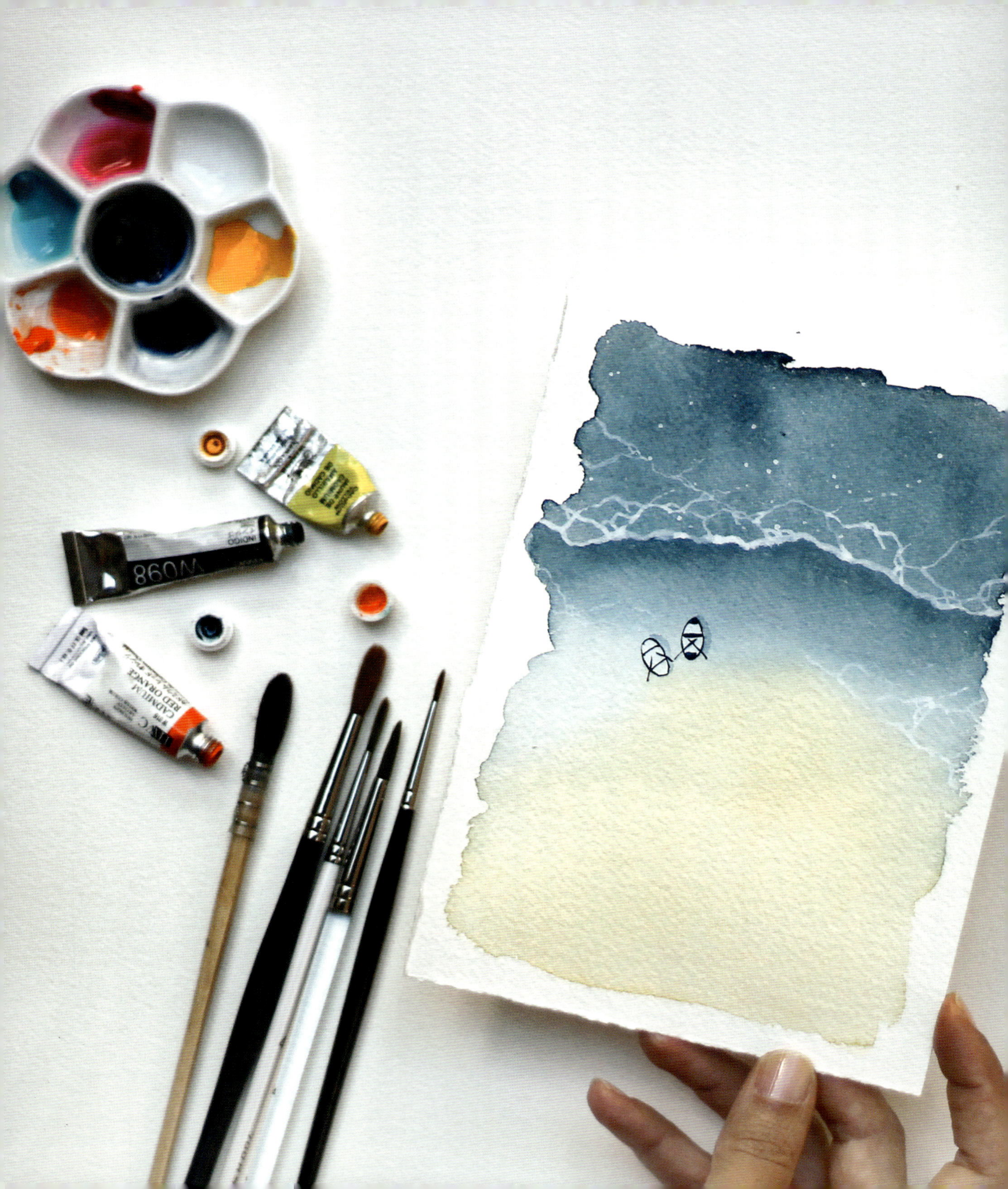
INDIGO
W098
CADMIUM
RED ORANGE

Contents

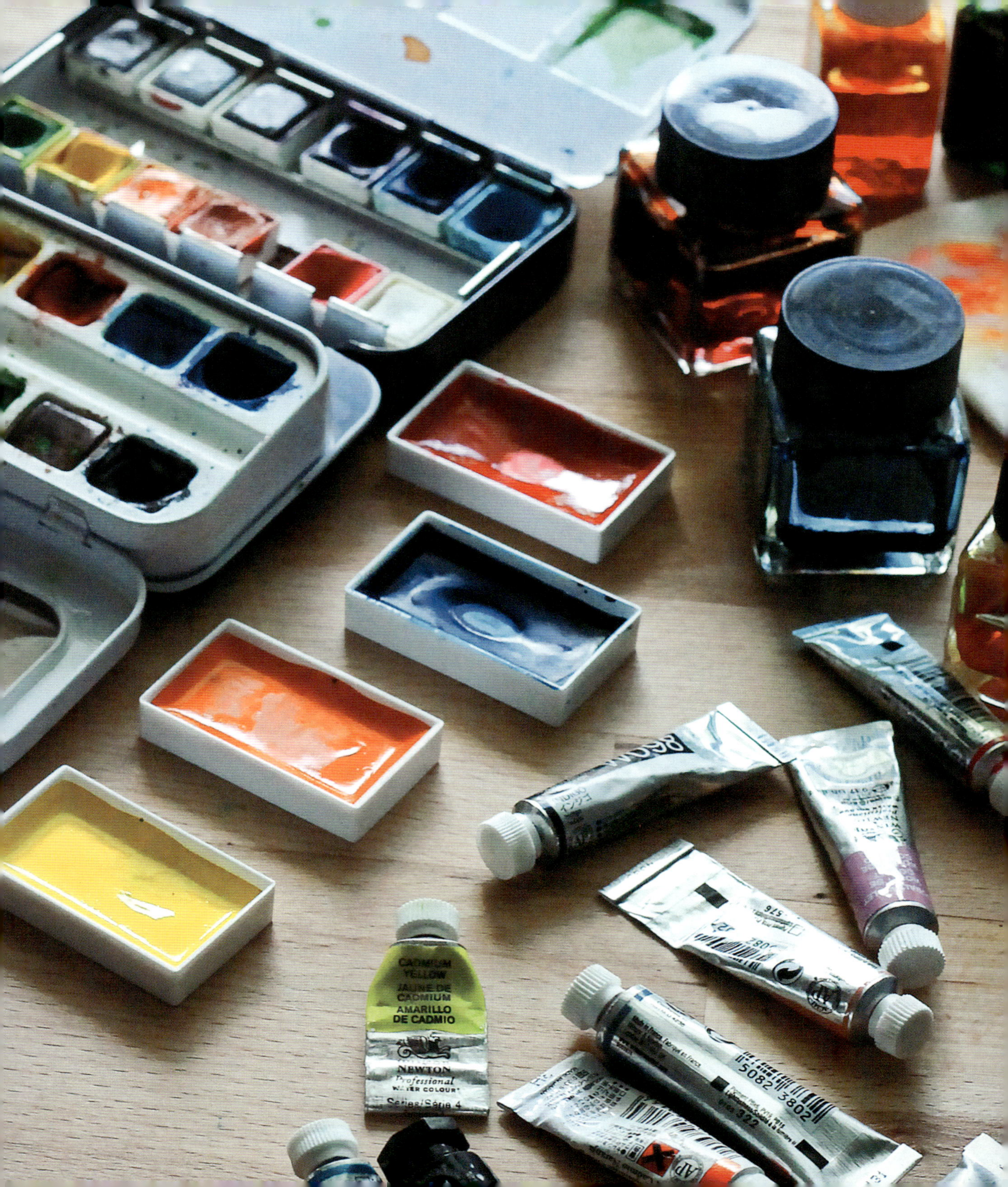
CADMIUM YELLOW
JAUNE DE CADMIUM
AMARILLO DE CADMIO
NEWTON
Professional
WATER COLOUR
Series/Série 4
5082 3802

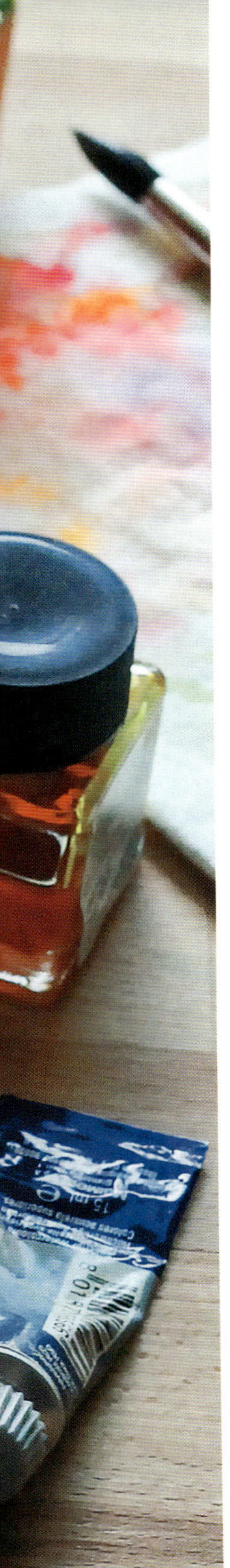

Introduction

Watercolor can seem scary and intimidating, but I promise you that it is absolutely not!

Starting with a new blank page can be paralyzing, but like Jay Shetty said, "Fortunately, a simple, powerful tool to short-circuit the panic response is always with us: our breath." Every single time I start a new painting or even a doodle, I take a deep breath in, and on the breath out, I let go of the panic and start painting something, anything. I always see it as a step forward in my art journey.

I was driven to watercolor because of its therapeutic and healing qualities. Every new painting gives me the opportunity to focus on my breath, assess my mental well-being and let go of anything that is not serving me at that moment in time.

The magic of watercolor is that it is soft, airy and magical and it flows effortlessly, creating transparency and fascinating blends and textures with very minimal effort. What I love most about watercolor is that you absolutely have to learn to let go. Let go of expectations, let go of control, let go of anything that does not serve you and, most importantly, learn to lean into the discomfort while you develop the skills to paint freely and in complete harmony with your brush. Always remember that through your journey, there are no mistakes; everything you paint is a step forward in your journey, and even if it feels small, it's a step forward nonetheless. Be kind and gentle with yourself as you go through your own learning process.

In this book, you will learn easy and beginner-friendly watercolor techniques that will help you learn muscle memory and simple brushstrokes, as well as focus on breathing techniques that will help you not only find a relaxing moment in your daily life but also create beautiful artworks that you can proudly share with your friends and family. Simplifying shapes with simple brushstrokes is key, and next thing you know you are a watercolor master!

Throughout my journey, I have found immense pleasure in teaching others wonderful and calming techniques, helping them find their flow, a moment of stillness and focus, find mindfulness, be amazed at their own creations and, most importantly, heal.

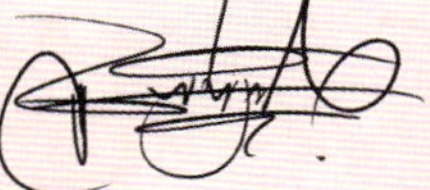

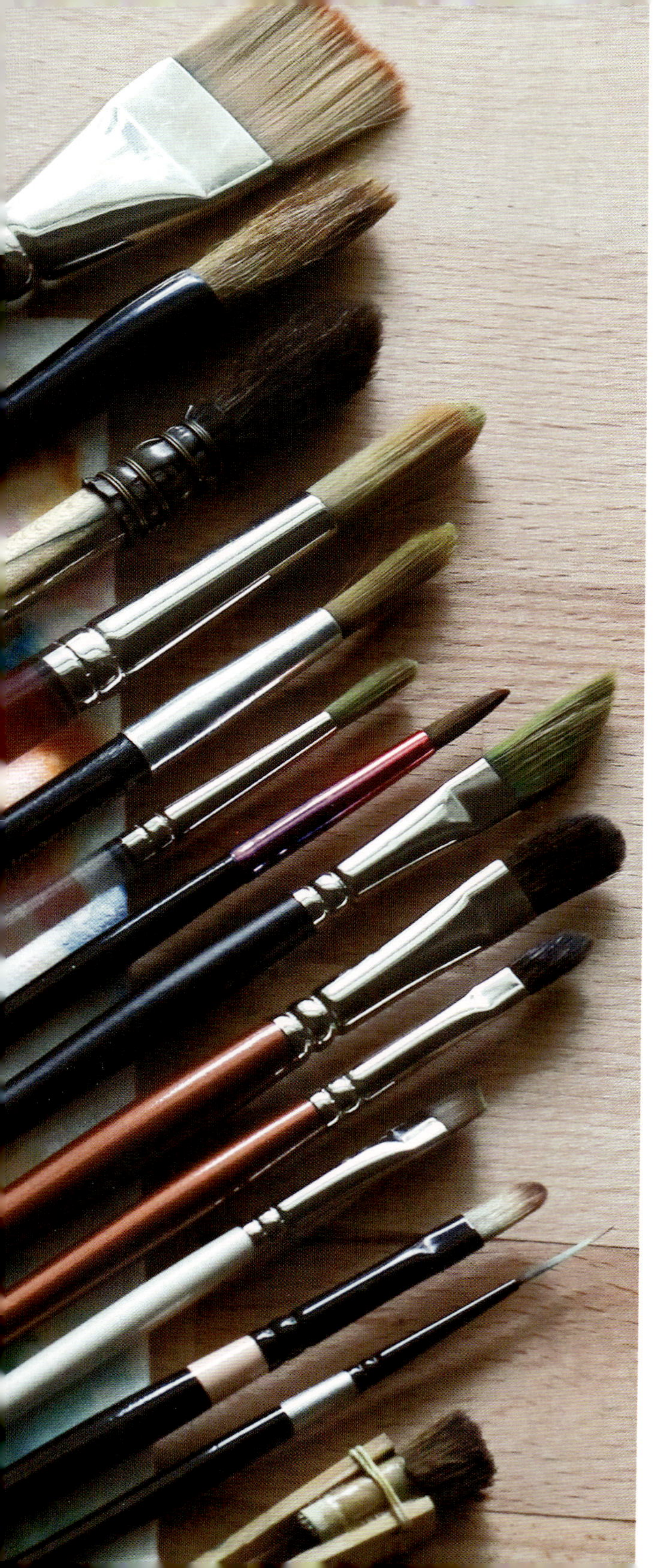

Materials

Brushes, paints and paper are the basic materials you'll need to start your journey. Moving forward in your artistic journey, there will be plenty more materials to introduce to your practice, such as colored pencils, pastels, markers and other mediums that help you experiment and create a variety of textures.

Brushes

I use two main types of brushes: synthetic and natural-hair brushes. The main difference is the way they hold water and the softness of the bristles.

When I want to paint something that requires precision, I tend to use synthetic brushes because they provide more stability in the way they move.

When I am painting more loosely, like a sky or soft shapes that require a ton of water, I tend to use the natural-hair bristle brushes because the paint just flows freely and they hold a ton of water and pigment.

There are plenty of brands out there to choose from. I do not swear by any particular brand because typically I just go to the art store and pick up a brush that won't break the bank. It was a trial-and-error process for me to find my favorite brushes, and I encourage you to do the same.

Some of the most versatile brushes are round synthetic No. 2 and No. 6 because you can pretty much paint anything with these two sizes.

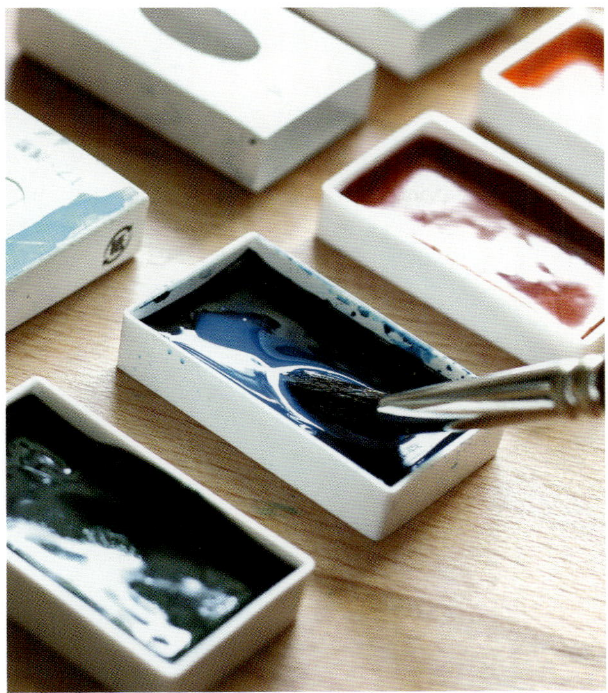

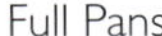
Full Pans

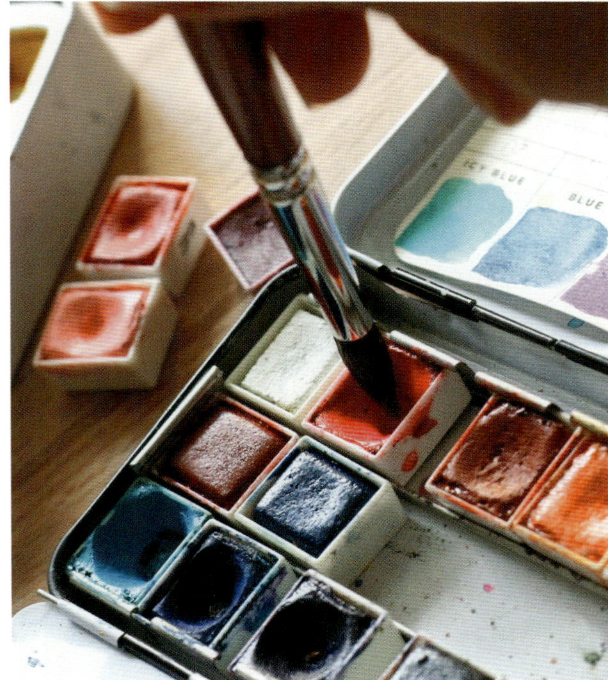

Half Pans

Paints

There are three main categories of paint: tubes (professional grade and student grade), pans (full pans [like Gansai] and half pans) and ink (for example, Ecoline and Dr. Ph. Martin's).

Tubes are some of my favorite kinds of paints because as soon as you push them out of the tube, they are ready to be used—no need to prewet.

Student-grade watercolors like Cotman are great to start, but as you move forward in your artistic journey, you will find the need for colors that are more richly pigmented and contain fewer synthetic binders or fillers. I tend to stay away from anything that has "hue" in it, as it is a filler. My absolute favorites for professional grade are Winsor & Newton and Holbein.

Pans are a great way to experiment with colors before moving onto tubes. A set usually comes with twelve colors to explore. They are also great for portability; I usually travel with a set of my favorite colors. The only two downsides to pans are that you typically find them in half-pans, which are the small kind, and they might ruin the tip of your brush trying to get all the paint out of the corners.

Second, you have to prewet pans before they are ready to be used. Some of my favorite pan sets are the Kuretake Gansai Tambi Watercolor set. They have long rectangular pans, and the colors are very rich.

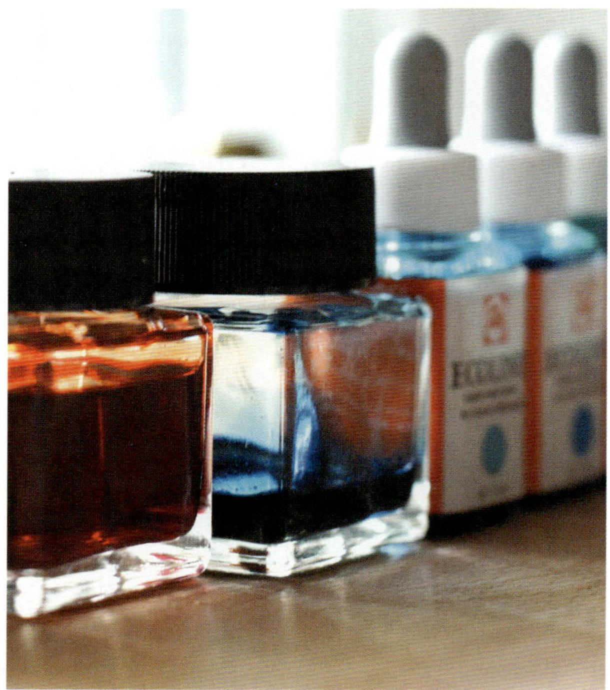
Ink Watercolors

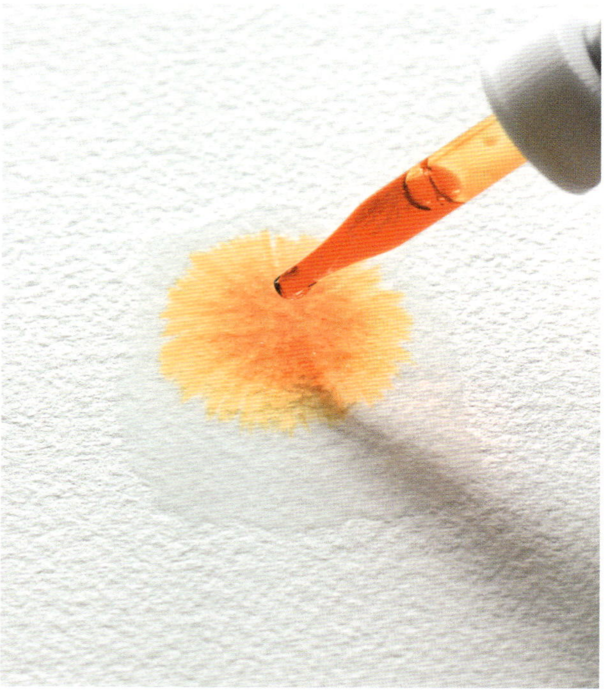
Ink on Cold Pressed Paper

Inks such as Ecoline or Dr. Ph. Martin's are super high in pigmentation. I use them very rarely because the intensity is hard to control. I typically have to do a lot of testing on the side before I decide on the water ratio for a desired intensity. The second you put ink on paper, it immediately stains it and sometimes it is hard to blend afterward. They are great if you are in need of a super-intense color.

Paper

There are two popular types of paper: cold pressed and hot pressed. In the most basic terms, cold pressed has texture, or tooth, which will give your paintings a beautiful texture. Hot pressed has a smooth surface and does not absorb water as fast. It is often used by artists that scan their paintings to digitize because it has less texture to clean up afterward.

Personally, I think paper is what makes or breaks your painting. After plenty of trial and error, I can honestly say that Arches® Cold Pressed 140lb (255gsm) is by far my favorite. It can be a bit pricey, but because of its high quality I usually paint on both sides of the paper, achieving the same fantastic results. Note that 100% cotton 140lb (255gsm) cold-pressed paper (roughly 5 x 7 inches [12.5 x 17.5 cm]) is what I will use for each project in this book.

Color Theory

Understanding the basics of color theory is key to the success of your compositions, but I will break it down to just a few key elements.

Primary Colors: yellow, blue, red. These are the three basic colors that you cannot make from any color combination; that is, you cannot mix any two colors to make a pure yellow.

Secondary Colors: green, orange, purple. These are the colors you get from mixing any of the primary colors. My favorite color combination is yellow and blue to make a beautiful green.

Tertiary Colors: yellow-orange, yellow-green, red-orange, red-purple, blue-green, blue-purple. These are the combinations of a secondary color and a primary color; that is, yellow and red make orange (a secondary color), then you mix a little more red and you get the most beautiful red-orange.

Complementary Colors: This is one of the most important and most used concepts in color theory. In essence, complementary colors are opposite colors in the color wheel. To find your complementary colors, simply draw a straight line across the color wheel and you will find your opposites. Those two colors will always look gorgeous together.

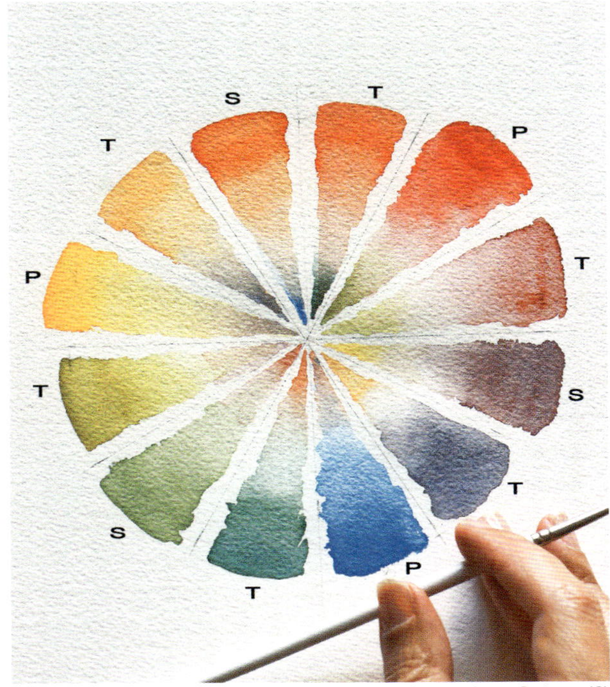

Color wheel showing Primary Colors (P), Secondary Colors (S) and Tertiary Colors (T).

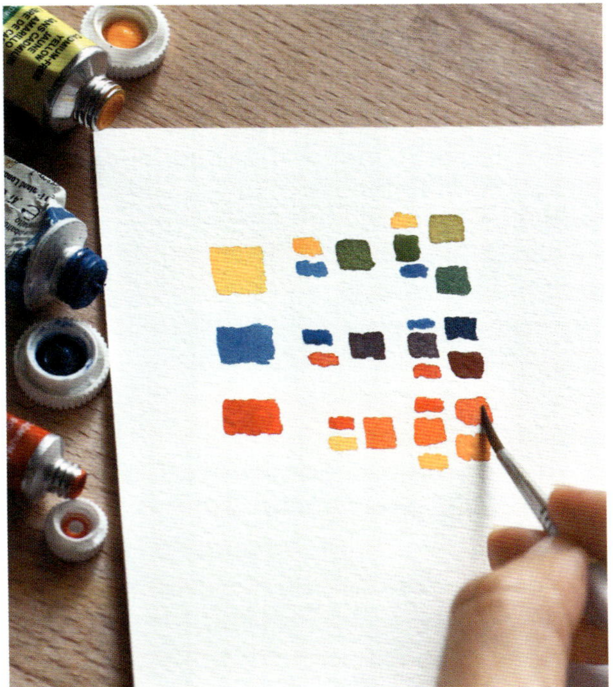
Mixing Colors

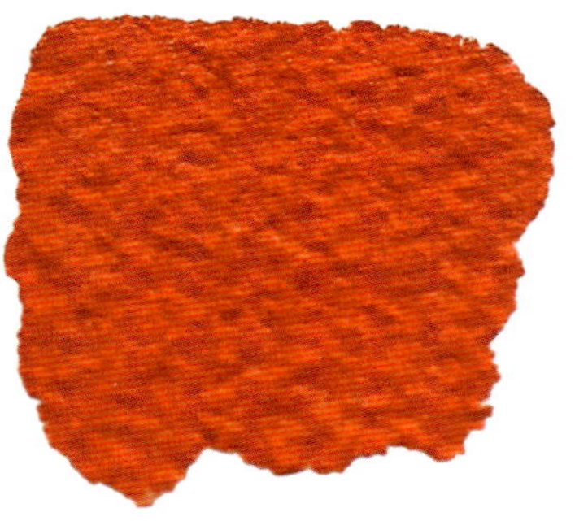 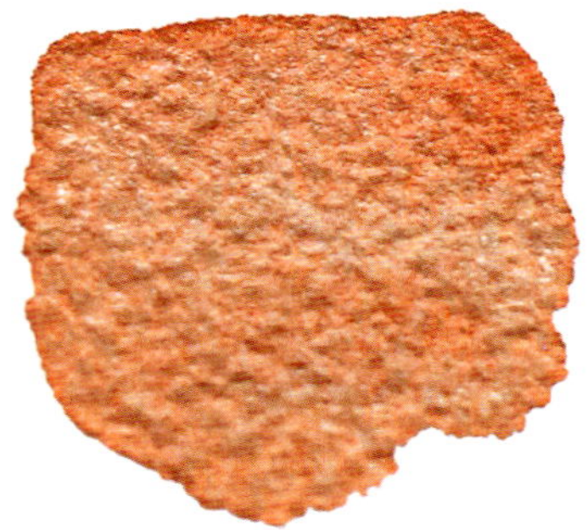 

Value

Value: This is how light or how dark the color is in its purest form. In watercolor painting, we adjust the value with the water ratio. This is a highly important word that will be used in every project in this book. Mainly, you will be using three values, dark, medium and light, as shown in the value photo.

The water ratios used in this book are as follows:

- **Dark Value: 1:1 ratio.** One dab of pure pigment to one dab of water from your brush.
- **Medium Value: 1:3 ratio.** One dab of pure pigment to three dabs (or dips) of water from your brush.
- **Light Value: 1:6 ratio.** One dab of pure pigment to six (or more) dabs of water from your brush.

Please note that you will have to test each color separately as you learn the water ratios for each pigment because some pigments are more intense than others. For instance, indigo is highly pigmented, so the ratios here work wonders, but a Cadmium Yellow might not need as much water to get a light value.

Monochromatic: Using one hue/color/pigment in its purest form with different variations of water ratio.

Color Temperatures: This concept leans a bit more on the psychology of color. I like to think of them as what the color feels like. I am sure there is a much more scientific approach to this.

- **Warm:** I like to think of these as the fun colors. You can find that red, yellow and orange are on one side of the color wheel and they make you feel happy and joyful and remind you of summer, sunshine or fire.
- **Cool:** For me, these are the calm and relaxing color temperatures. You can find blue, green and violet on the opposite side of the warm colors. These evoke tranquility, mystery, water or the ocean, green grass of the meadows or gloomy landscapes.

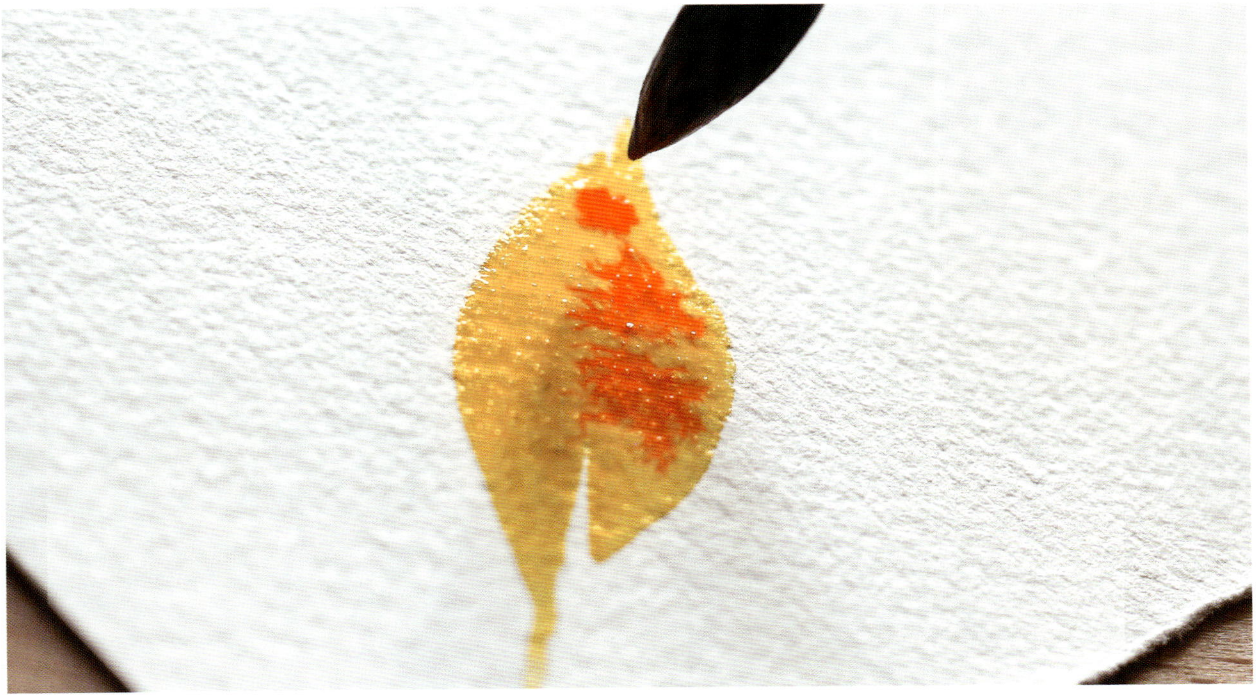

Wet-on-Wet

Basic Techniques

Understanding and practicing these basic techniques will give life and energy to your paintings.

Wet-on-Wet: This technique is the fundamental technique of watercolor painting and, of course, it is by far my favorite technique. In essence, wet-on-wet is starting your painting with a wet surface—be it another pigment or just clean water. This creates fantastic color textures on the paper and beautiful gradients. These gradients are best achieved when you take the time to blend the colors with consistent, steady and soft movements within the shapes that you paint.

Wet-on-Dry: I most often use this technique for painting details or creating layers. You have to wait until a first layer of pigment is dry to move on to painting on top of it.

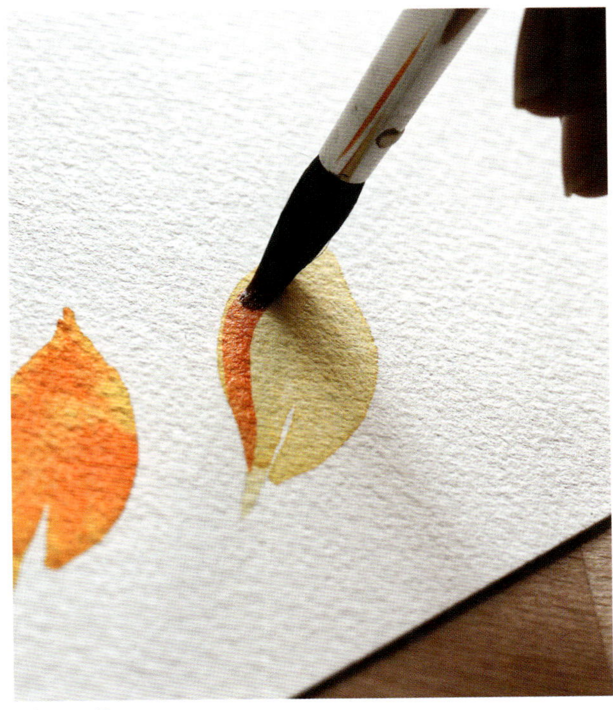

Wet-on-Dry

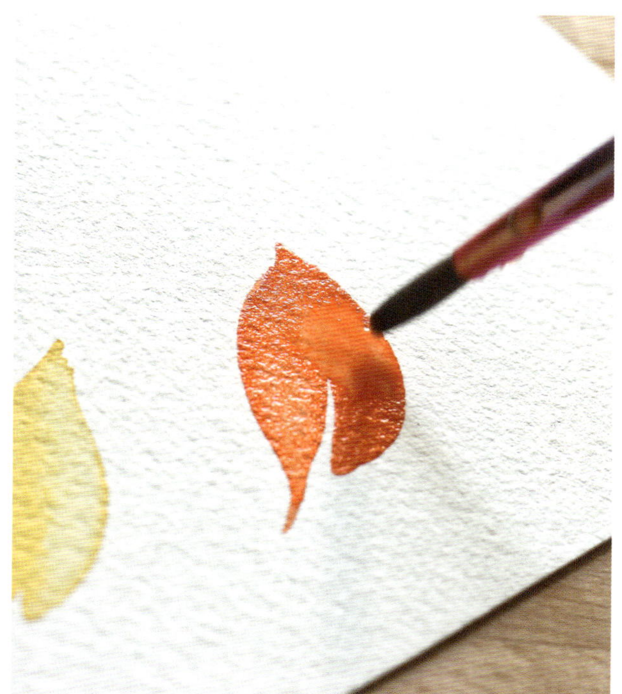
Blooms

Blooms: I love blooms! They are a somewhat uncontrollable technique where you just let watercolor flow where it wants to flow. This is done by adding a drop of water or pigment to a wet surface and letting it dry. Do not blend, do not touch, just let it expand and flow.

Lifting: This is often used when creating a light source or a highlight. Using a clean, damp brush, drag the brush on the color surface where you want to create the highlight and the brush will absorb the pigment.

Transparency: This is the concept of creating see-through layers. Using a very light value pigment (lots of water), you will paint the first layer of your subject. Let it dry completely. Repeat the first step with the same value consistency. I often use this technique when I want to create something very light, airy and soft.

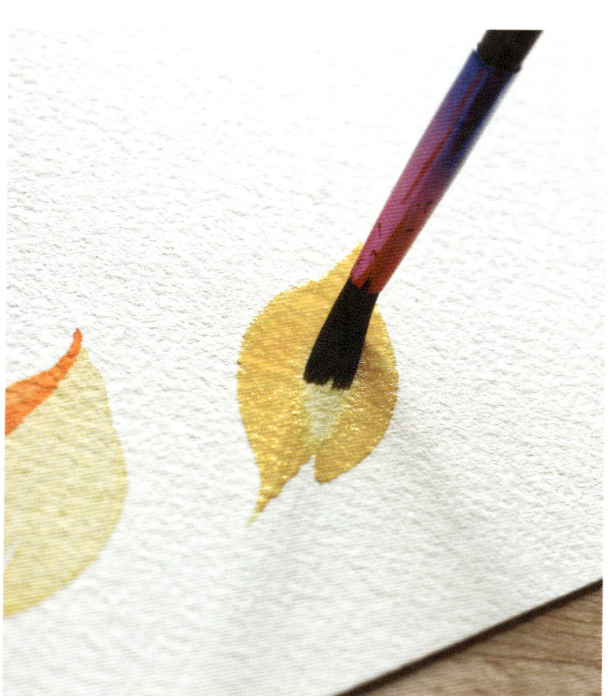
Lifting

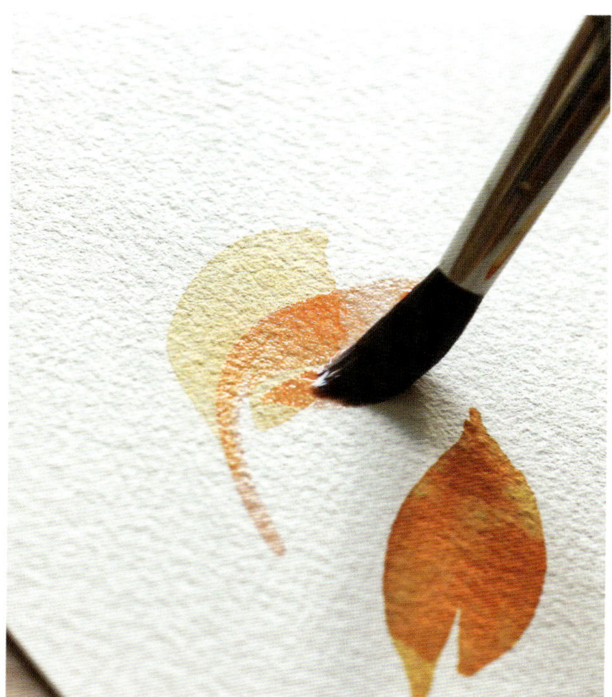
Transparency

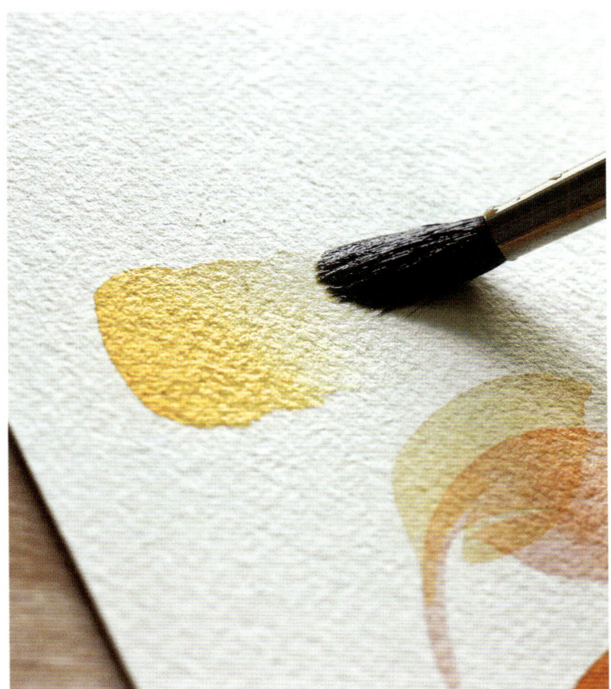

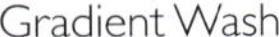

Gradient Wash

Blended Wash

Gradient Wash: A wash is used to diffuse a color from a dark value to its lightest value seamlessly by blending it with water and moving the pigment around in a consistent direction. It is important to not add copious amounts of water to the gradient; instead try to push the pigment into the white area by adding only enough water to help the pigment move softly.

Blended Wash: This technique is used to blend colors seamlessly in a consistent direction. Ideally, the colors will be of the same value to create a consistent gradient. Moving the first pigment from its darkest value to its lightest value toward a central point and then using a second pigment and repeating the same step in the opposite direction will create a seamless transition of colors.

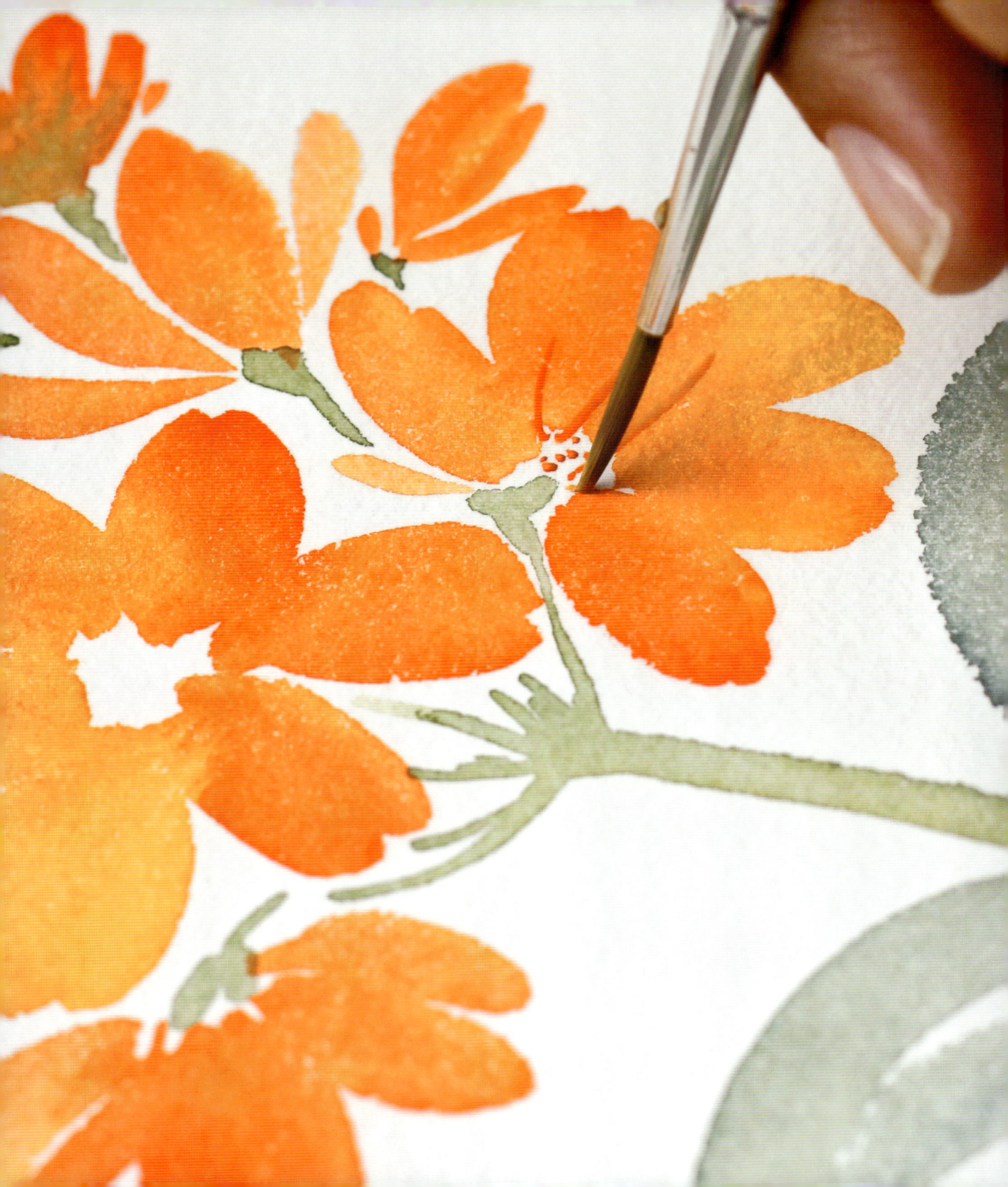

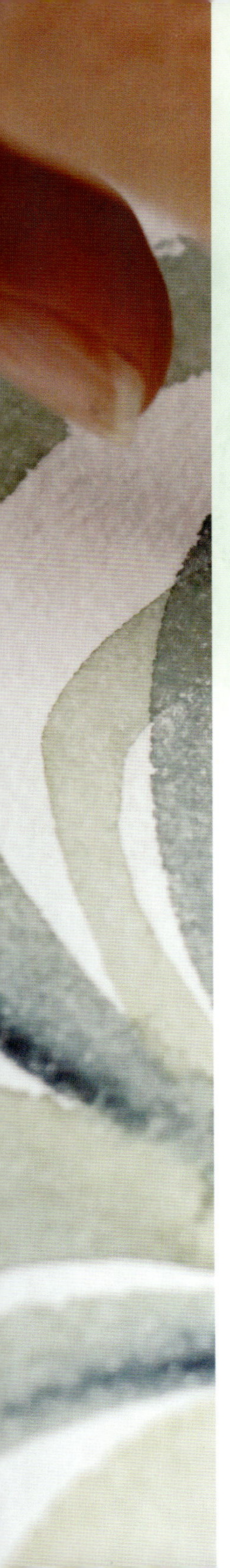

Soft and Gentle *Botanicals*

I want to begin our watercolor practice with botanicals because of their soft and airy nature. These simple but important exercises will help you build muscle memory, gain confidence in your practice and feel relaxed and joyful by creating something simple yet absolutely gorgeous.

I started my journey with soft botanical work and found that the slow and soft movement of the pigment produced a very calming feeling that set my day up with a mindfulness approach to the day's challenges.

The very first project of this book is truly how I started my practice a few years ago and to this day is my go-to exercise when I only have five minutes to myself and still want to create something beautiful and get a sense of small progress in my art journey.

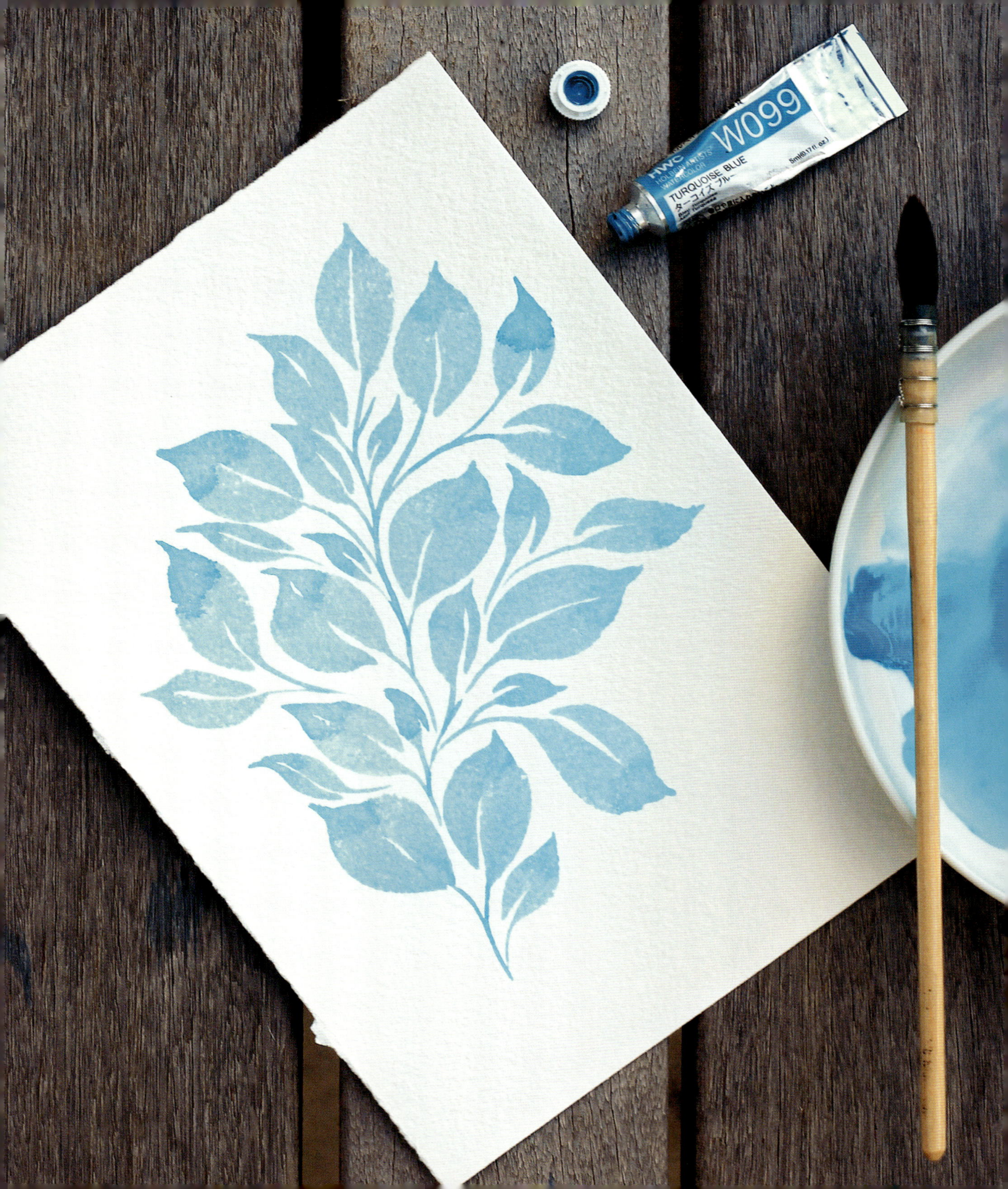
HWC
W099
TURQUOISE BLUE

Soft and Flowing Leaves

This leaf exercise is my go-to when I feel stuck or frustrated about something or when I get the "I can't paint" feelings. With each soft brushstroke my mind starts getting clearer and I feel more relaxed. I breathe in and out with each stroke and next thing I know, the annoying thoughts or feelings dissipate and I feel much better. The best part is that you get so lost in the soft movement of the brush that it almost feels like it's dancing on its own. I highly recommend that you choose a color in the range of the cool tones such as indigo, violet or turquoise to put yourself in a calmer and more relaxing mindset.

Materials

- Your favorite pigment (mine is a soft turquoise)
- Soft round brush No. 4 or No. 6

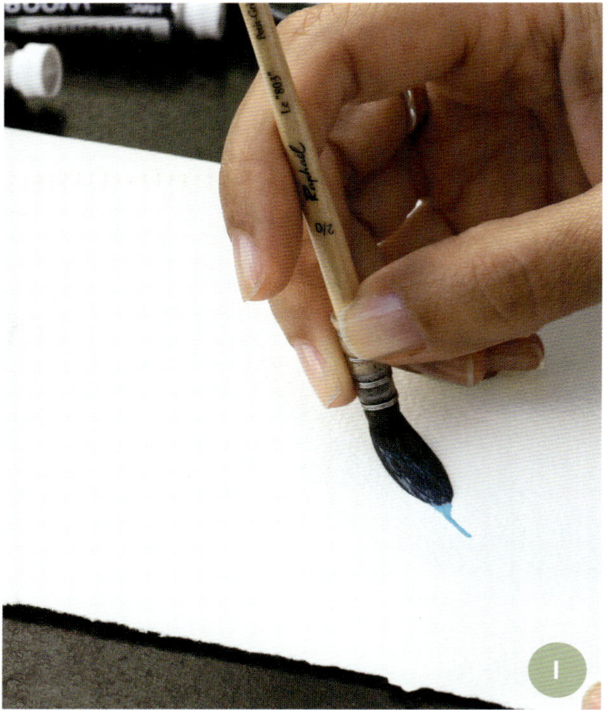

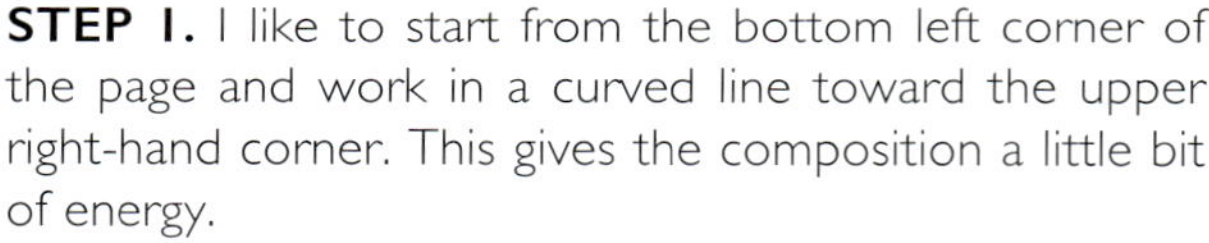

STEP 1. I like to start from the bottom left corner of the page and work in a curved line toward the upper right-hand corner. This gives the composition a little bit of energy.

You will be working on this project one leaf at a time. Let them take you wherever they want to go.

Start by wetting your soft medium brush No. 4 or No. 6 with clean water and then loading it up with your chosen pigment. I like for my pigment to be soft by diluting it with water. Make sure all the bristles are wet and have some pigment. Please note that the stem and leaf will blend into a single brushstroke. With the very tip of the brush, create the short stem from which the first leaf will grow, then, to form the leaf, gently push and drag the brush and lift it at the top of the leaf. As I start this process, I also start focusing on my breath and match it to the movement of my brushstrokes. The stem becomes my in breath and the gentle dragging of the brush becomes my out breath.

STEP 2. Leaving a gap between the first and the second brushstroke in the middle of the leaf is very important as it creates a natural highlight and gives the impression that the leaf has a midrib. Repeat step 1 for the other side of the leaf.

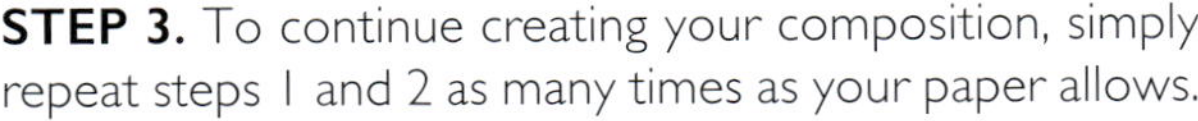

STEP 3. To continue creating your composition, simply repeat steps 1 and 2 as many times as your paper allows.

As you continue to paint more leaves, remember to paint each stem growing out of another one. You want to keep them looking as connected as possible.

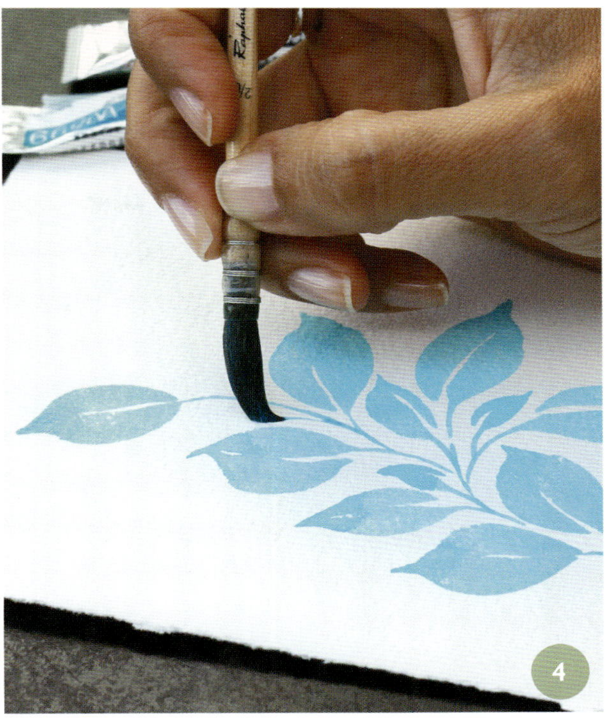

STEP 4. As a final touch to the composition, you can add smaller leaves using mostly the tip of the brush, gently pushing the brush and then lifting it up.

Tip: Remember to hold your brush as if it is made out of a fragile material. This helps the brush flow more naturally. I hold my brush so lightly that I've dropped it on the painting a few times, and that is okay—the splatter becomes a happy mistake.

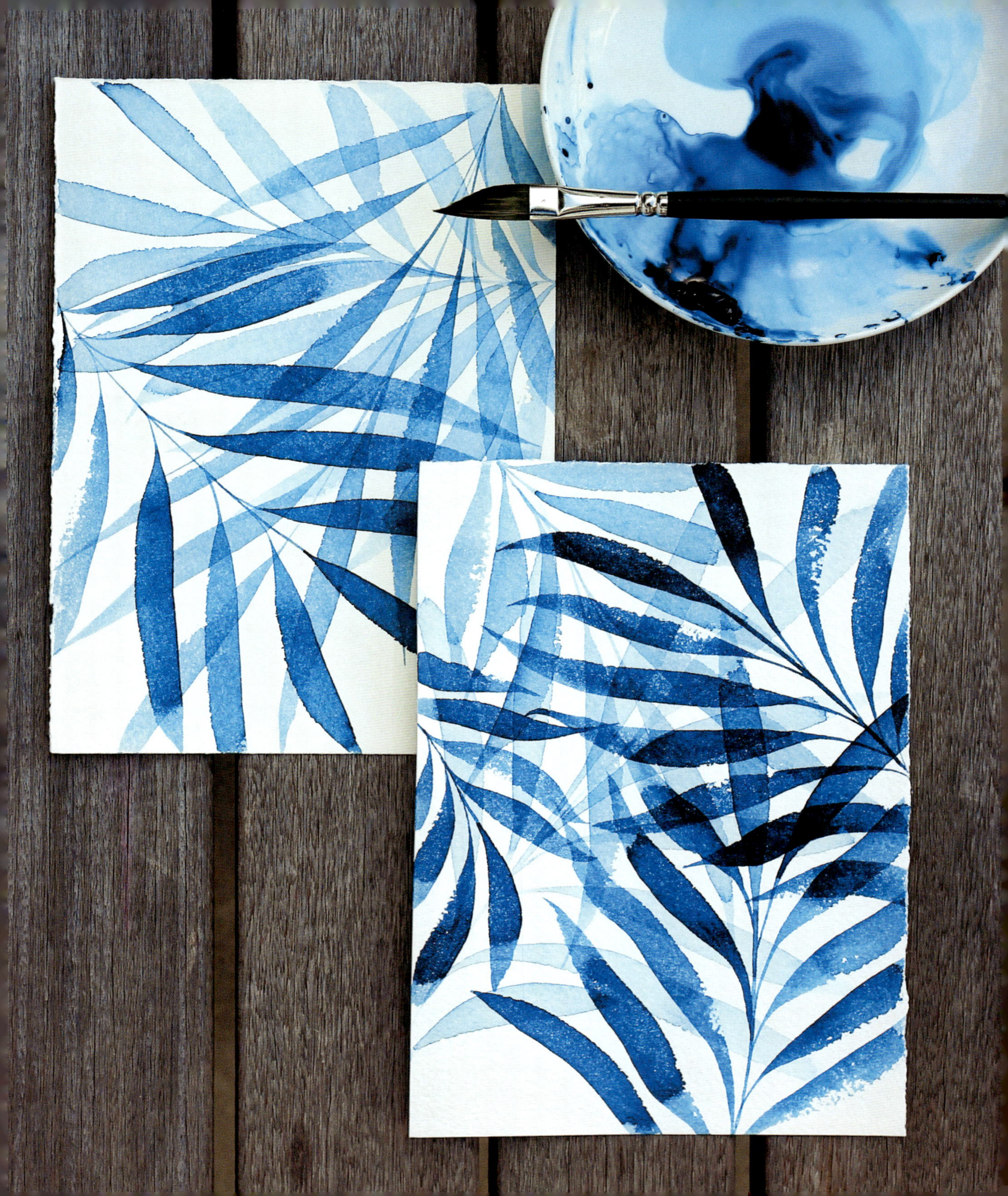

Relaxing Transparent Leaves

One of the most magical qualities about watercolor is that you can paint over it as many times as you like. This is called layering and in this next project you will learn this technique and create a pattern of leaves. As with the previous project, your brush will move softly on the paper as you paint soft and gentle palm leaves.

Because these are longer brushstrokes, my exhales also get longer; this helps my hand get steadier. Don't forget to breathe though—there have been times when I catch myself holding my breath for no reason at all! It is important to find your own flow of breath versus brushstroke.

Materials

- Indigo
- Dagger brush No. 8

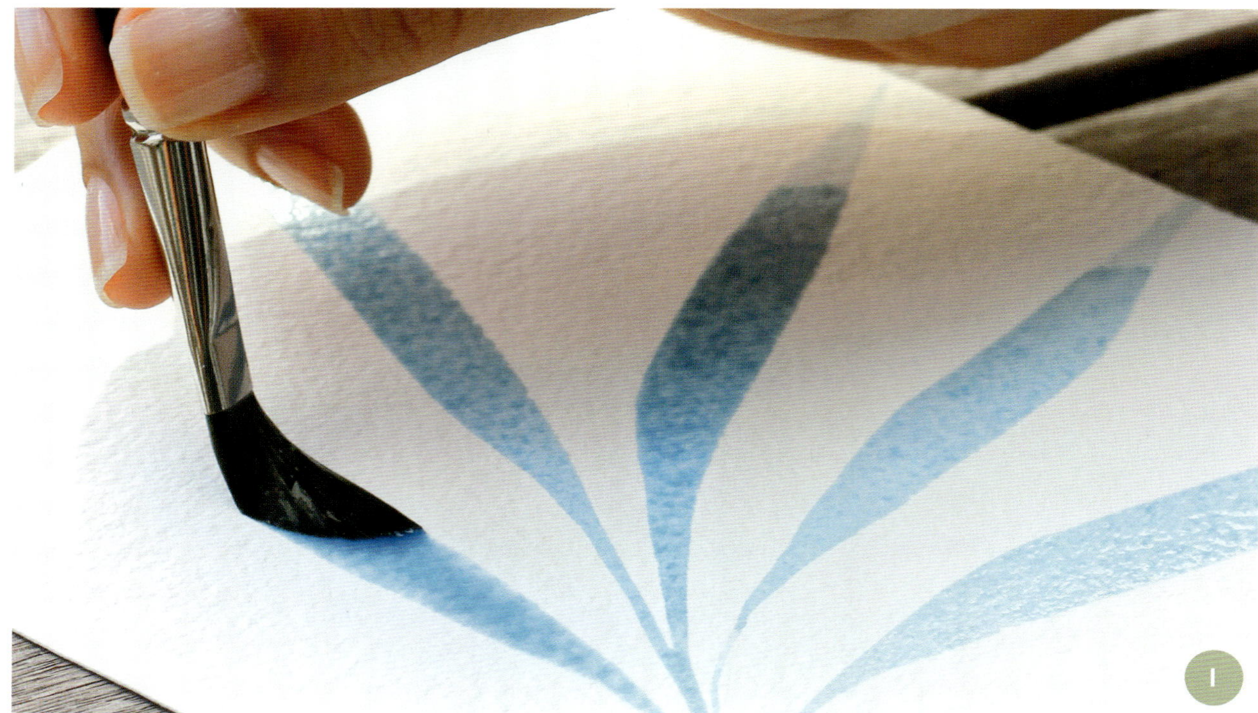

STEP 1. In this project, you will be putting to practice the wet-on-dry technique as well as practicing value variation and mindful brushstrokes. This monochromatic painting will have a variation in value but not in pigment. The first layer will be a watered-down indigo that will produce a soft blue. For the second layer, you will add more pigment. The last layer will be the darkest value pigment. Of course, you can add as many layers as you like, but always remember to work from light to dark.

How do you get your water to pigment ratios correct? Always start from light to dark.

Grab a small amount of pigment with the tip of your dagger brush No. 8 and put it on a small plate (like a saucer), then add about five dabs of water to the pigment and mix thoroughly. This will be your lightest value. To achieve darker values, gradually add small dabs of pigment to the existing mix without adding any more water. Please see the Color Theory chapter (page 11) if you are in need of more clarification.

The first step is to start with a clean and dry piece of watercolor paper, grab your dagger brush and load it with your lightest value pigment and start your first layer. Starting from the bottom left-hand corner, use the tip of the brush to paint the stem and then gently push and drag long strokes of pigment onto the paper toward the outer edge of the paper. Repeat this step four or five times, always painting your leaves from a central stem outward.

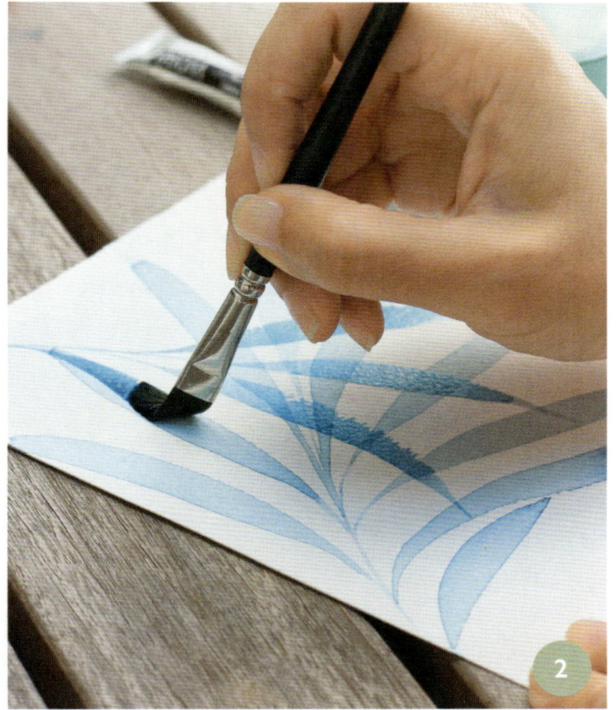

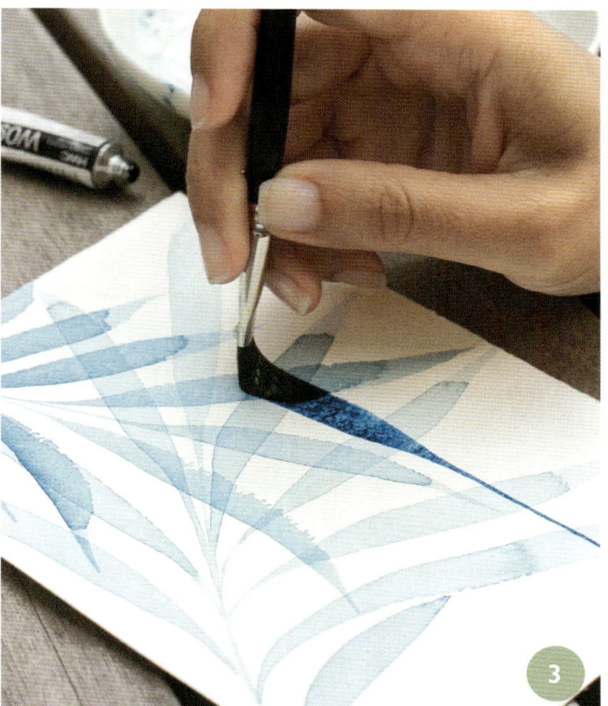

STEP 2. Once the first layer is completely dry, you can move on to the next layer. Load up your brush now with the medium value indigo and start dragging your brush in the same long brushstrokes, finding the movement of the brush calming and gentle. I like to start the second layer from an opposite corner of the paper so the leaves have a better chance of overlapping in a more energetic manner.

Tip: The more your long leaves extend past the edge of the paper, the more interesting the composition. So go ahead and paint outside the lines!

STEP 3. For the third and last layer, you will be using the darkest value indigo. Look for any empty spaces and try to fill those with the long brushstrokes.

I truly hope you found the practice of long and soft brushstrokes relaxing and calming. The longer the leaves, the deeper your breaths and the more relaxed you will feel.

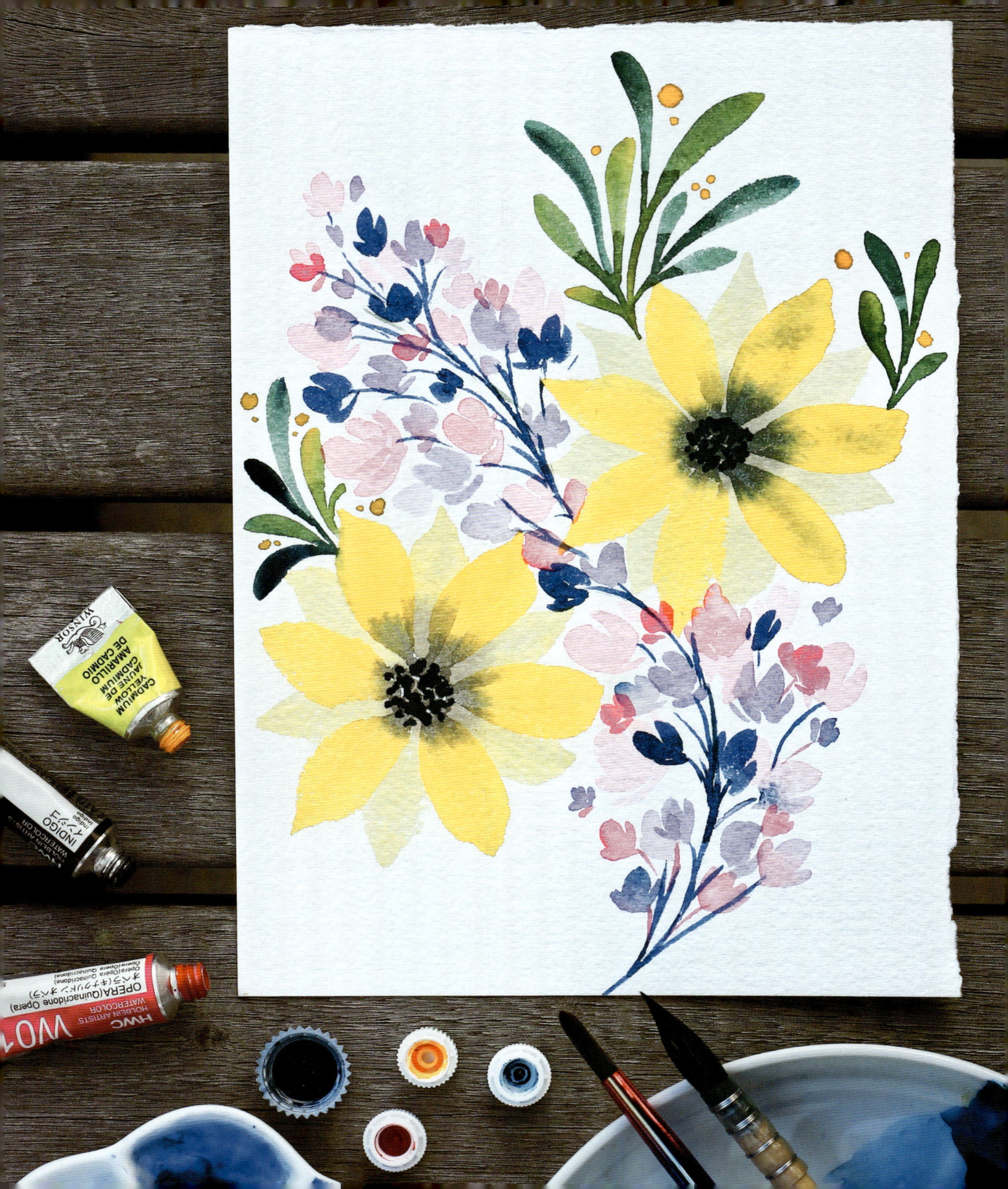

WINSOR
CADMIUM YELLOW
JAUNE DE CADMIUM
AMARILLO DE CADMIO
INDIGO
WATERCOLOR
HWC
HOLBEIN ARTISTS' WATERCOLOR
OPERA (Quinacridone Opera)

Mellow Wildflowers

In this project you will venture into the wonderful world of mixed compositions. You will be painting a Black-Eyed Susan, a Lupine and Wild Filler Leaves.

As with most compositions that I paint, I like to picture myself in a place where my creation will take place or where I would like to be. For instance, I lived in Los Angeles for almost a decade and I never actually took the time to go see the wildflowers in Death Valley or travel north to see the wild blue Lupine near San Francisco. So I like to imagine that I am there listening to the sound of the wind bringing me the wonderful scent of all the wildflowers swaying in unison.

Practice each flower type separately. Once you have the hang of it, create your own composition.

Materials

- Brown (a mixture of indigo and orange will give you a deep brown)
- Cadmium Yellow
- Cobalt Violet
- Indigo
- Soft round brush No. 1
- Soft round brush No. 4
- Soft filbert brush No. 4
- Synthetic round brush No. 2

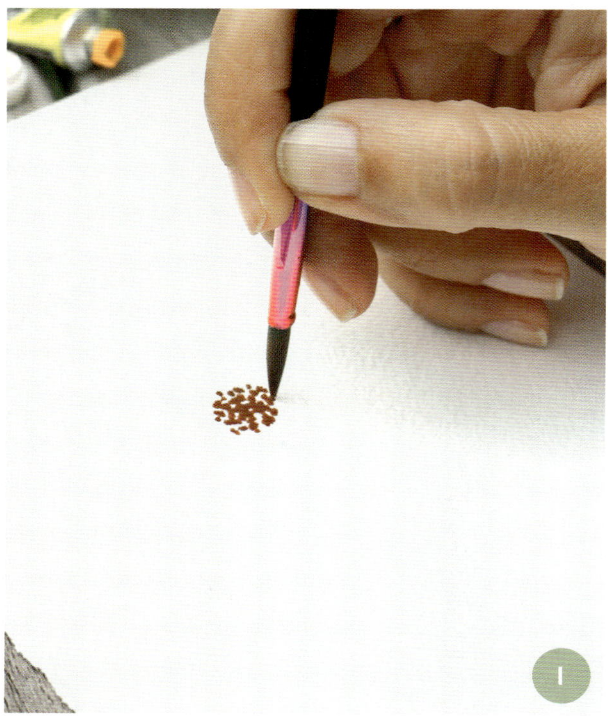

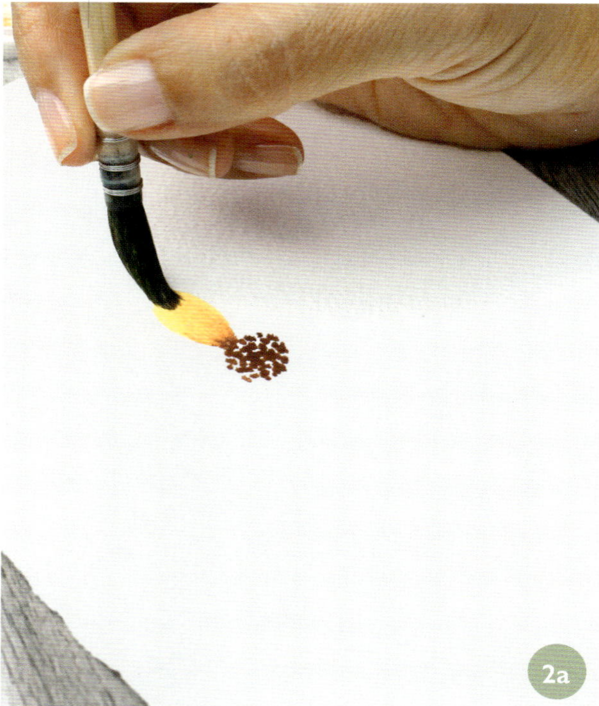

Black-Eyed Susan

Now that you are familiar with the soft and gentle leaf strokes, starting with the Black-Eyed Susan should ease you into the composition for this project.

STEP 1. Starting with a clean and dry piece of watercolor paper, take a deep breath, relax and envision your soft brushstrokes on the textured paper. Now that you are ready, load up your round brush No. 1 with a dark brown (remember that indigo and orange make brown in a 1:1 ratio) and start softly stippling the pigment to create the center of the flower.

STEP 2. After you've created your center, it is time to paint the first layer of petals. Before the brown center dries, grab your soft bristle brush No. 4, load it up with a medium value of Cadmium Yellow and gently drag the first petal of your flower from the center, touching the brown pigment ever so slightly and dragging the brush outward softly, pushing it into the paper and gently lifting it as you reach the end of the petal. Note the blending effect that the petal has with the brown at the center of the flower. Please do not rush through the process. Keep in mind to work fast enough to not let the center of the flower dry. Work around the center of the flower, leaving some generous gaps in between each petal for the first layer.

STEP 3. Once this first layer is completely dry, repeat the first and second step right on top of the flower you just created, but this time fill in the gaps you left on the previous petals. This will give the flower a bit of transparency and lightness.

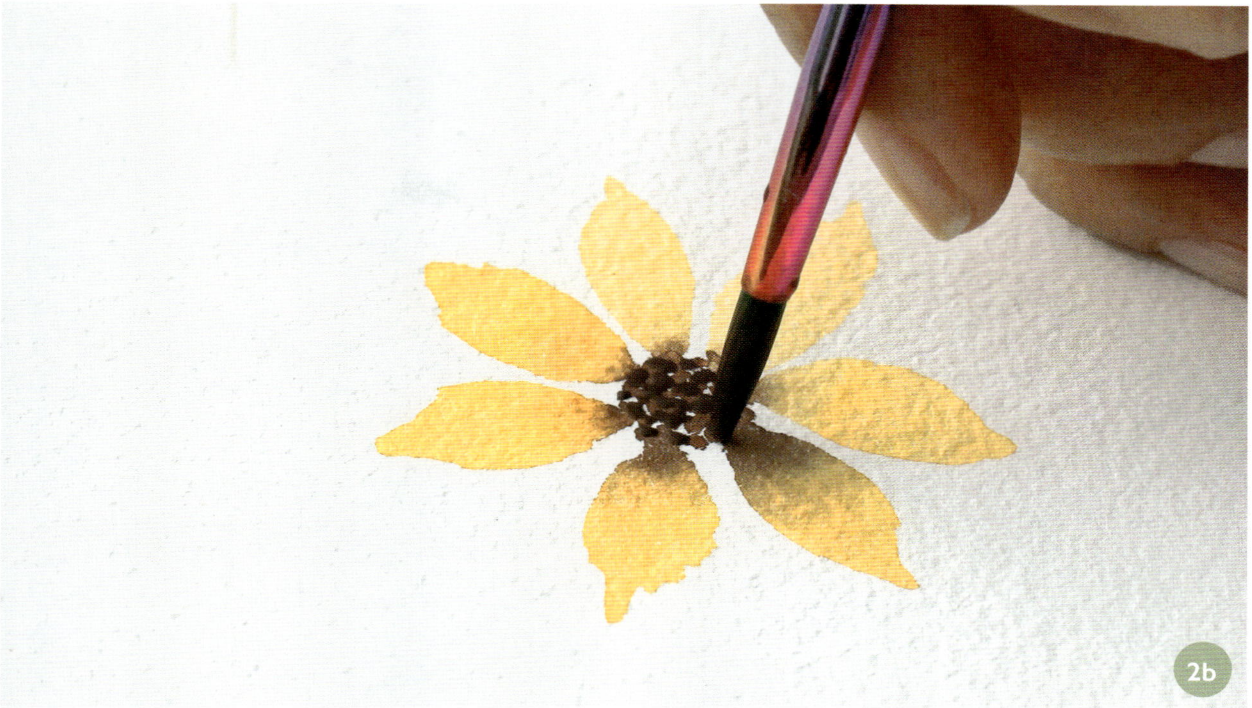

2b

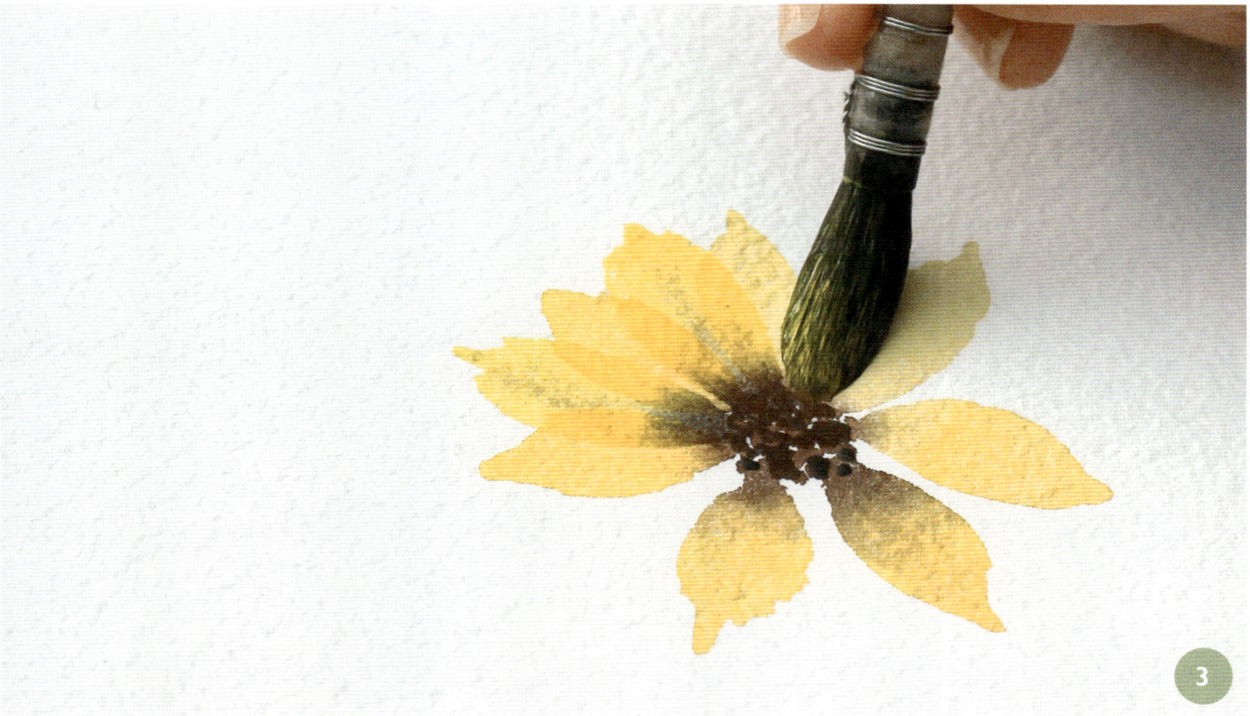

3

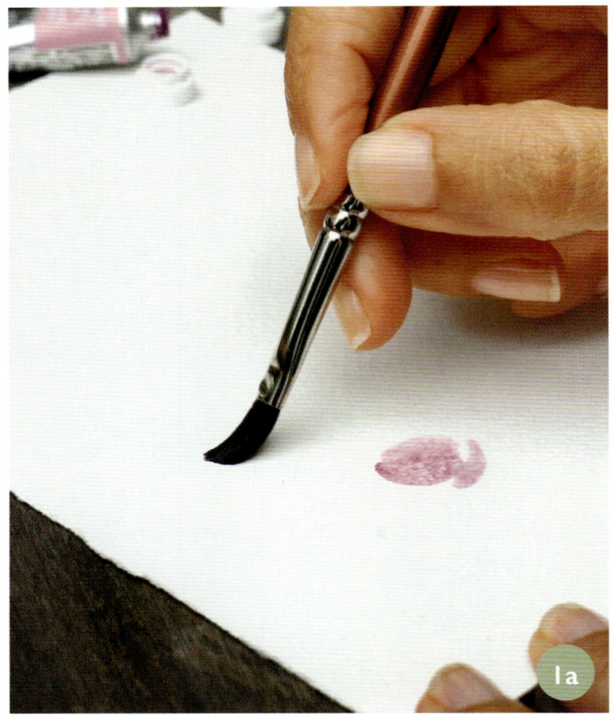

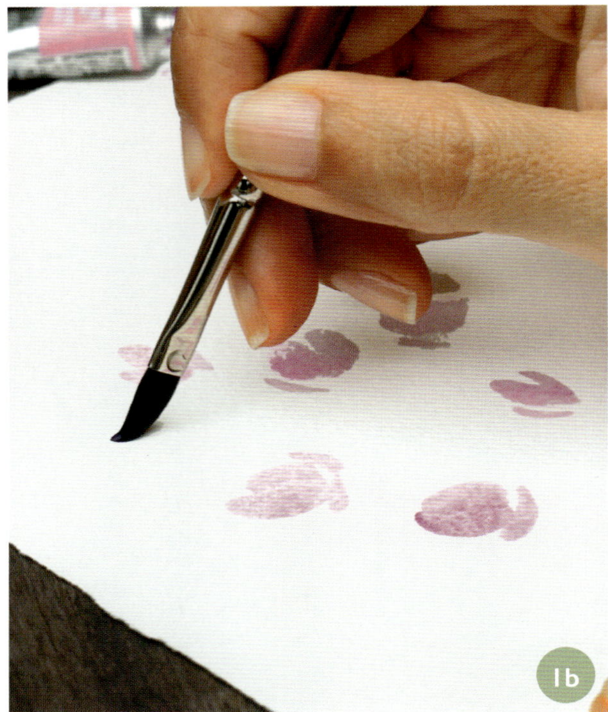

Lupine

Moving on to the Lupine, you will need the filbert brush No. 4 and a light value of Cobalt Violet for the first layer. The Lupine will require four layers, so you need to practice your patience while the paint dries between each layer. Because the brushstrokes are small in nature, they will not dry as quickly as a long flower petal would.

STEP 1. Start with the most transparent and light layer of petals. Water down your Cobalt Violet pigment to its lightest value and load up your filbert brush with it. Use the flat part of the brush to start painting small round petals in a random diagonal formation. Some petals can be bigger and some smaller—the more variation, the better (you can pencil in a curved line to help you envision a central stem).

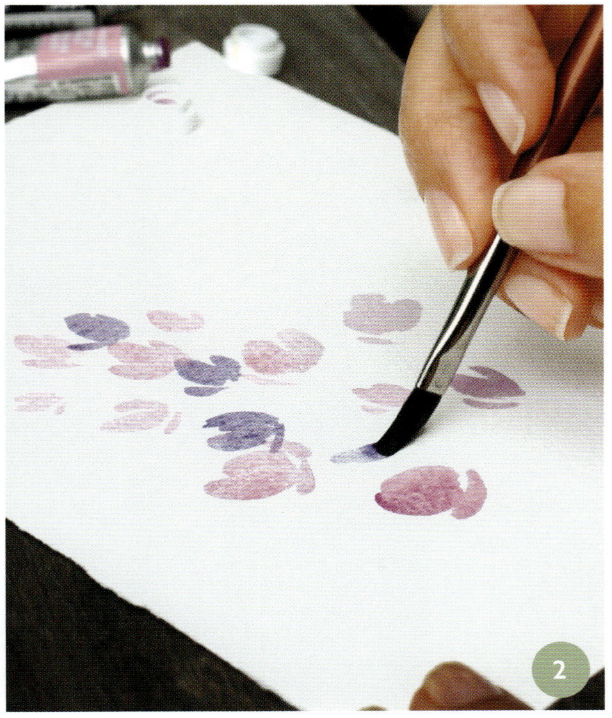

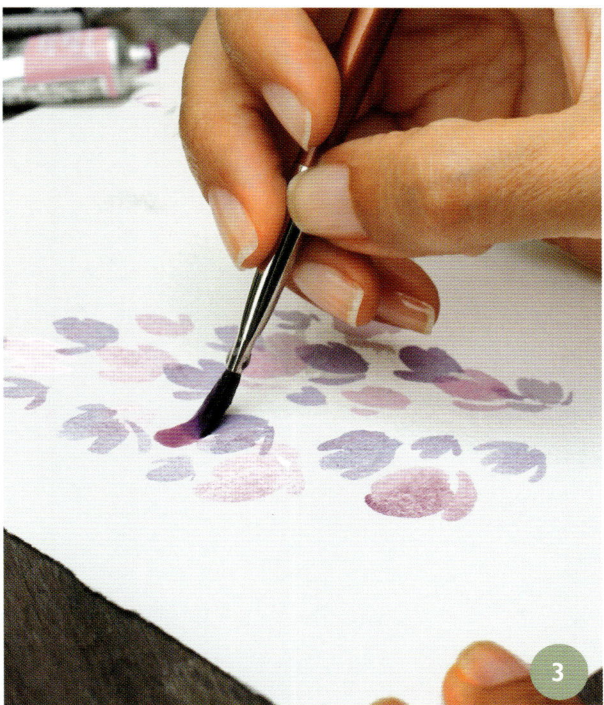

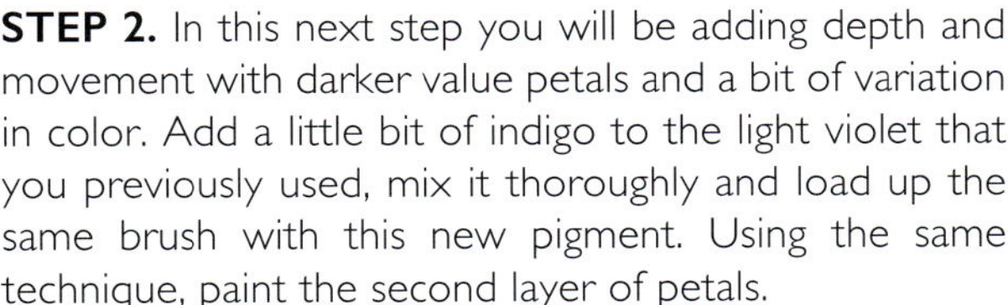

STEP 2. In this next step you will be adding depth and movement with darker value petals and a bit of variation in color. Add a little bit of indigo to the light violet that you previously used, mix it thoroughly and load up the same brush with this new pigment. Using the same technique, paint the second layer of petals.

STEP 3. The third layer uses only Cobalt Violet, but in its darkest value, and overlaps all the white spaces that look empty. You can use a variation of small to large petals to give the appearance that some petals are just buds or some petals are sideways.

STEP 4. The fourth and last step is to bring this flower together by painting little stems that somewhat meet at a central, larger stem. Use a medium value indigo and the round brush No. 1 for the final detail of adding the stem. Try to maintain a central stem where smaller ones grow from, but do not worry too much about making it perfect or realistic. You are not aiming for perfect; you are aiming for wild and pretty.

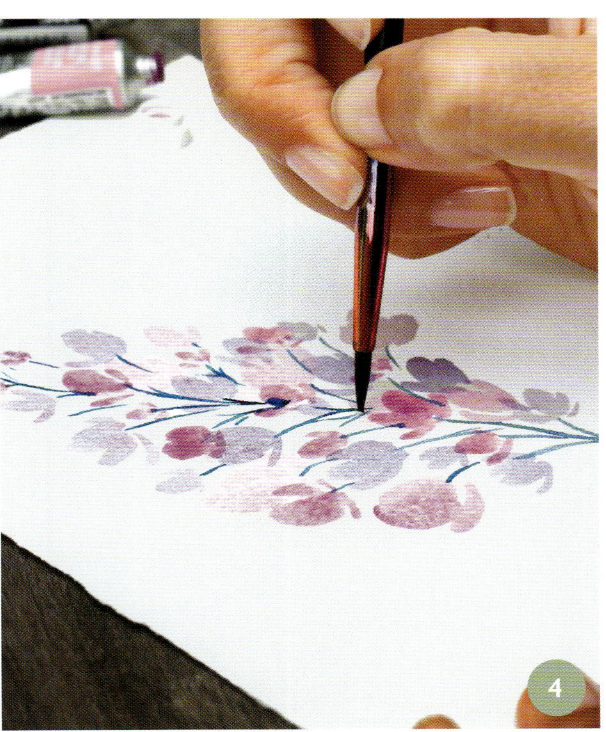

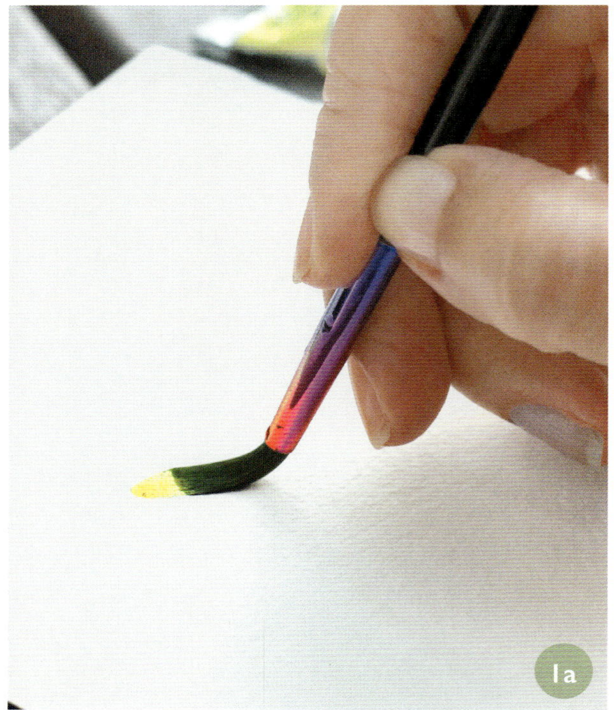

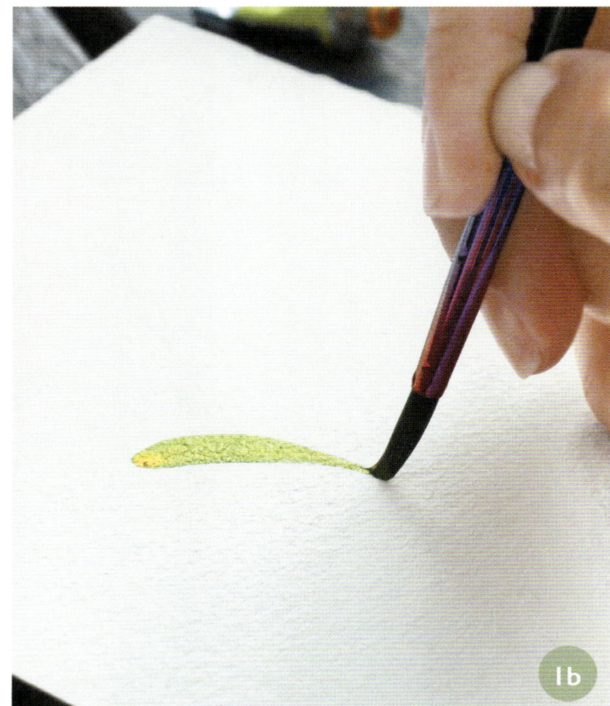

Wild Filler Leaves

For the last part of this project you will be painting what I like to call wild filler leaves. They are just an abstract representation of wild grown leaves that help a composition look more dynamic.

STEP 1. Load up your synthetic round brush No. 2 with a dark value Cadmium Yellow and have a medium value indigo ready for dipping the tip of your brush. Start with a push and drag motion, moving your brush downward and gently lifting it up as you finish the leaf to create the stem.

Tip: As you paint more leaves from the outside toward the main stem, add a little bit of indigo to the tip of the brush and watch it mix and perfectly blend in the paper as you drag the brush downward.

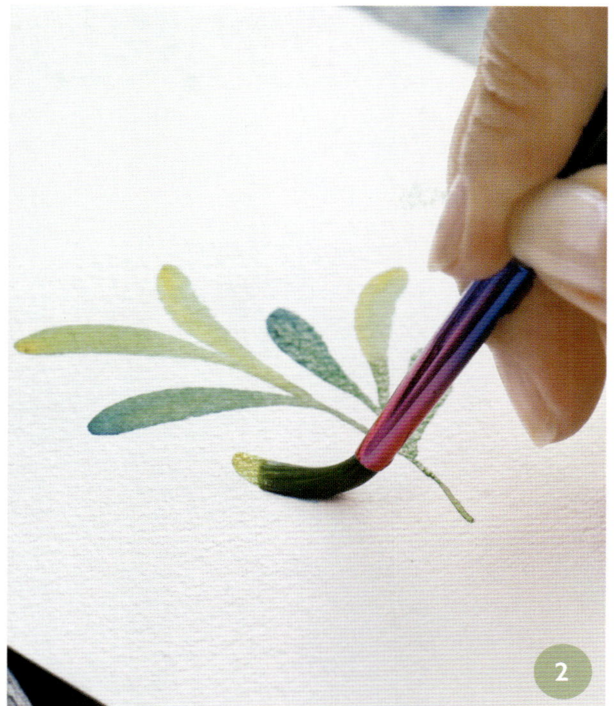

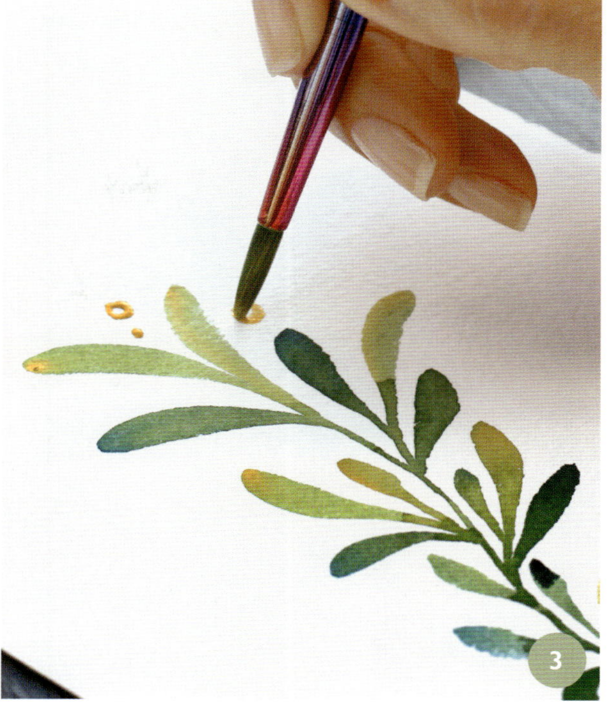

STEP 2. Using the same technique as the first step of push and drag, curve some leaves in the opposite direction, but still attach them to the same stem. This will add variety and movement as if the leaves were moving softly with the wind.

STEP 3. As a final detail, you can add small dots of Cadmium Yellow or indigo or a combination of the two in no particular placement. Be as spontaneous as you want with this.

Now that you have learned how to paint these three different flowers, you can go ahead and create a composition of your own that you can use for a greeting card or to frame on your desk.

I truly hope that with this project you were able to find a moment of relaxation as you watched your paintbrush dance with each different flower. The colors are vibrant and the shapes full of energy. Please add as many variations and details to your own compositions and most importantly feel proud and happy of your bouquet arrangements.

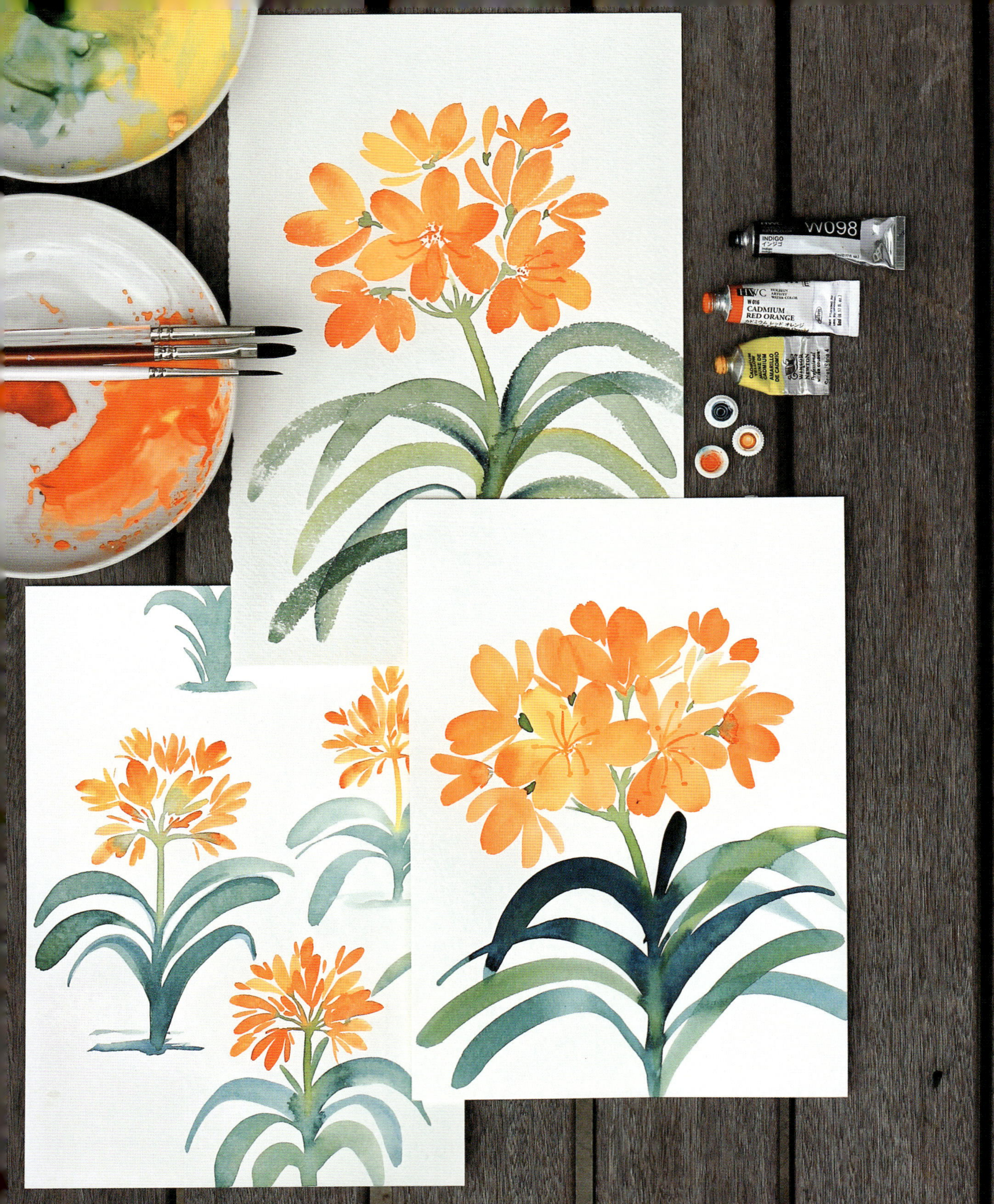
W098
INDIGO
CADMIUM
RED ORANGE

Happy Clivia

This flower just makes me so happy! Orange is one of my favorite colors, and its natural contrast with the deep green leaves fills my heart with so much joy. When thinking about mindfulness, I don't just think about relaxing and being in a calm state of mind but also about what specific thing brings me joy. This flower is a perfect example because of the soft round nature of the petals and the playfulness of the long leaves. Its vivid and warm colors help me understand that loud, playful and chaotic moments are also joyful and are just as important as the calm, meditative ones. The essence of this project is to bring joy with playful brushstrokes and warm, joyful colors.

Materials

- Cadmium Red-Orange
- Cadmium Yellow
- Indigo
- Soft filbert brush No. 4
- Synthetic round brush No. 2
- Synthetic round brush No. 1

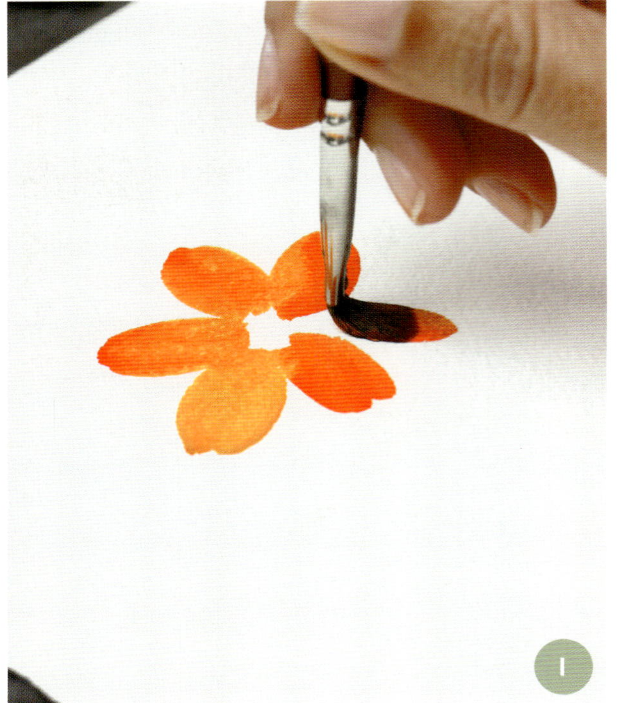

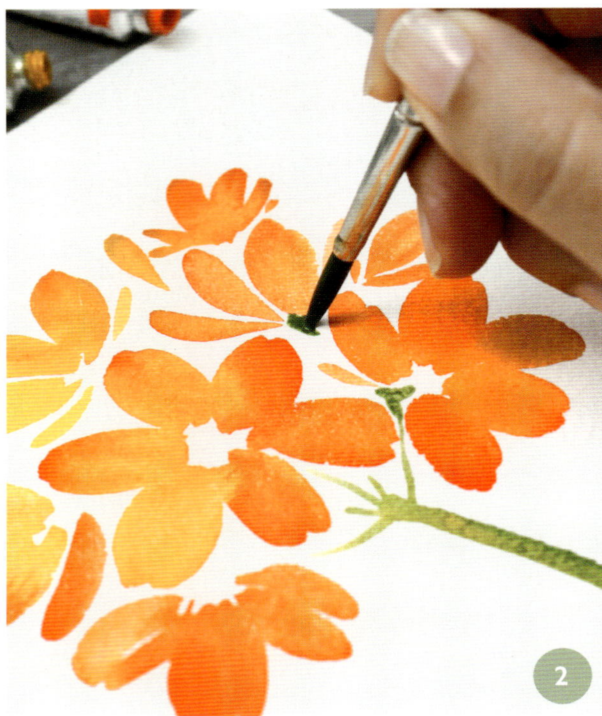

STEP 1. Start with your paper completely dry, load up your filbert brush No. 4 with a dark value of Cadmium Red-Orange and with the flat side of the brush, push and drag the paint inward toward an imaginary central point in a single brushstroke.

While the paint is still wet, you can add a dark value of Cadmium Yellow to the petals either where they stem from the center or at the edge of the petals to give them a light contrast by lightly dabbing the pigment on the already painted yellow petal.

Tip: To paint thinner petals, use the smaller side of the same filbert brush and remember to maintain a central imaginary point from where the flower grows.

STEP 2. Using the synthetic round brush No. 2, on a separate plate, mix a little bit of indigo with the Cadmium Yellow, close to a 3:1 ratio or one part medium value indigo to three parts Cadmium Yellow. This will give you a soft yellow-green that leans more toward yellow than green to paint the stem of the individual flowers.

Using your synthetic round brush No. 2, and with a very gentle touch, paint the main stem from the bottom of the flowers toward the bottom of the paper. Using the same mixture of paint and brush, go ahead and paint the smaller stems as if they were growing from the previously painted main stem.

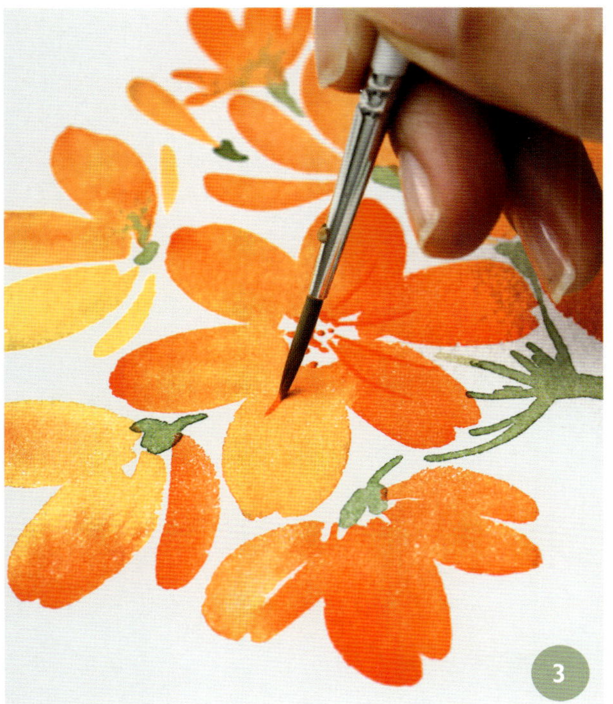

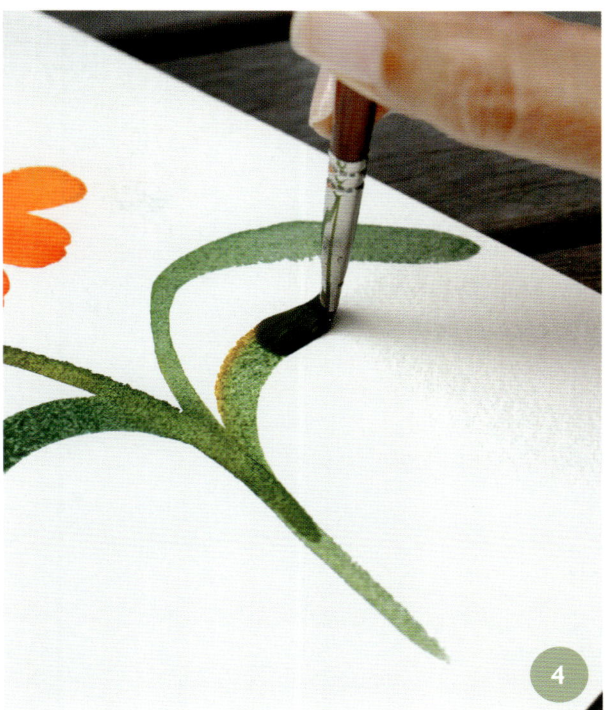

STEP 3. Make sure the orange petals are completely dry before adding the stamen with your synthetic round brush No. 1 and a dark value of Cadmium Orange-Red. Because this step requires a bit of precision, it is a perfect opportunity to keep practicing mindfulness toward your breath and how it can synchronize with the movement of your brush. Take a deep breath in, and as you drag the brush slowly to create the stamen, take a slow and steady breath out.

STEP 4. This last step is the most satisfying and relaxing one. This is a great opportunity to continue practicing your breath. You can use the same mixture with which you painted the stem of the individual flowers, but for this step, add a dark value indigo that will give you a deep green. This step can also be very playful because you can gently drag your filbert brush from the stem of the flower outward, or you can start with the flat part of your brush on the outside and drag it toward the stem. Either approach works, so don't be afraid to play with the strokes a little bit.

I hope you found this project as playful as it was relaxing and had the opportunity to practice your breath synchronization to find yourself focused, energized and ready for the next project at hand, be it another watercolor painting or some complicated brainstorming session at work.

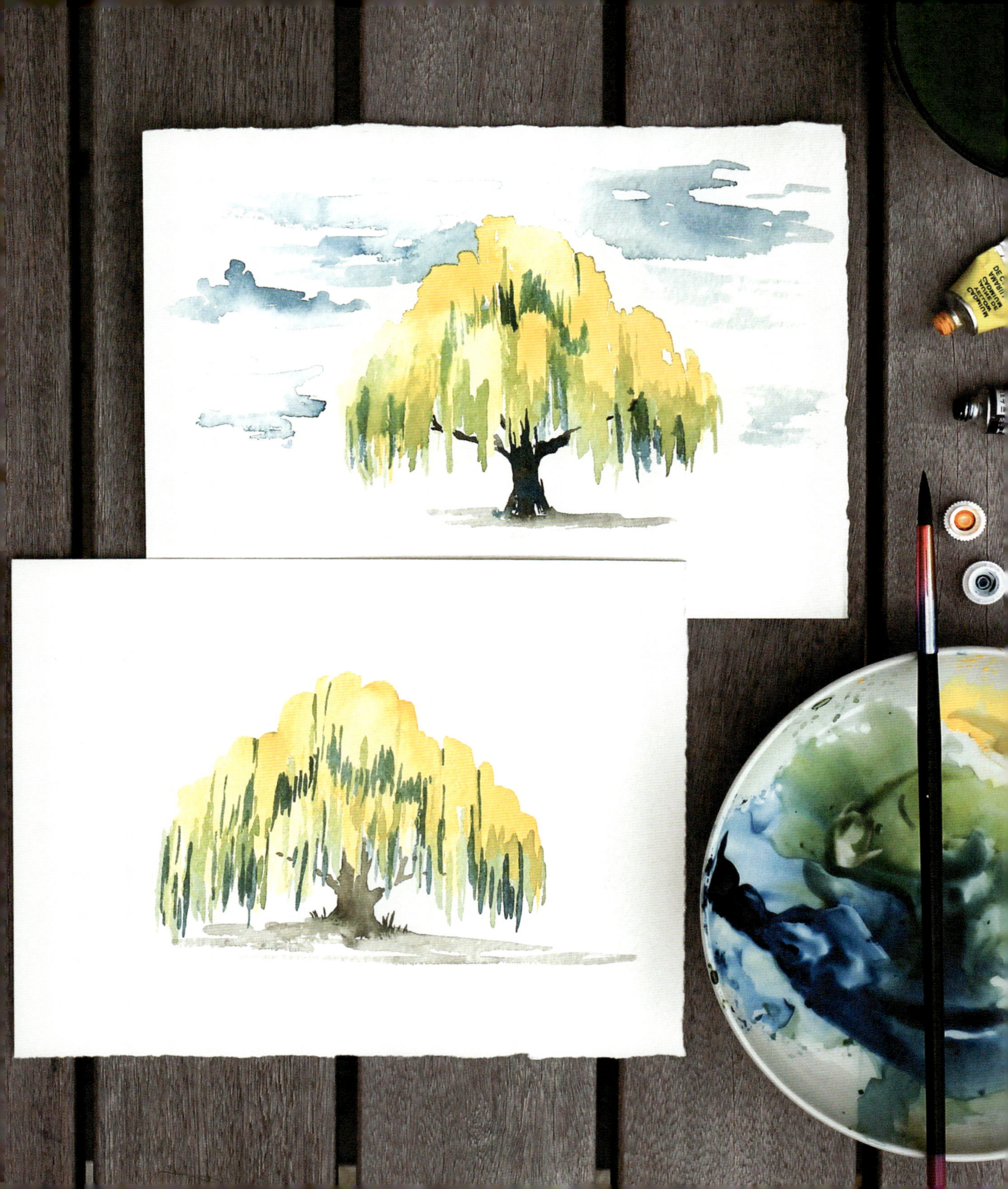

Graceful Weeping Willow Tree

In reality, this tree is grandiose in size but soft, airy and gentle, and that is exactly the state of mind that the shapes and colors in this next project intend to evoke. There is no need to stress about the exact shape of the tree—remember that this is a flowy kind of tree. The more you immerse yourself in letting the pigment flow on the paper, the more you will feel yourself focused on the present moment and forget for even just a split second the worries of the day or that grocery list that is never ending. Stay present and stay focused on that gorgeous yellow-looking blob.

At the end of this project, I hope you find yourself with a calm heart and a sense of accomplishment in painting one of the most fascinating trees there are.

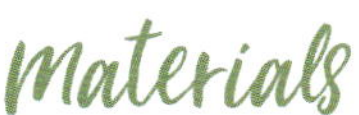

- Cadmium Yellow
- Indigo
- Brown (remember that indigo and orange make brown in a 1:1 ratio)
- Synthetic round brush No. 6
- Synthetic round brush No. 4

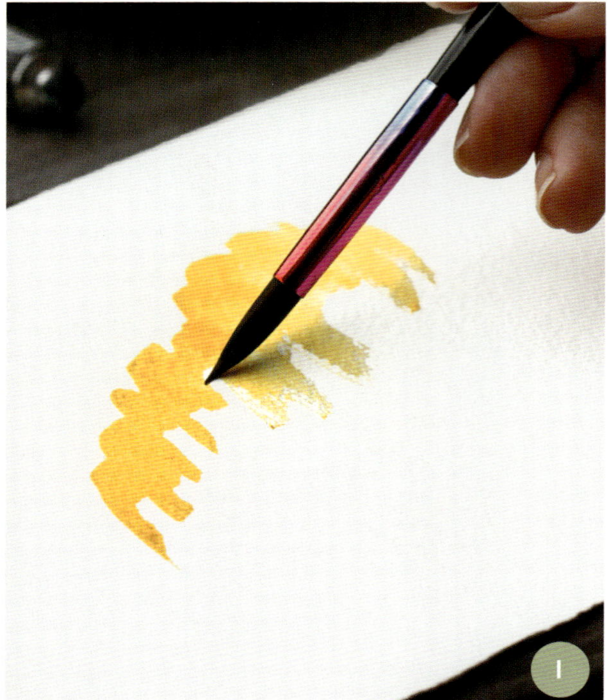

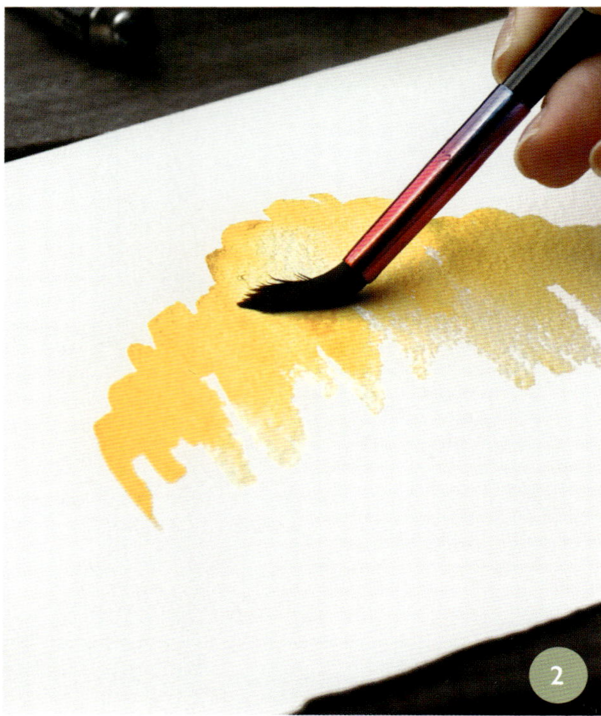

STEP 1. The first step in this project is to create the basic shape of the tree. Starting with your paper completely dry, load up your synthetic round brush No. 6 with a medium value of Cadmium Yellow and paint the top of the willow tree with downward strokes. Start the strokes in different places and make it vaguely cloud-shaped. Relax your hand and let the brushstrokes lead the way.

STEP 2. While the paint is still wet, go ahead and clean your round brush No. 6, remove the excess water with a paper towel and lift up some of the yellow pigment softly to create the illusion of transparency or lightness.

While you wait a minute or two for most of the yellow pigment to get absorbed into the paper, on your mixing plate, mix one part light value Cadmium Yellow and one part light value indigo thoroughly to create a soft lime green that you will be using in the next step.

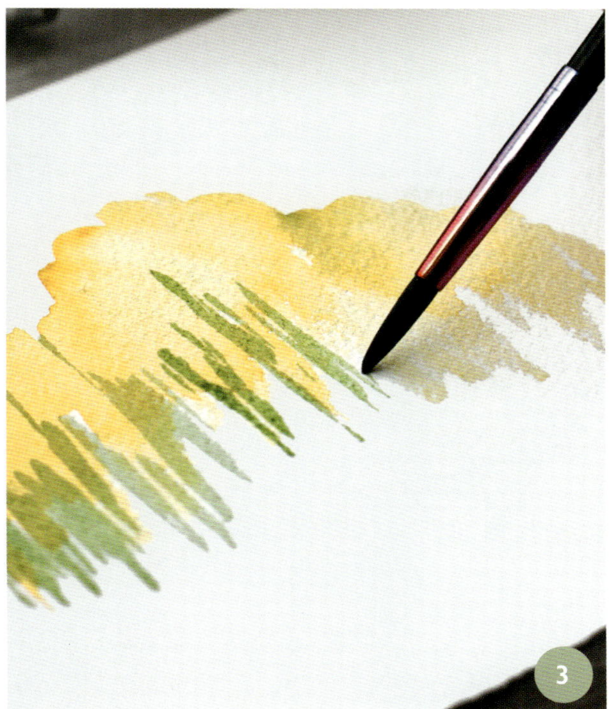

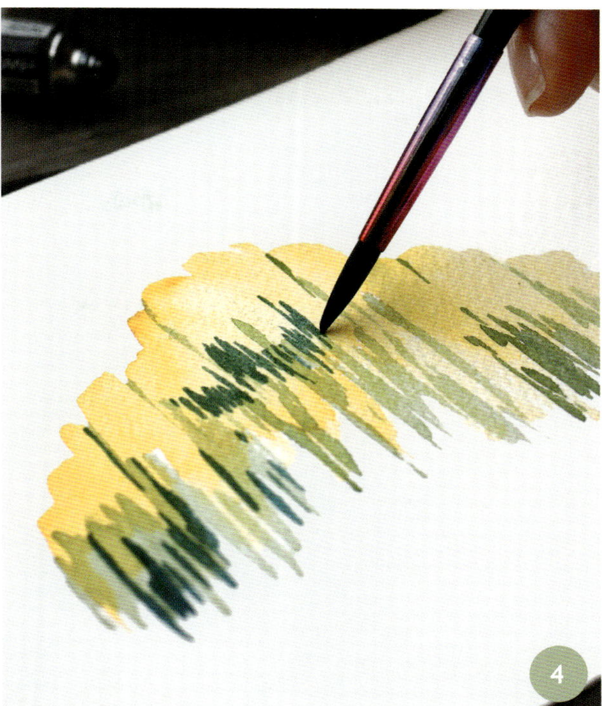

STEP 3. It is time to add dimension to the tree by adding shadows. Even if the yellow shape is not fully dry, you can still continue with this step. Using the light green mixture of paint that you created in the last step, load up your synthetic brush No. 4 and start painting lines in random places, starting roughly from the bottom half of your tree. These soft but repetitive movements will allow you to find a moment of calm and help to dissipate any stress that you may be carrying. Should some of the green stripes blend with the not fully dry yellow, do not worry—these small blended areas will give the tree an even softer look overall.

STEP 4. Add the final layer of shadow to the tree. Using the same brush No. 4, add a bit more indigo to your lime green mix until you have a dark value green. Repeat step 3 with this new pigment focusing on empty spaces, sometimes overlapping the previous stripes but always remembering to leave vast areas of yellow untouched. Remember that the willow tree's natural shape flows downward, and this is why you want to keep your brushstrokes flowing downward as well.

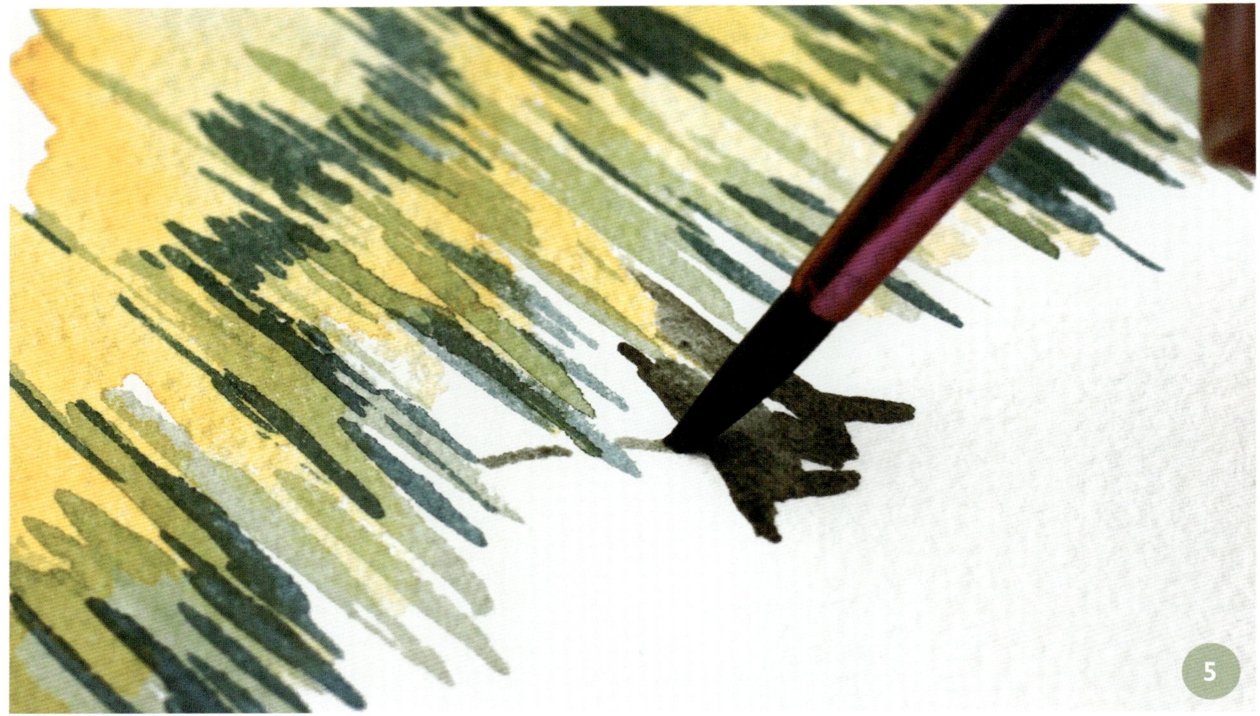

STEP 5. Now, to make this really look like a tree, add a trunk and some branches. Grab your round brush No. 4 and load it with a medium value brown (remember that indigo and orange make brown in a 1:1 ratio). Starting from the middle bottom of the tree shape, paint a short trunk and some small branches in any open space you can see between the previously painted long brushstrokes. You can also add a few brushstrokes horizontally at the bottom of the trunk to create a ground level. You end up with a wonderful, soft and gentle willow tree!

Now, take a second to appreciate the wonderful tree you just created! Soft shapes, vibrant colors and a relaxed state of mind.

Serene and Delicate Sakura in Water

This project brings back memories of when I lived in Japan and got to experience Sakura for the first time. These flowers are so delicate that the slightest wind causes the petals to fly away so gently it almost looks like snow. I love painting these flowers in water because they are typically along a river or a lake and the petals are so fragile that you will find large amounts of them floating just on the surface of the water, creating a white and soft pink blanket of petals. For this particular project I make myself a lovely matcha tea latte, channel some Kyoto vibes and start preparing my paint for this lovely project.

Materials

- Indigo
- Turquoise
- Acrylic White Titanium (1:4 water ratio)
- Opera Pink
- Soft round brush No. 6
- Soft filbert brush No. 4
- Synthetic round brush No. 1

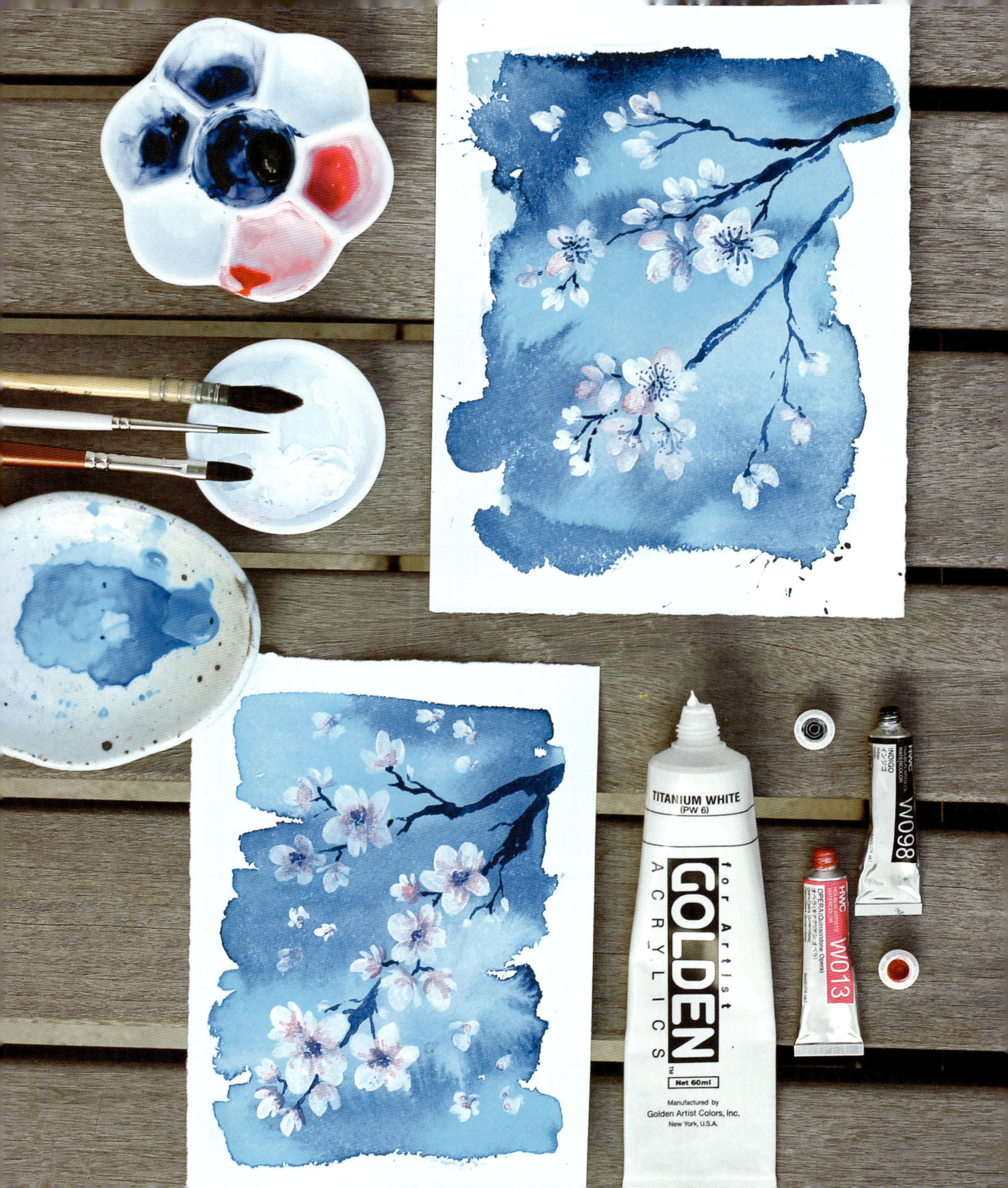
TITANIUM WHITE
(PW 6)
for Artist
GOLDEN
ACRYLICS
Net 60ml
Manufactured by
Golden Artist Colors, Inc.
New York, U.S.A.
HWC
INDIGO
W098
HWC
W013

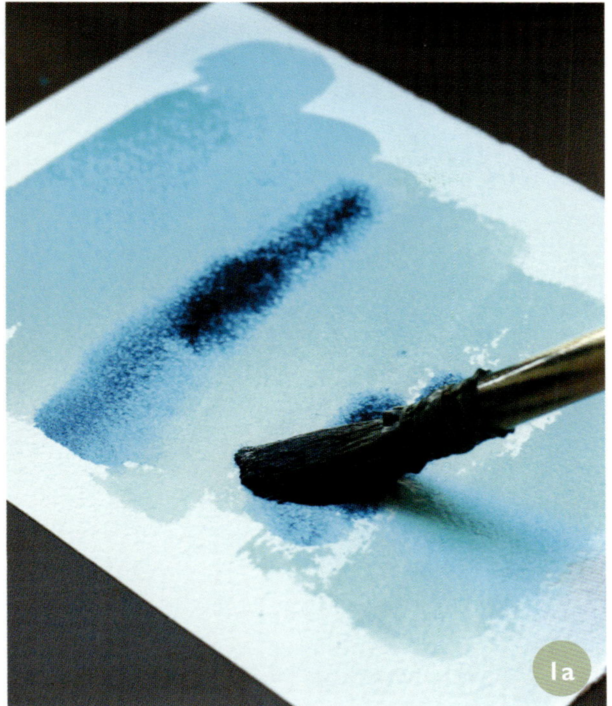

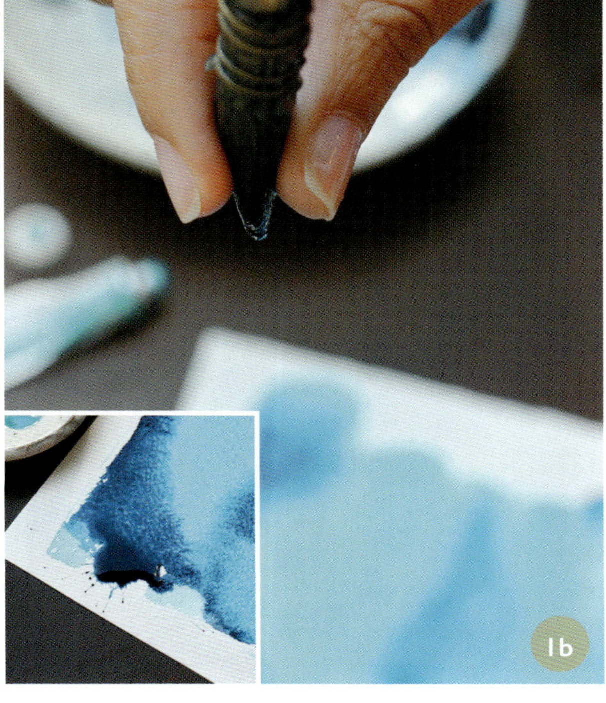

STEP 1. Create the background, which will be a mixture of indigo and turquoise.

Start by wetting the entire surface of the paper slightly to achieve a glossy surface. I like to leave the edges of the paper dry for ease of holding the paper should I need to move it and also because it gives the painting a looser vibe. Now, with the soft round brush No. 6 you will distribute the turquoise paint on the wet/glossy surface in long horizontal and quick brushstrokes on the entire paper. It is okay to leave some white spaces. While the turquoise layer is still wet, add a few horizontal stripes of a dark value indigo in random spots, also in a horizontal movement. This difference in hue will give the impression of depth in the water. If there are any puddles of paint or water at the edges, simply absorb them with a napkin or paper towel by gently touching the puddle with the edge of the napkin.

Note: Please notice that I am neither taping nor caring about the edges of the paper. The more loosely you work, the more relaxing and enjoyable the painting experience will be.

To emphasize the relaxed approach of the composition, hold your soft brush, which is already loaded with indigo, in a vertical position about 6 to 8 inches (15 to 20 cm) away from the paper and squeeze the pigment out of it to make a splash on one or two edges of the paper.

Take a moment to simply watch how the turquoise and the indigo blend and how the pigment gently moves and settles into the paper. I absolutely love watching watercolor dry and get lost in the movement of the pigment. I hope you do this as well.

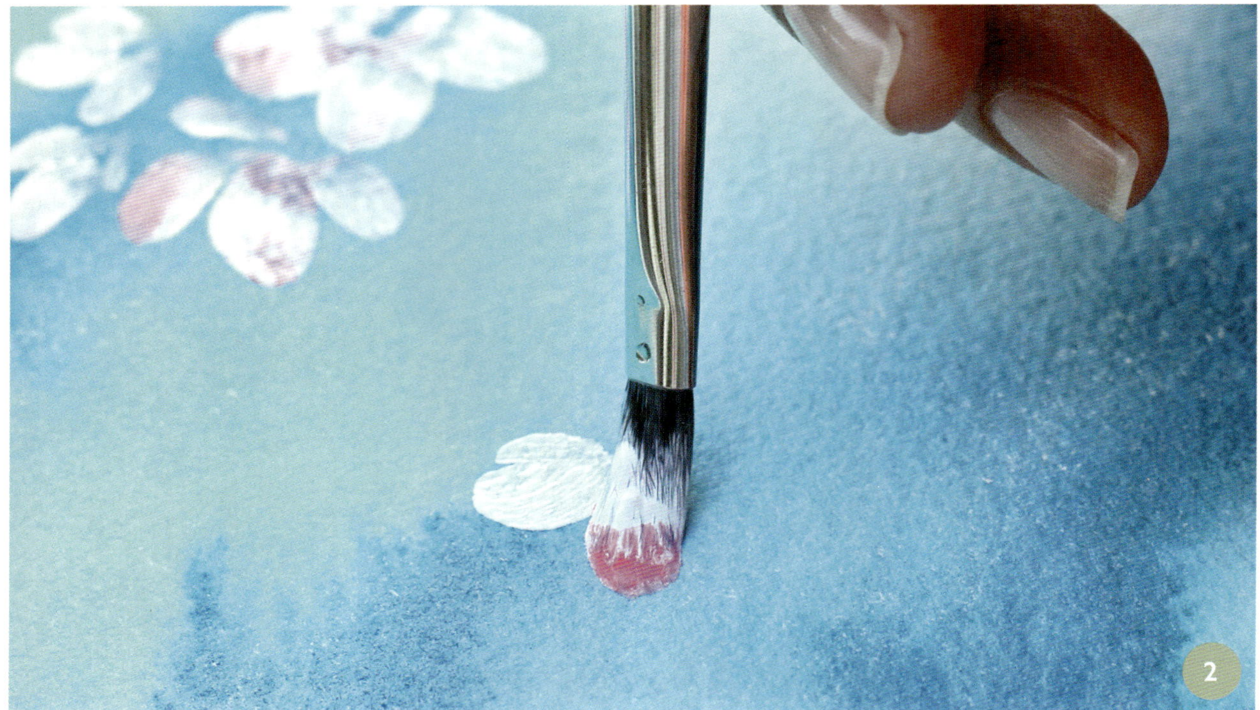

STEP 2. Add the flowers and a few random petals that have fallen in the water.

While you wait for the background to dry, on a small saucer, dilute some of the Acrylic White Titanium paint with water roughly at a 1:4 ratio, just enough to make it soft and flowy. Also make sure you have a dark value of Opera Pink ready. Load up your filbert brush No. 4 with the soft white acrylic and only touch the Opera Pink with the very tip of the brush. Start painting the petals with the flat part of the brush and a push and drag brush motion toward an imaginary center. Remember that the open flowers have five petals and Sakura grow in small groups—kind of like small pom-poms—so try to gather four or five flowers in one spot. To give the impression that some petals have fallen in the water, paint some loose petals in random places, maybe toward the edges of the paper.

While you paint your Sakura petals, take a moment to focus on the gorgeous blending between the Opera Pink at the edge of the brush and the white acrylic from the belly of the brush. This effect brings me so much peace because the colors just flow together so beautifully and effortlessly. Watching the petals become small flowers is somewhat magical.

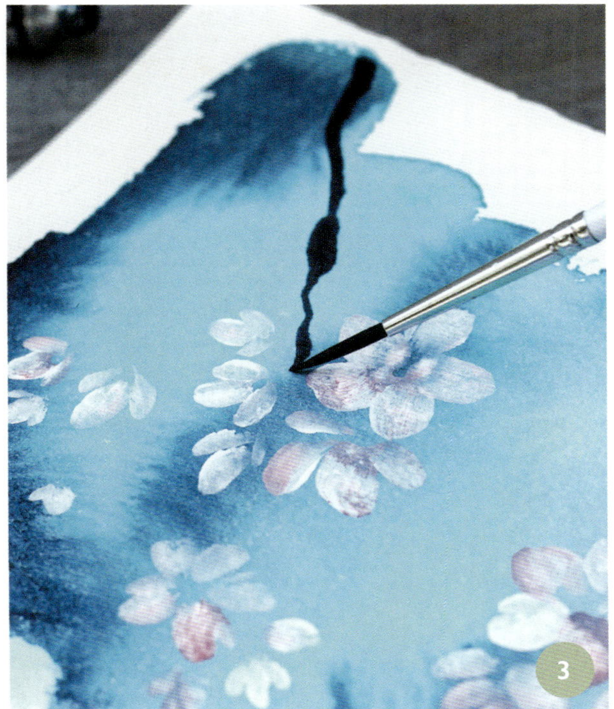

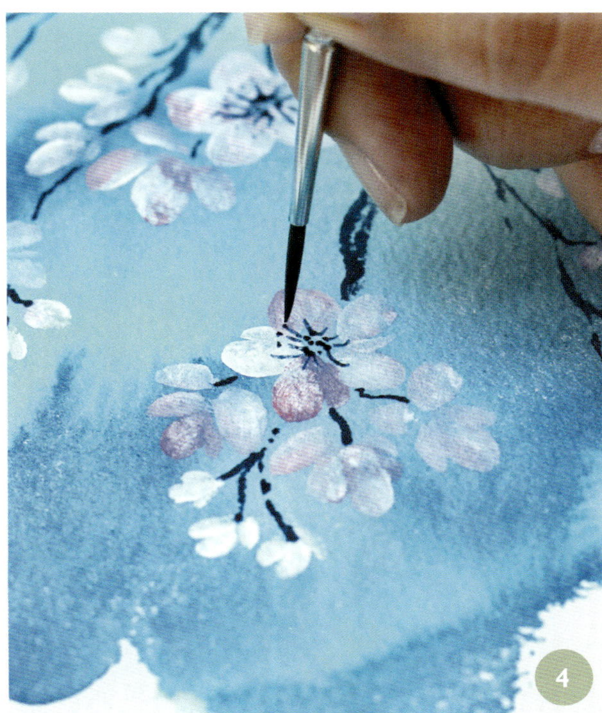

STEP 3. Add the branches that connect all your gorgeous little flowers together and put together the entire composition.

After waiting a minute or two for your flowers to dry, use the synthetic round brush No. 1 and load it up with a dark value indigo to start painting the branches from which the flowers grow. Start painting a wiggly line from the upper left corner downward toward where the flowers are and try to connect them using the tip of your brush, especially the buds. The wigglier the line, the better. Remember to not connect the branches with the petals that are "floating" in the water.

STEP 4. Paint the stamen of the flowers. Using the same brush and the same indigo, softly paint small, curved lines starting at the center of the flowers, moving outward and adding a few dots at the end of each line.

Once everything has dried, take a moment to appreciate the soft and simple shapes of the flowers and assess your calm and relaxed mood as you look at your gorgeous flowers.

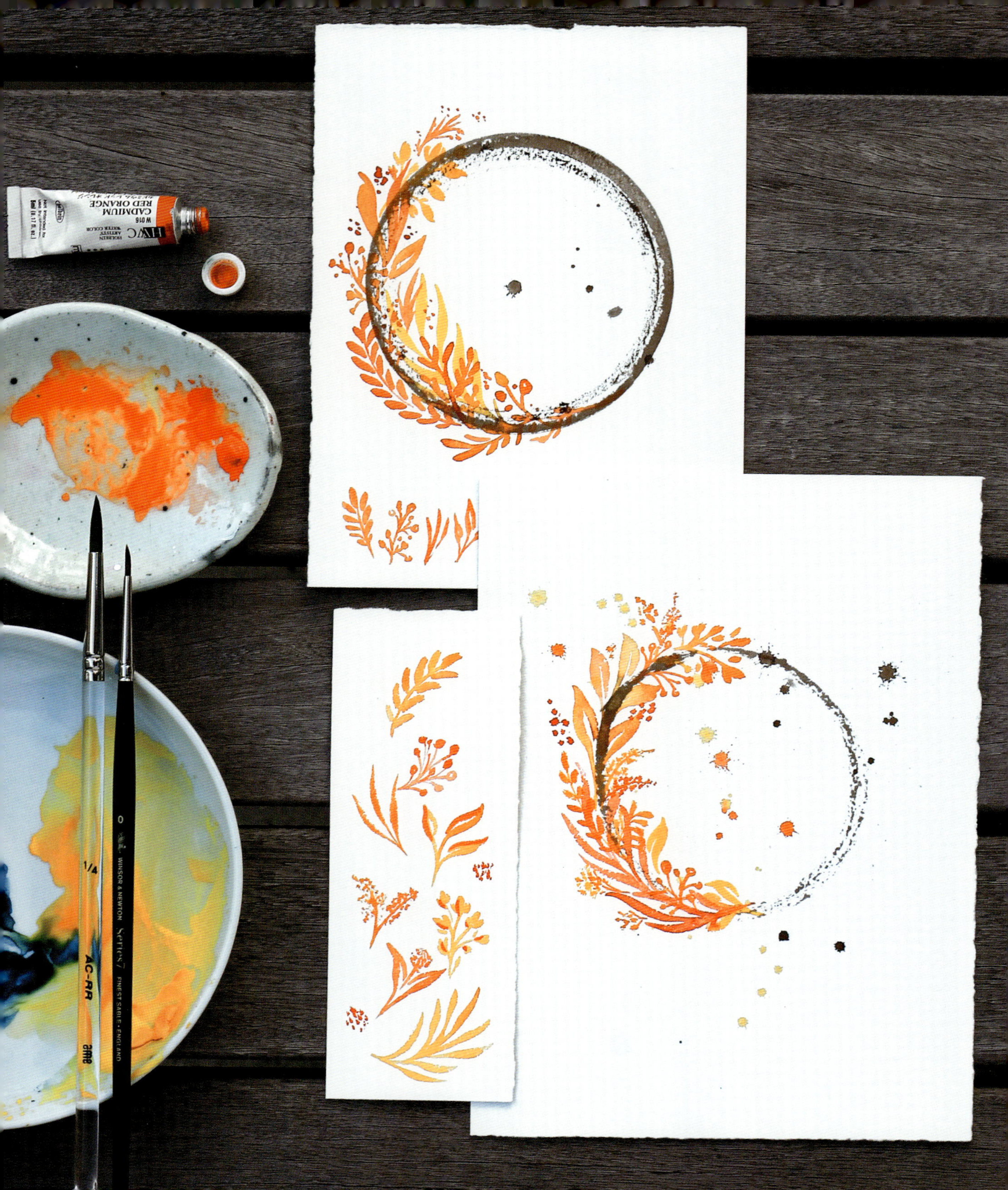
HWC
CADMIUM RED ORANGE
WINSOR & NEWTON
Series 7
FINEST SABLE · ENGLAND
AC-RR

Loose Autumn Wreath

This next project is perfect for finding your flow, as you can paint almost abstractly and will not have to worry about anything looking perfect or creating a perfect representation of nature. The fact that you will be using only three colors frees you up to the endless possibilities of flower or leaf shapes. You will indeed practice some of the soft, gentle leaves from the first project and the long movements of the palm leaves of the second project, but on a much smaller scale.

Materials

- Brown
- Cadmium Yellow
- Cadmium Red-Orange
- Synthetic round brush No. 0

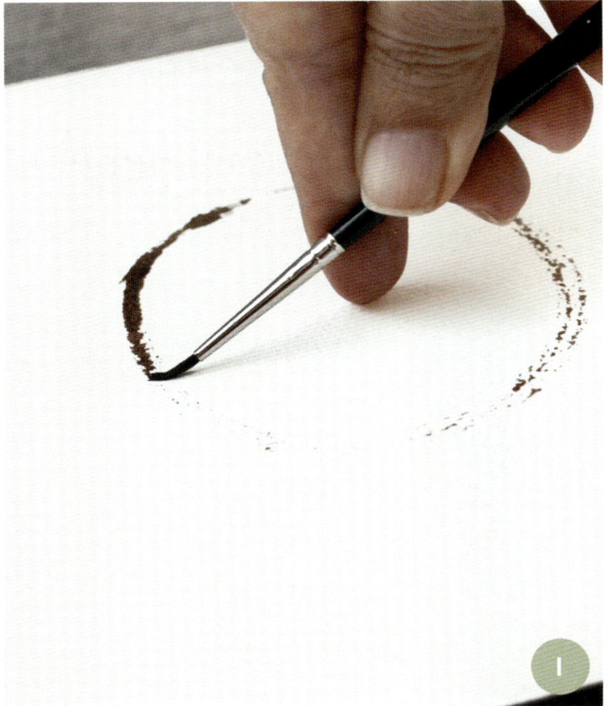

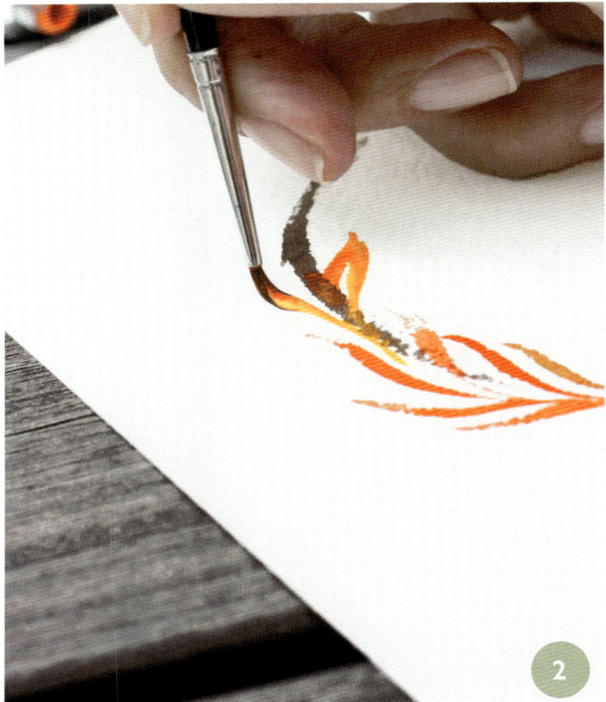

STEP 1. This first step is very relaxing and freeing as there is absolutely no need to create a perfect circle. Starting with your paper completely dry, load up your brush No. 0 with a dark value brown (remember that a 1:1 ratio of indigo and orange make brown), hold it as shown in the picture and move the paper to create the circular shape. You might want to do this a couple of times to create the illusion that there is more than one branch from which the leaves will grow. Painting these loose circular shapes is a very relaxing exercise in itself, and I hope you enjoy this process.

Note: The technique in the first step is called the dry brush technique and it is used when you want to create texture with minimal effort, making your brush do most of the work for you.

STEP 2. Paint loose leaves that grow from the circular branches as a base layer.

Once the circular shapes are dry, go ahead and clean the brush completely and then load it with a dark value Cadmium Yellow. Dipping only the tip of the brush in the Cadmium Red-Orange, start painting the first soft leaves with a gentle push, drag and lift motion that grows outward from the circular branch.

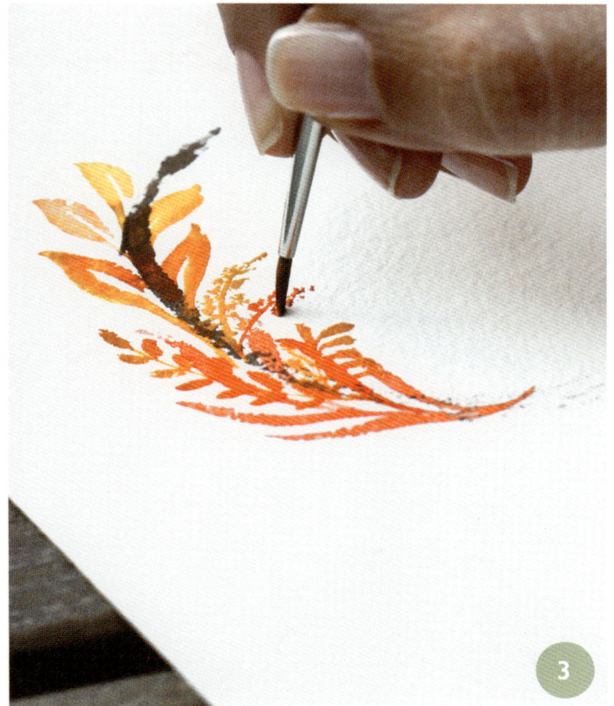

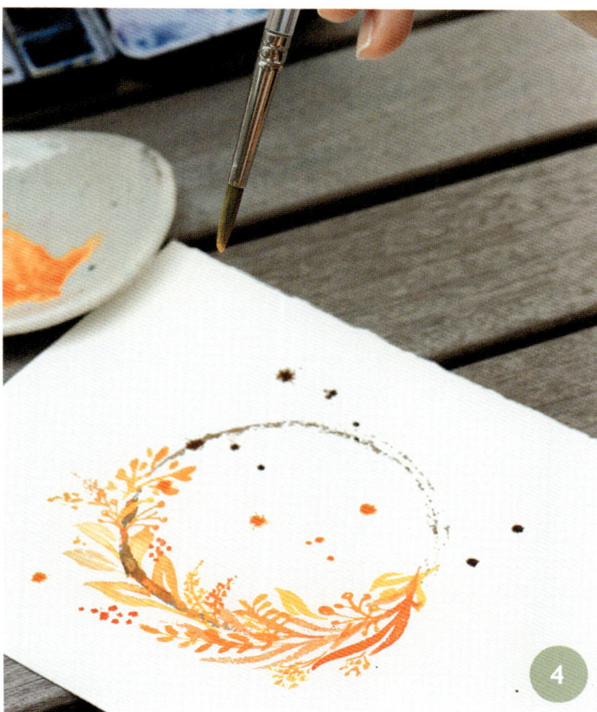

STEP 3. Paint all the abstract flowers to your heart's content. You might want to practice on a scrap piece of paper until you get comfortable with the abstract shapes.

Painting four or five small round shapes next to each other with a stem creates an abstract flower; painting a single, long, curved and thin brushstroke with stippled dots at the end will create an abstract version of baby's breath; and making little oval shapes joined by a single stem will create filler leaves. You might want to make some a little more orange and some a little more yellow to add variety. You can also overlap them once you see some of the previous leaves have dried. Once you feel comfortable with your leaves and flower shapes, go ahead and paint them around the circle.

STEP 4. As a final touch of energy, you can splatter some Cadmium Yellow and Cadmium Red-Orange paint onto the paper. Loading your brush first with a dark value Cadmium Red-Orange, do a first layer of splatter by gently taping it with another brush about 8 inches (20 cm) away from the paper. Clean your brush, load it with a dark value Cadmium Yellow and repeat step 4 to create the second layer of splatter.

Learning this new technique of painting circular shapes with a dry brush technique gives you the satisfaction that you are learning new things every day as well as making great progress in your watercolor journey. I hope painting this lovely wreath was a very relaxing and quick project for you.

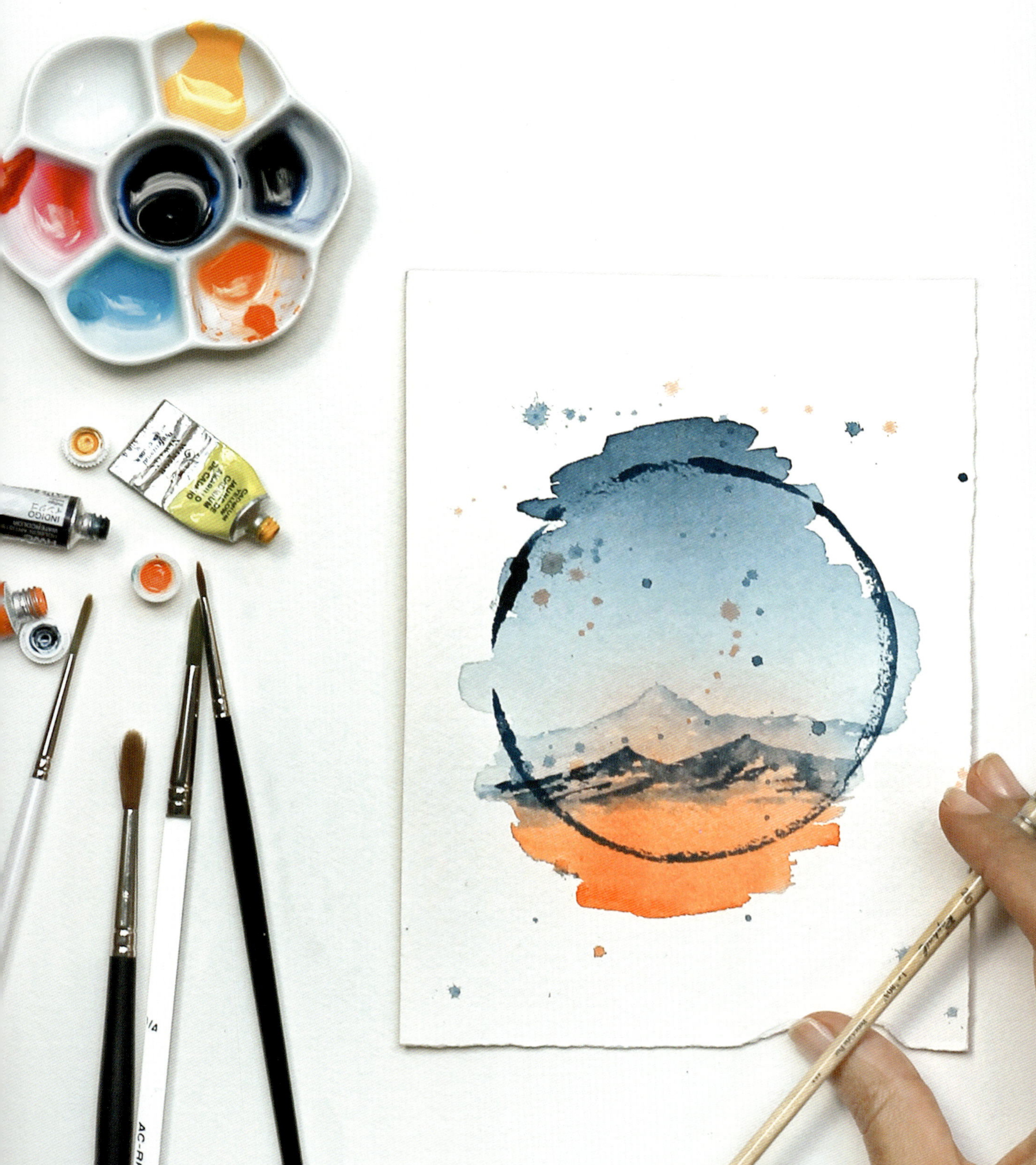
INDIGO
AC-RR

Magical Landscapes

I tend to travel to places that induce a sense of peace and calm. Don't get me wrong, I love big metropolitan cities, but within those places I also find myself searching for the parks, botanical gardens or a peaceful skyline. I have been fortunate enough to have lived in and traveled to many places. Some of my favorite places to paint and get lost in are the rainy or foggy mountains of the north of China, relaxing beach landscapes that remind me of the warm sea breeze of the Maldives or the lush forest landscapes of Japan. All of these places allow me to focus on and appreciate the present moment, and painting them guides me to a meditative state of mind as I watch the paint slowly flow, blend and create textures or get lost in the smaller details.

In this chapter I will take you to some of my favorite places, and I hope to transmit the feeling that I once experienced in these fabulous locations.

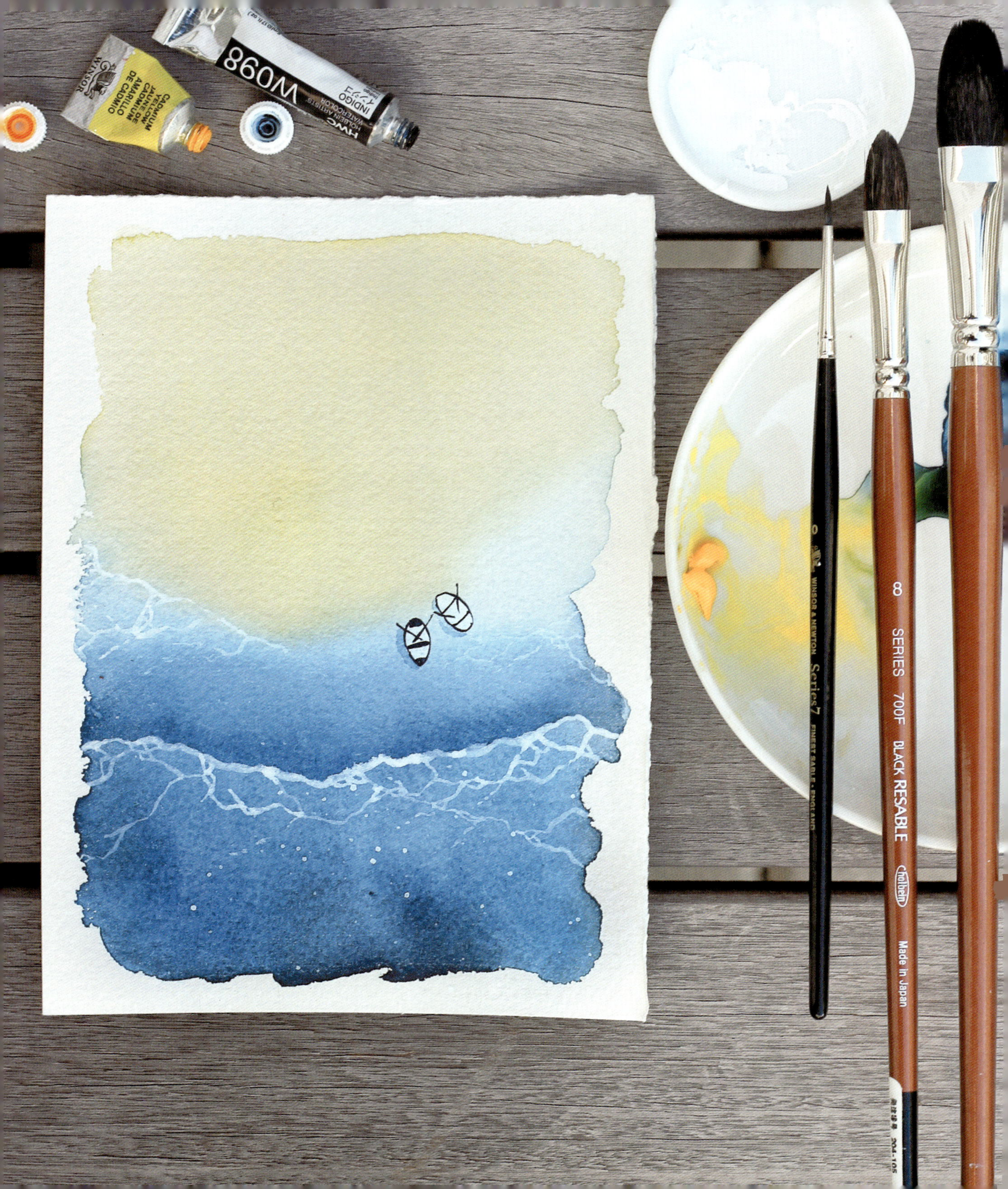

W098
INDIGO
HWC
HOLBEIN ARTISTS' WATERCOLOR
WINSOR
CADMIUM YELLOW
AMARILLO CADMIUM
DE CADMIO
WINSOR & NEWTON
Series 7
8
SERIES 700F
BLACK RESABLE
holbein
Made in Japan

Relaxing Day at the Beach

There is nothing more relaxing than grabbing your favorite new novel, finding a quiet spot at your favorite beach and reading with ocean sounds as your background music. By far, one of the most peaceful and relaxing places I have ever visited was the Maldives, specifically the island of Iru Fushi in the Noonu Atoll. The fact that you have to take a seaplane to get to this remote small island really emphasizes the fact that you are in the middle of the Indian Ocean far away from any civilization. This sense of separation has been one of the most freeing and peaceful moments of my life. Now, channel that happy, warm and cozy place in your mind and take a slow, deep breath in and a slow, deep breath out, put on some ocean wave sounds and let the paint flow.

Materials

- Indigo
- Cadmium Yellow
- Acrylic White Titanium (1:2 water ratio)
- Large soft filbert brush No. 12
- Synthetic round brush No. 0

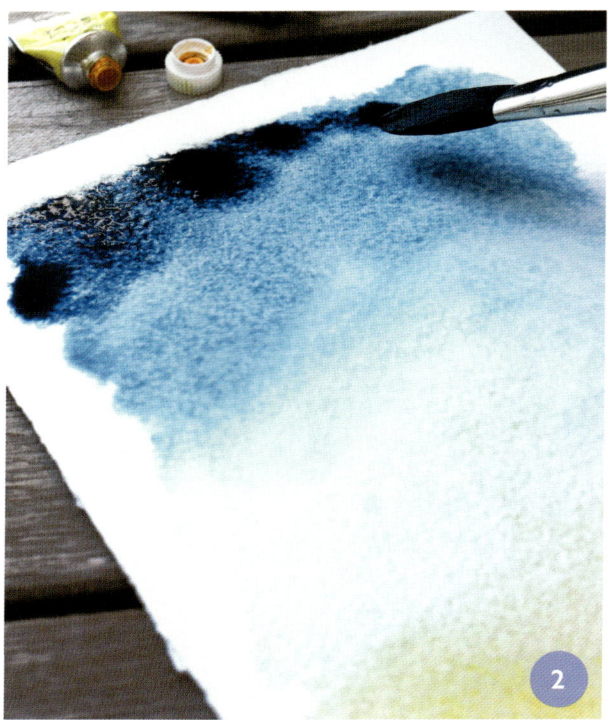

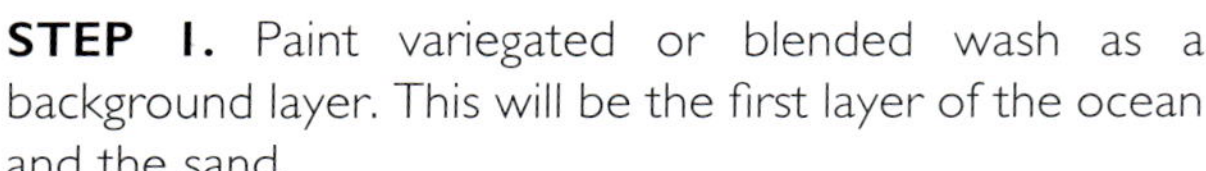

STEP 1. Paint variegated or blended wash as a background layer. This will be the first layer of the ocean and the sand.

Working with a wet-on-wet technique, you will very lightly wet the entire paper with clean water until it has a sheen on the surface. If any small puddles form, remove them by gently touching them with the edge of a paper towel.

With your soft filbert brush No. 12, dab some dark value indigo at the top edge of the paper, tilt the paper vertically slightly and let the pigment flow downward to about the middle of the page. Take a minute to watch the pigment flow and move around the paper. It almost feels like the soft waves of the calm ocean coming in and out, just gently touching the surface of the sand.

With the paper still wet, clean your brush and now use the Cadmium Yellow to repeat the previous step, but from the other side of the paper, creating the sand layer of your composition.

STEP 2. Add depth to your background.

With the paper still wet, dab a little bit more indigo to the indigo section of the painting to add depth to the ocean. Move the paper around just a little bit and let it dry completely.

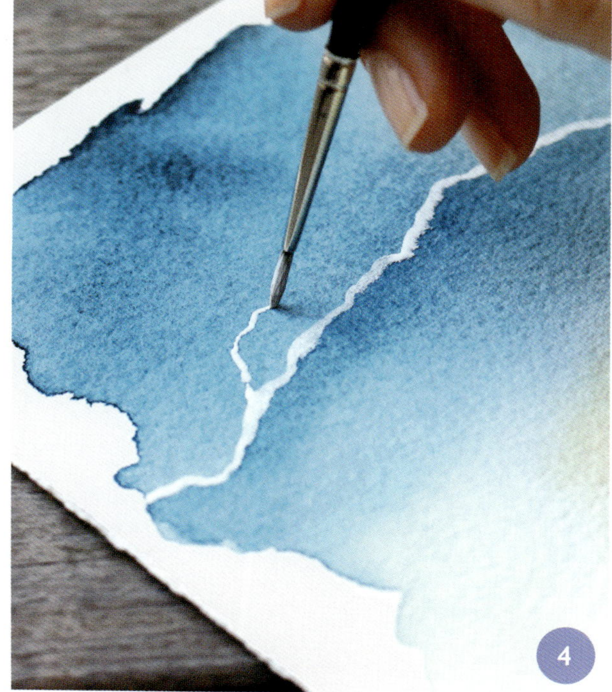

STEP 3. Add variation to the depth of the ocean by working with the wet-on-dry technique.

With the paper now completely dry and with your soft filbert brush loaded with a medium value of indigo, paint a second layer of ocean at about a quarter of the way from the top of the paper down. This will help define the waves coming into the surface of the sand. Gently push the paint toward the yellow, but make sure by the time the indigo reaches the yellow that you have diluted or washed the indigo to a very light value so as to almost disappear into the sand.

STEP 4. Add texture to the ocean surface by adding small waves or sea foam.

Now that the washes are completely dry, using the synthetic round brush No. 0 loaded up with some diluted Acrylic White Titanium, paint a line following the exact edge that you created with the second wash of indigo. Once you have the edge of the wave painted, start making random wiggly lines on the upper side of the edge to create different-sized uneven bubble-like shapes. This gives the impression of the natural soft foam that comes with the waves. You can take the next couple of minutes to relax your mind and let your hand just flow. There are no mistakes to be made—the more random the lines you create, the more organic your wave will appear.

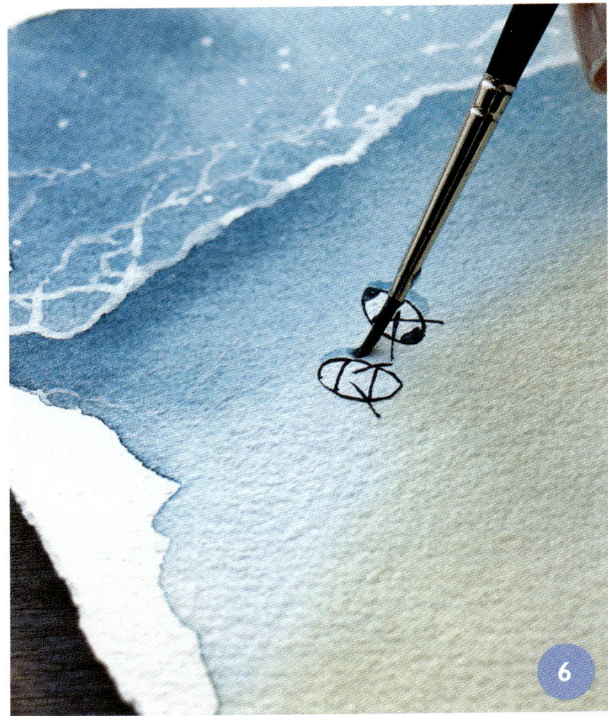

STEP 5. Paint the two little boats that will give your painting that magical feeling of tranquility and peace as if you and your best friend were the only ones on this fabulous secluded beach.

With the small brush No. 0 still loaded up with the Acrylic White Titanium, paint two small oval shapes on the edge of where the sea meets the sand and let them dry. While these shapes are drying, make sure to completely wash the acrylic off your brush as you will be using it to define the edges of the boats in the next step. By all means, have fun with these two little boats and the composition. You can paint kayaks, or maybe just one boat, or you can paint them in fun colors if you have other colors of acrylic or gouache available, or you can even paint some beach towels.

STEP 6. Add just a few more details.

With the small brush No. 0 loaded with a dark value of indigo, softly outline the oval shapes of the boats, draw a few lines in the center as to appear like a little bench, paint a few oars, give the boats a little shade with a light value of indigo and voila! You have the cutest little boats to complete your relaxing beach composition.

Step back, look at your painting and imagine the warm, soft ocean breeze that this painting evokes. I hope that practicing your blending wash and getting lost in the repetitive motion of painting the sea foam brought a sense of calm and mindfulness to your practice.

Calm Ocean Night

People do not often think of Japan as a beach destination, but if you get to visit the Yaeyama Islands of southwestern Japan, you are in for a treat! I had the opportunity to go to the small island of Ishigaki in Okinawa Prefecture, and it was absolute paradise. Its soft, sandy beaches and azure waters were a much-needed and refreshing break from living in a large city like Osaka. Watching the paint flow on this painting will leave you with a sense of calm that only the stillness of the night brings.

Materials

- Indigo
- Acrylic White Titanium (1:4 water ratio)
- Soft round brush No. 8
- Synthetic round brush No. 2

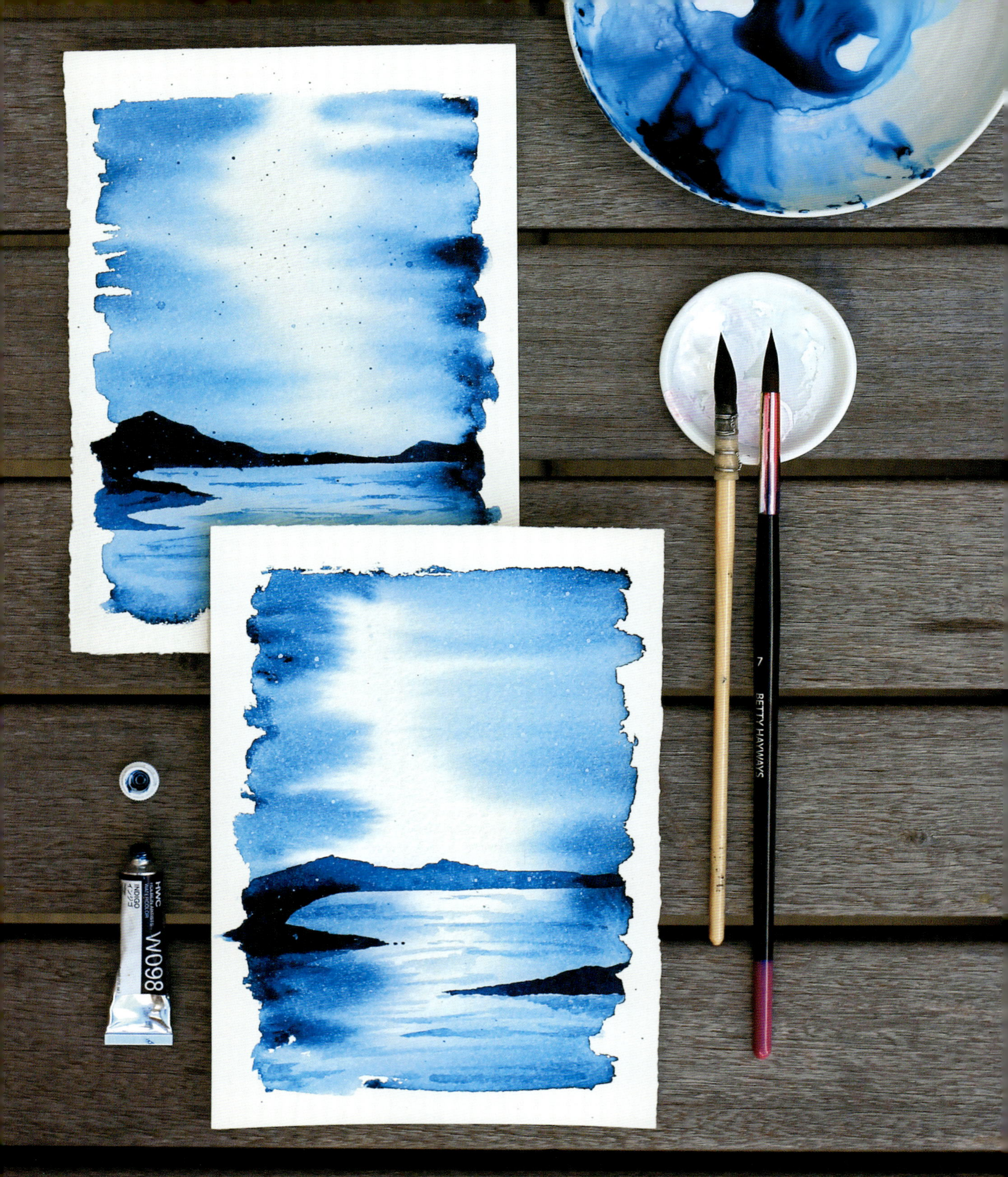
HWC
WATERCOLOR
INDIGO
インジゴ
W098
7
BETTY HAYWAYS

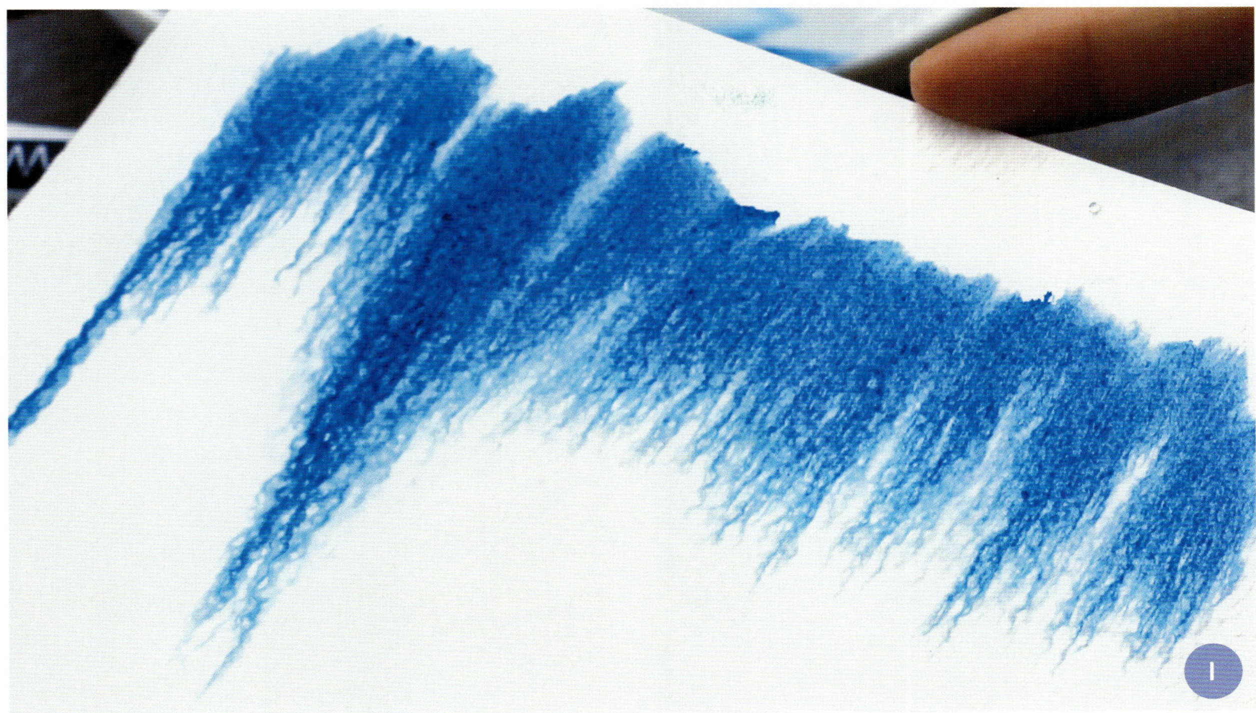

In this project you will practice your wet-on-wet technique as well as wet-on-dry and splatter techniques.

STEP 1. Wet your paper to achieve a glossy surface overall. Leaving about ½ inch (1.25 cm) of dry surface on all edges of the paper will give you a bit of space to hold the paper when you have to move it as well as create a loose compositional approach. Load up your medium soft round brush No. 8 with a dark value of indigo and dab the pigment along the right edge of the wet surface of the paper. Move the paper sideways so the paint slides toward the left side.

Take a moment to appreciate and get lost in the movement of the indigo as it slowly moves across the page. It only takes a few seconds to take a deep breath, watch the paint flow, assess your state of mind and let go of anything that is not serving you at the moment.

Note: Please note that I apply the paint unevenly along the edge of the wet surface to create the illusion of the moonlight in the middle of the paper. Remember that the white of the paper is your source of light.

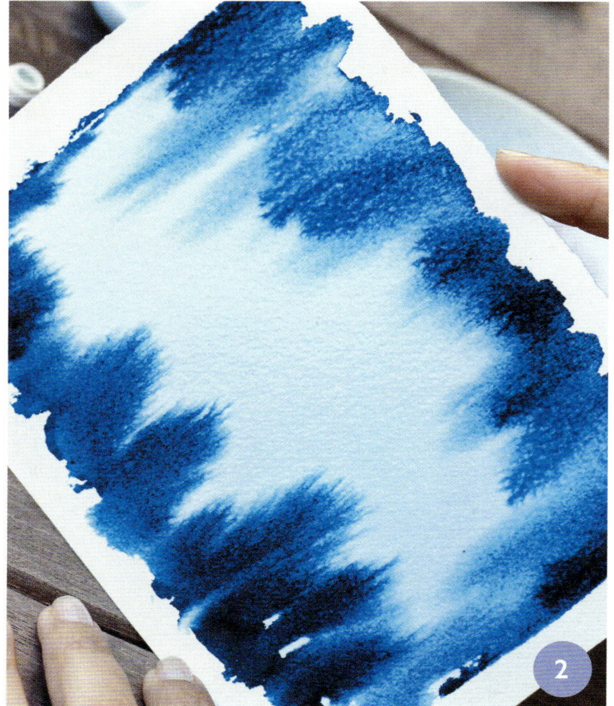

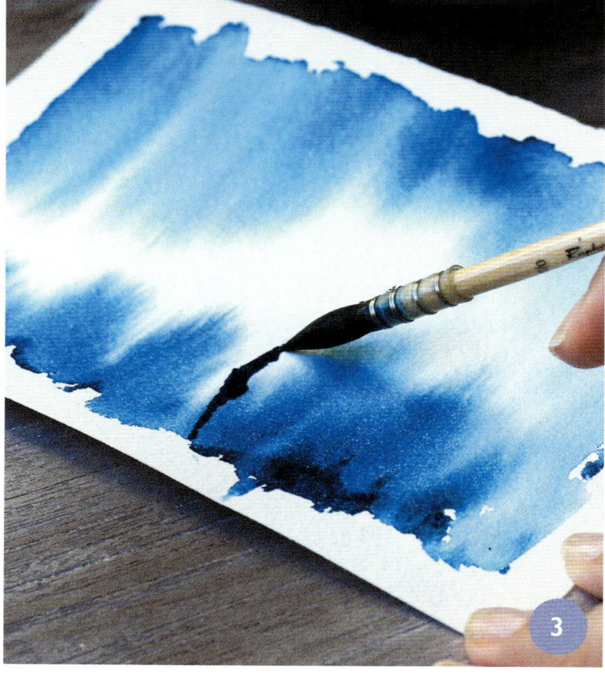

STEP 2. While the surface of the paper is still wet, repeat step 1 but on the other edge of the paper, and keep moving the paper in a horizontal manner, letting the paint flow but not completely mix and cover the entirety of the paper, creating an organic but central light source.

Tip: While the paper is still wet, you can dab a few more spots of dark value indigo along the edges but at different places to add depth to the sky or water surface.

Once you are satisfied with the look of the light source in the middle, let it dry on a flat surface.

STEP 3. Paint the mountains that will break the horizon line and create your landscape.

Load up your medium synthetic round brush No. 2 with a dark value of indigo and start painting a wiggly line all the way across the paper horizontally—this will be the top of your first mountain shape. Make sure you paint a somewhat straight line at the bottom of your mountain to give it a clear separation between mountain and water surface.

Now that your mountain shape is done, you can move on to the fourth step and create the water ripples to give texture to the ocean surface.

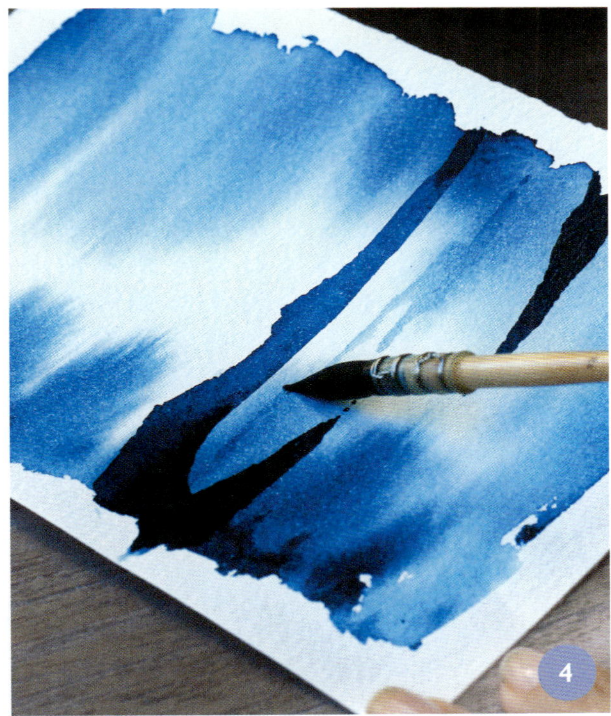

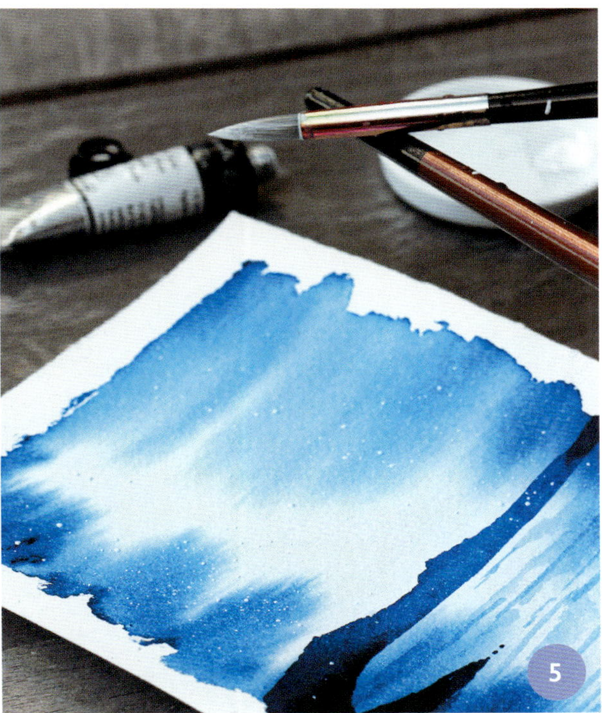

STEP 4. With your soft brush loaded with a very light value of indigo, hold your brush very softly and with horizontal soft brushstrokes paint the ripples in the water. Let it dry for a few minutes and assess the painting. If you feel like you need a few more mountains, go right ahead and add little ones with a dark value of indigo at the bottom of the painting. This gives the painting a little bit more depth.

The fifth and last step of adding stars by sprinkling a diluted Acrylic White Titanium mixture adds a magical touch to your composition.

STEP 5. Load the synthetic brush No. 8 with the Acrylic White Titanium and gently tap it with another brush about 8 inches (20 cm) away from the paper. It is important to first test on a separate piece of paper how much water your brush is holding so as not to splash big droplets onto the painting.

Note: It is important to use a synthetic brush because the bristles will hold the pigment better, and when splashing the pigment on the paper the droplets will be small and consistent. A soft brush will release larger water droplets and they will not look like stars.

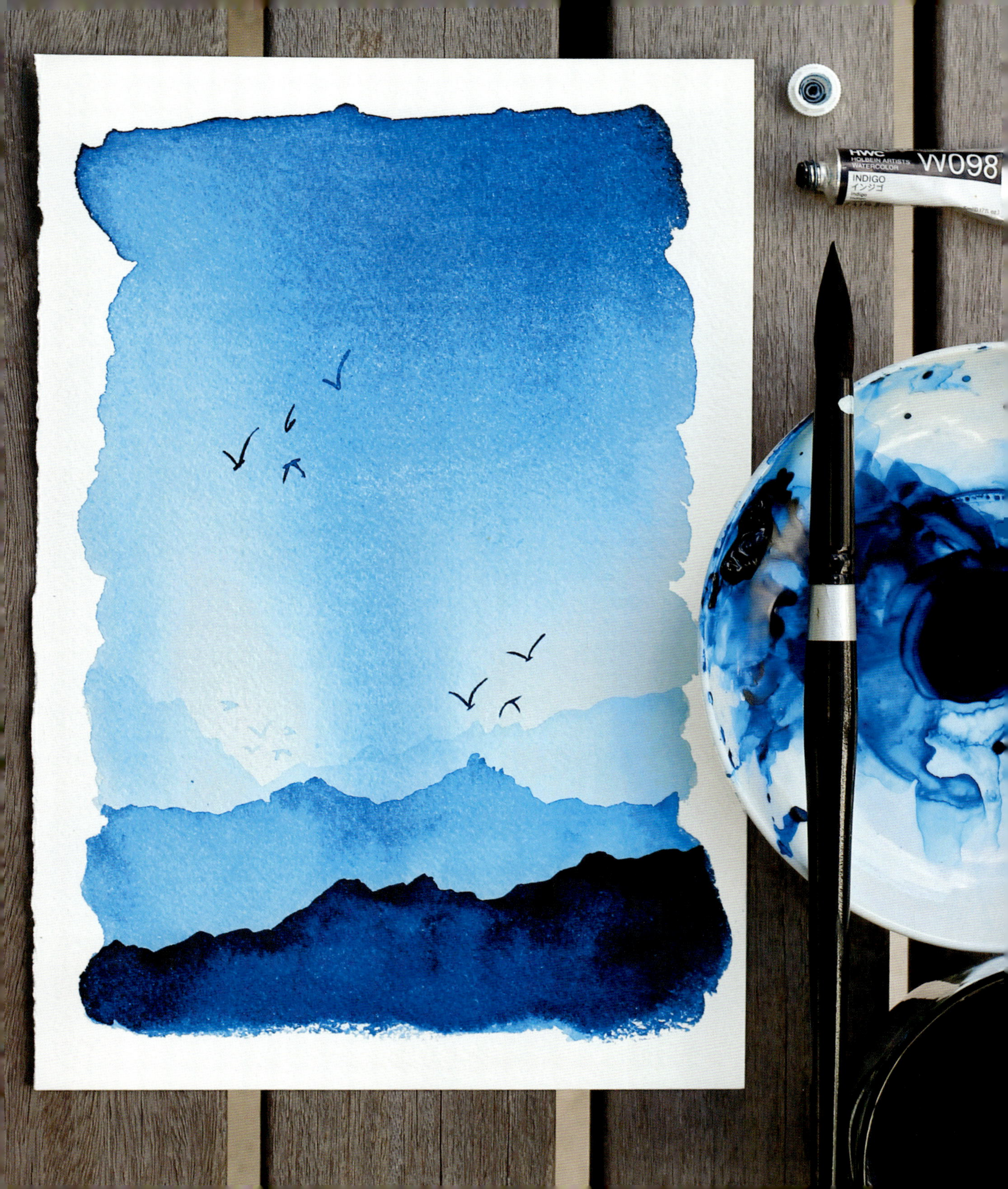
HWC
HOLBEIN ARTISTS' WATERCOLOR
W098
INDIGO
インジゴ

Serene Rainy Mountains

Traveling to Mianshan in central Shanxi Province in the north of China was like transporting myself 2,000 years into the past. Sitting for a few minutes on the balcony of a temple embedded in the mountains and looking out into the glorious mountain range as the fog slowly dissipated was intimate, peaceful and mind blowing all at the same time.

This next project is intended to captivate that moment of stillness and mindfulness you get when staring at the immaculate perfection of nature. One of the most fascinating aspects of a landscape painting is the depth perception that you can capture in a single sheet of paper. The simple concept behind this is to make the objects in the background very soft and airy and little by little increase the value of your pigment to bring the objects to the foreground.

Materials

- Indigo
- Soft round brush No. 10
- Soft round brush No. 4
- Soft round brush No. 1

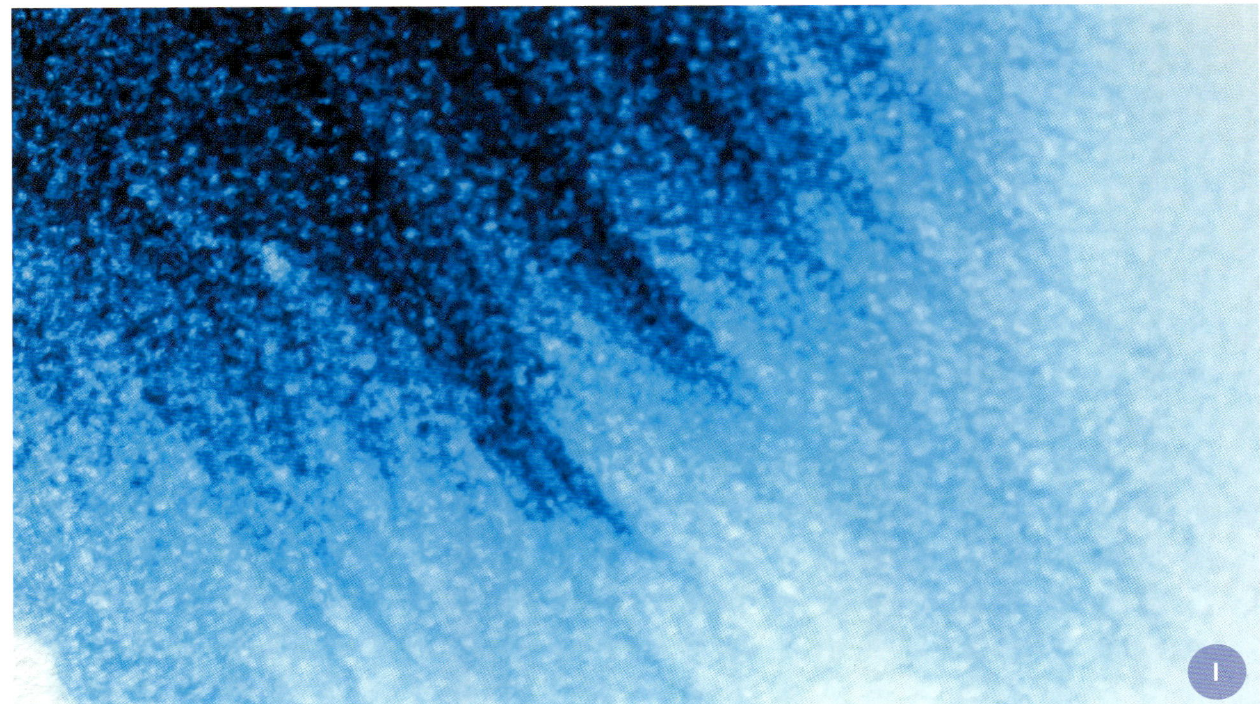

In this project you will practice the wet-on-wet technique as well as further understand the value scales to create a monochromatic composition.

Before you start with the first step, it is important to prepare a dark value of indigo beforehand so the surface of the paper when it is wet does not dry while you prepare the pigment.

STEP 1. Once you have your pigment ready, put it aside for a minute while you wet the entire surface of the paper with water, using your large soft round brush No.10, until it is glossy. While the paper is still wet, with the same soft brush No. 10, add the dark value pigment horizontally to the top of the paper. Move the paper around—primarily vertically—to let the paint travel through the top two-thirds of the paper. This is one of the steps I enjoy the most because there is a very calming sensation when you just watch pigment run on the paper. In order to create a "rainy" atmosphere, make sure to focus more on moving the paper vertically up and down multiple times until you see that the pigment is not traveling anymore and lay it on a flat surface to dry.

Note: One of the reasons why I do not tape the border as a preparation step of my process is because it implies that the painting must be perfect; hence, I will get more stressed out if my painting does not achieve said concept of perfection. Watercolor for me is much more of an approach of letting go of expectations and letting the paint and water do its magical thing. Let it flow and let it go.

STEP 2. Once the paper is completely dry, you will start painting the mountain that is farthest away in the distance. This is a perfect use for the wet-on-dry technique, and you will be working from light to dark to create atmosphere.

To make the mountain seem far away, it will be very light in value. For this step you will need a separate clean plate to water down your pigment until it is a very light value. Use the same value pigment you mixed for the first step, but on a separate plate add the pigment and lots of water. This will create a very soft, light value indigo. Load up your medium soft round brush No. 4 with this light value indigo and paint a wiggly line across the paper at about one-third the distance from the bottom, then drag the paint softly toward the bottom of the page. This will create a soft mountain that almost disappears in the fog.

Note: This step can be tricky because we have a tendency to want to create a perfect mountain. You may think "a wiggly line is not a mountain." Well, in this step I practice very much the idea of letting go of any ideas of what a "mountain" should look like. A wiggly line will be just perfect.

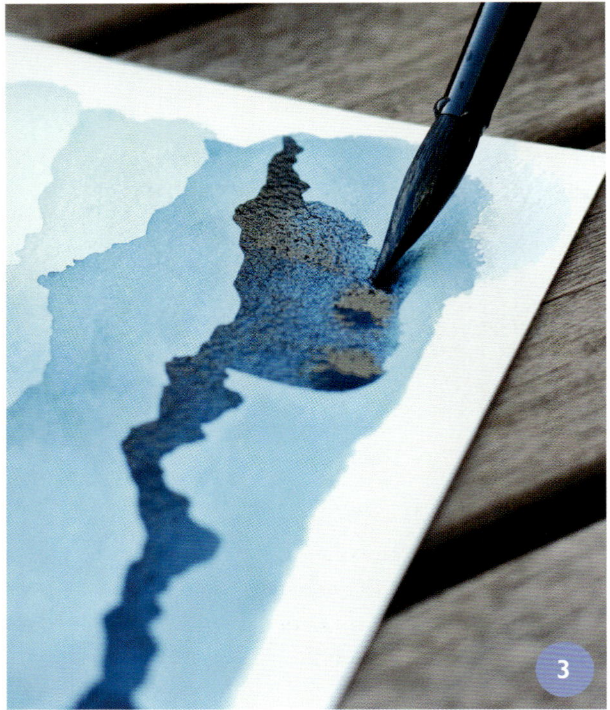

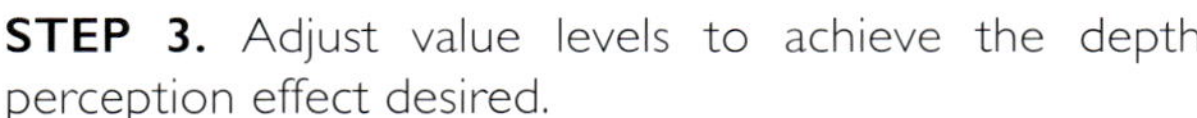

STEP 3. Adjust value levels to achieve the depth perception effect desired.

Let the first mountain completely dry. Add a bit more pigment to your plate with the light value indigo to achieve a medium value indigo and start painting the second mountain using the same brush. You can start from the opposite end and move a little up and down to create variation in the mountain range. Last, add yet another dab of pure pigment to your pigment plate and try to get the darkest value indigo you can, but make sure the paint still flows nicely. Add a third mountain with said dark value indigo. You can repeat these steps as many times as you like to create a richer landscape.

STEP 4. Add the details and oh boy! This last step just brings the composition together so magically!

Nothing better than a few little birds flying in the vastness of the great mountain ranges that Mother Nature does so majestically.

You will be practicing the same concept of aerial perspective where the birds farthest away will be small and painted with the lightest value of indigo and the ones closer to you will be a little bit bigger and painted with the dark value indigo. Using your detail soft round brush No. 1 start painting "V" shapes with a slight curve to them all over the sky. I like to paint the birds in groups of three or four because birds usually fly in flocks. Adding these little birds makes your composition look like actual animals live in this wonderful misty forest you just painted.

I really hope you found yourself lost in the process of letting water and pigment do its magical dance. Remember to not attach yourself to any preconceived idea of what this should have been but rather enjoy the masterpiece you just created.

Sunset View in the City

One of my favorite things to do when I get home after a long day at work is to make myself some tea, get in my comfy sweatpants, go to my balcony and watch the world slowly wind down with me. The sun slowly setting behind the mountains and tall buildings creates a wonderful array of vibrant colors in the sky as the lights of the buildings one by one start to illuminate the skyline. I could sit there for hours and imagine the people getting home to their families or watch the ones jogging alongside the river to get their daily exercise.

In this project, I invite you to create a vibrant yet serene sunset view of the city of your choice.

Materials

- Cadmium Yellow
- Cadmium Red-Orange
- Dark purple
- Indigo
- Synthetic square brush No. 8
- Synthetic angle brush No. 2

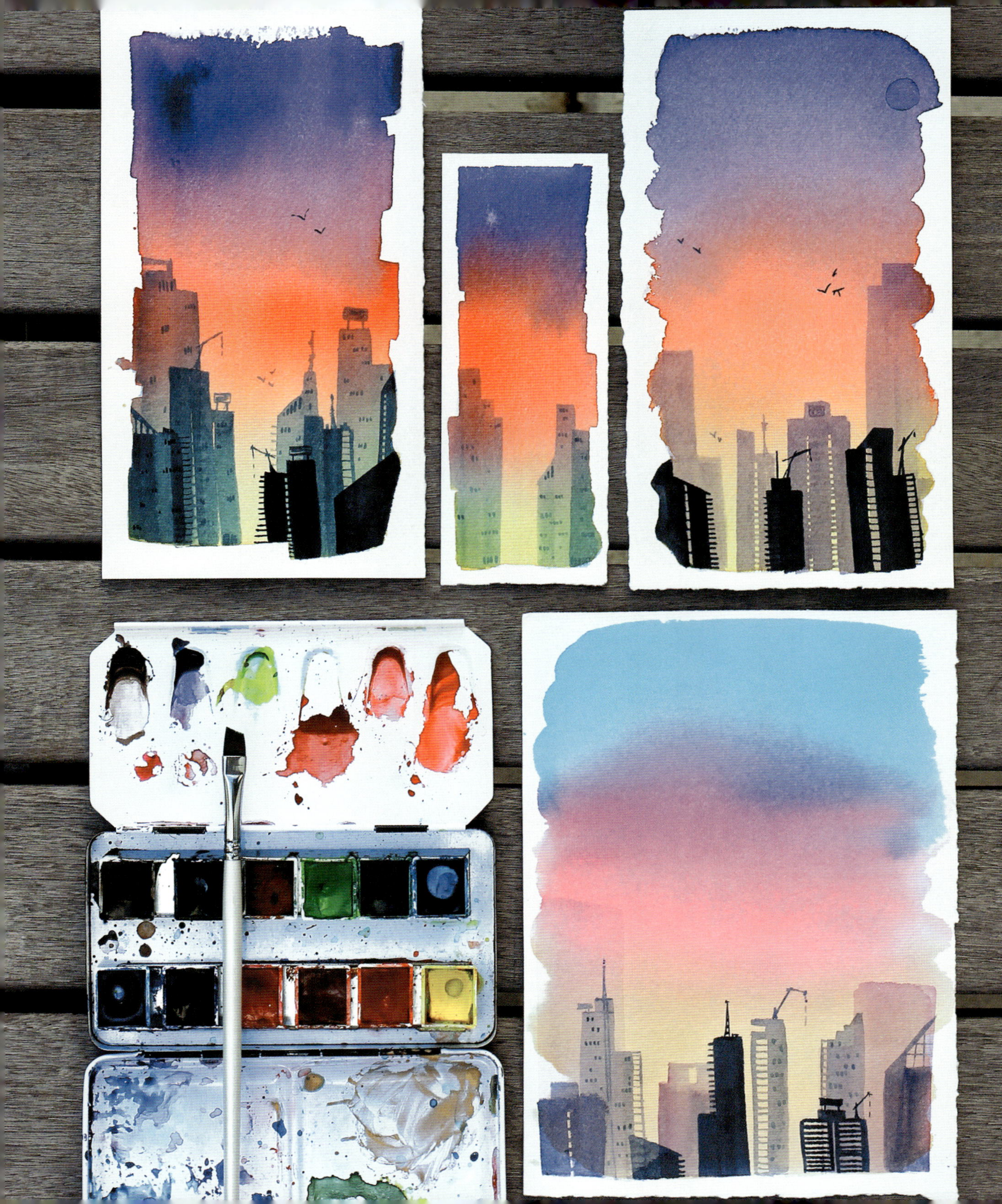

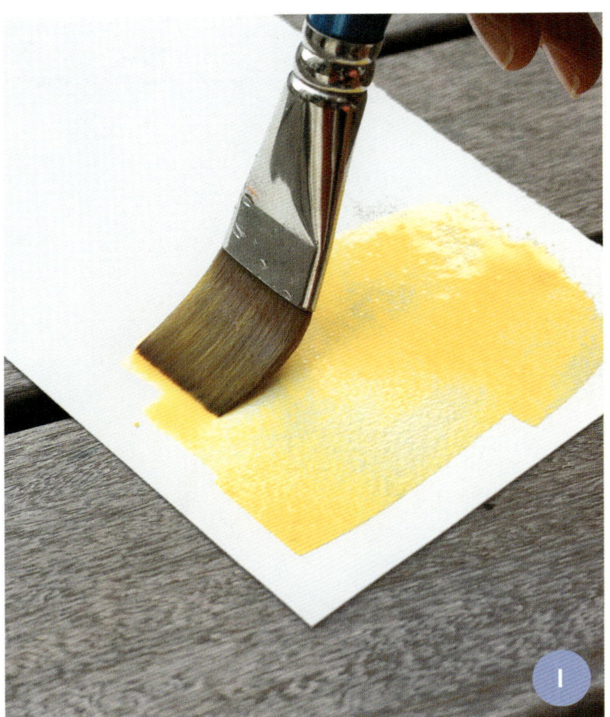

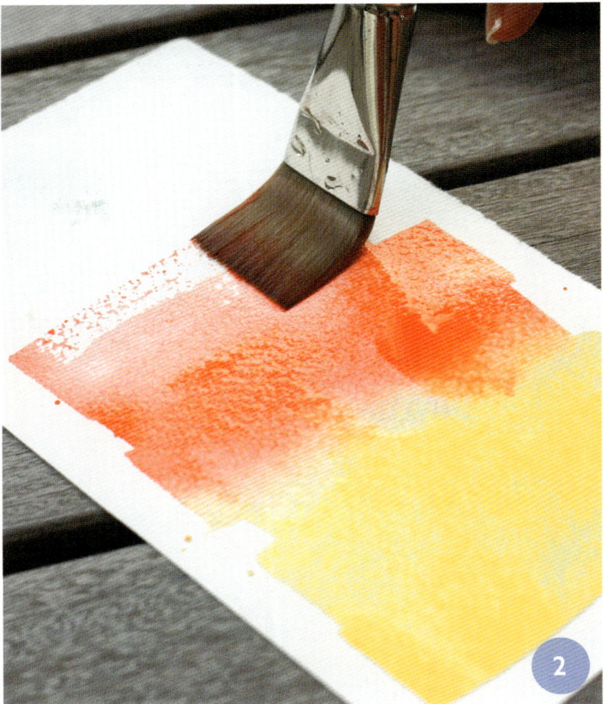

Note: Painting this composition vertically will give more space to the sky and still have room for layers of tall buildings.

Working with a wet-on-dry technique will allow the intensity of the pigments to stay vibrant and not look devalued and muted. Always remember that watercolor dries lighter than when you apply it on the paper. For this project it is also very important to have a small amount of diluted pigment ready to allow for better blendability between colors.

Painting the three-color wash of the sky is a three-step process, but it is very relaxing as you watch the pigments blend seamlessly and softly. Get lost in the flow of the colors and then watch the paint slowly settle.

STEP 1. Start painting the sky from the bottom up with a dark value of Cadmium Yellow. With your paper completely dry, use the large synthetic square brush to paint the bottom third of the paper with this vibrant color in horizontal brushstrokes.

STEP 2. Wash your brush in clean water and load it up with your dark value of Cadmium Red-Orange. You will then paint the middle section of the paper and softly blend it with the previously painted yellow section.

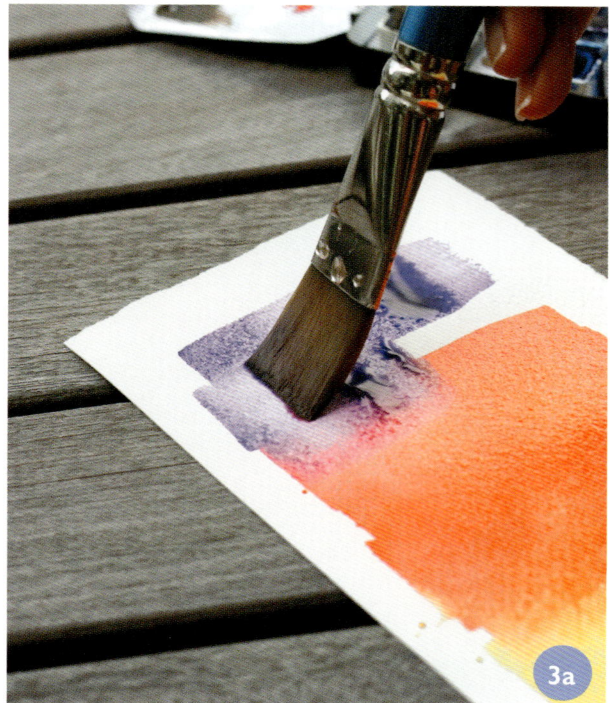

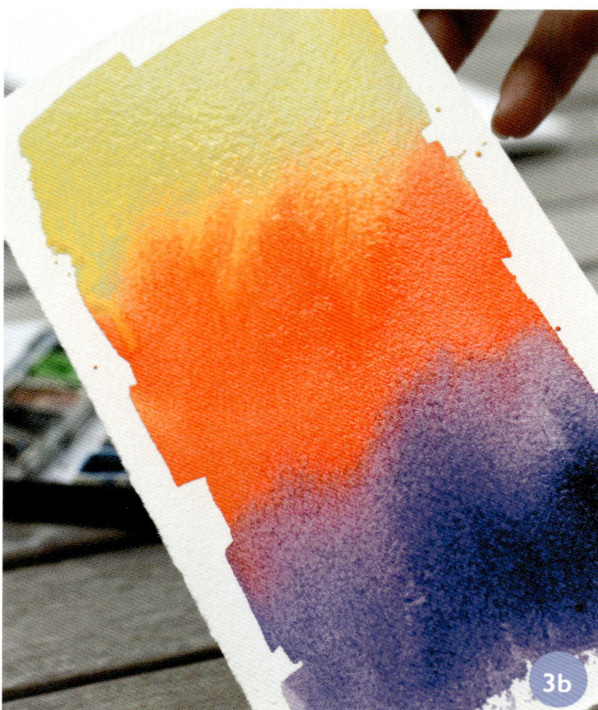

STEP 3. Again, clean your square brush and then load it with the dark purple. Paint the top section of the paper in the same horizontal brushstrokes and softly blend with the orange section. Just a few blending brushstrokes will do the trick.

To create a smooth transition between colors, move the paper around in horizontal and vertical motions and watch the pigments gently blend with one another. Do not try to blend it too much or the colors will become muddy. Once you are satisfied with the gentle blend of colors, let it dry completely. Leaving the paper to dry naturally on a flat surface will allow the pigment to settle and finish blending on its own.

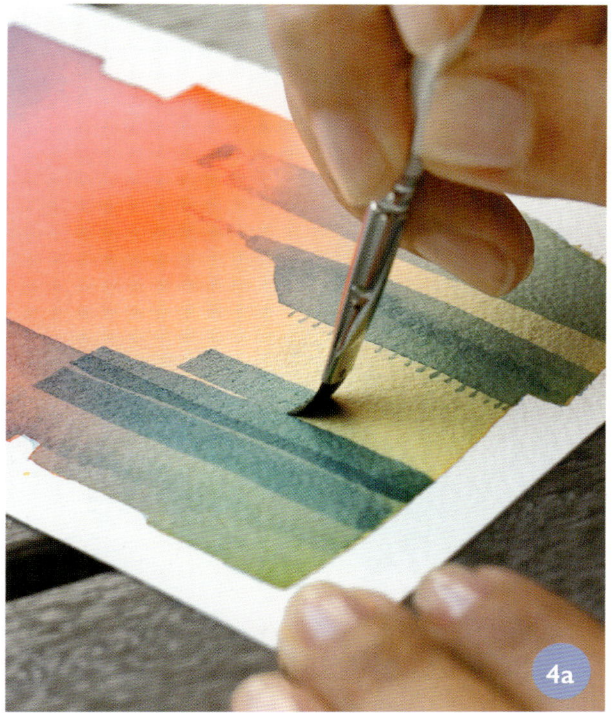

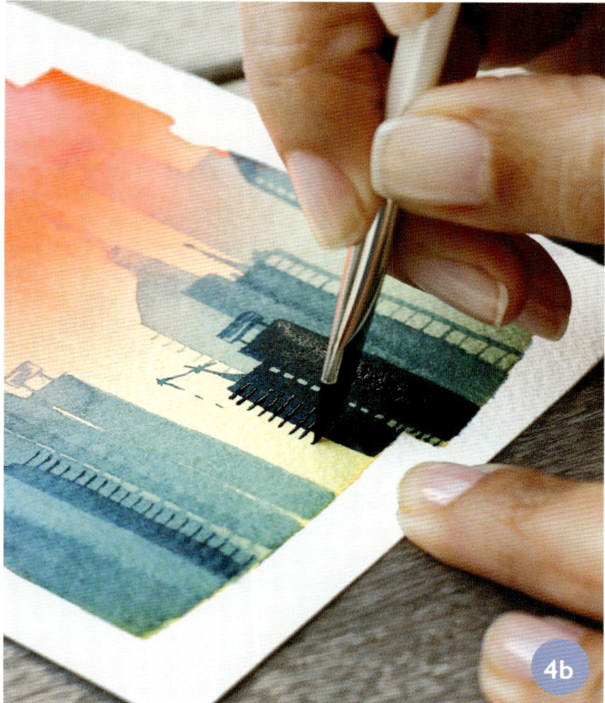

STEP 4. Next is painting the skyline. This step will be done in three layers starting with the lightest layer in the back and gradually moving toward a darker value layer in the front.

Using a very light value of indigo and the small synthetic angle brush, paint long rectangular shapes that resemble buildings. Some can be wider, some can be shorter and some can have angled roofs.

Tip: Leave some spaces between shapes so as to not lose the bottom color of the sky.

Repeat this step two more times, each time adding a bit more pigment to your indigo mix. Always remember to let each layer dry completely.

Now, to make these shapes really look like actual buildings, you have to paint balconies, terraces, windows and even some construction cranes if you like, but not to worry—there's no need to be an architectural genius to achieve this. You are just giving the impression and feel of life to your painting. The simpler the shapes the better.

This step can be very relaxing because its repetitive nature can be an instrument for five minutes of focus and meditation while you paint.

Using the flat part of the angle brush to paint the balconies helps with steadiness and consistency.

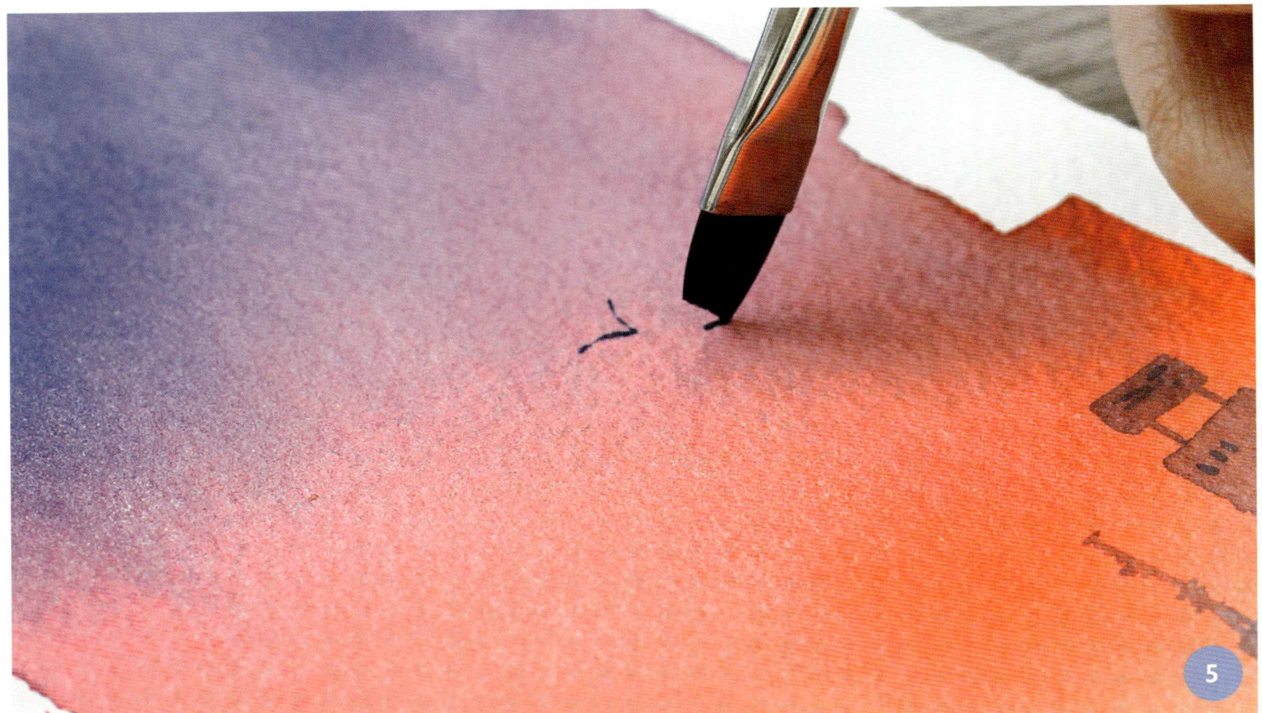

STEP 5. Add the energy of a few birds and the impression that some windows are beginning to light up. Using the very tip of the brush, dab a few small lines in the background building shapes to give the impression of windows. Last, paint some birds in the sky by lightly painting small "V" curved shapes in the sky.

Add as many details as you like and get lost in this beautiful city sunset view that you just created.

Getting Lost in the Forest

As a creative person it is very important for me to stay connected to nature, and one of the most memorable experiences of my life was hiking eight hours from the base of Mt. Fuji to Base No. 5 with my nephew. Getting lost in the forest was such a magical experience that I wanted to capture this feeling of true connection with nature in this painting.

In this project, you will create a magical landscape in which you too can get lost and find a sense of coexistence with nature. You will use both wet-on-wet as well as wet-on-dry techniques. You will also focus on botanical details that you have learned in previous exercises such as the Loose Autumn Wreath (page 49) or the washes from Relaxing Day at the Beach (page 55).

Materials

- Cadmium Yellow
- Indigo
- Soft round brush No. 16
- Soft round brush No. 8
- Synthetic round brush No. 1

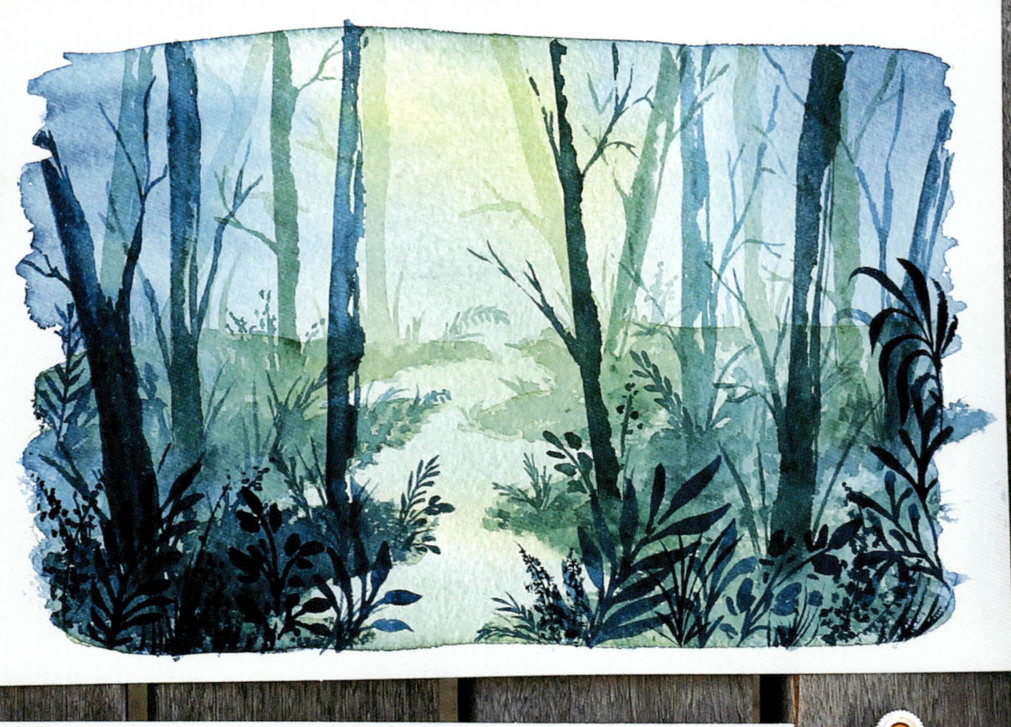

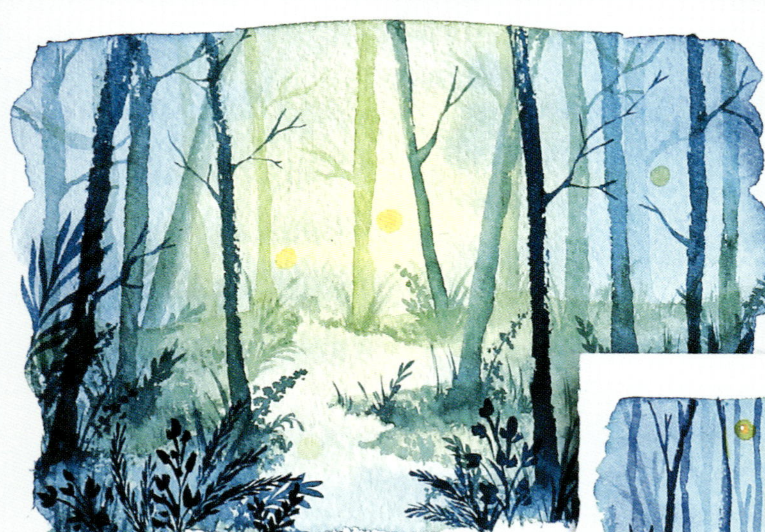

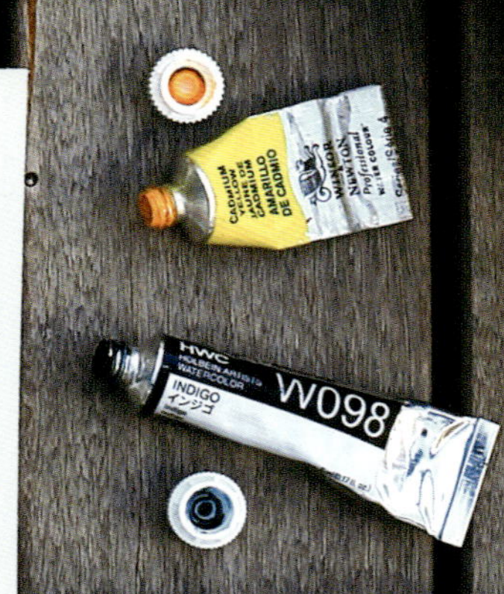
HWC
INDIGO
W098

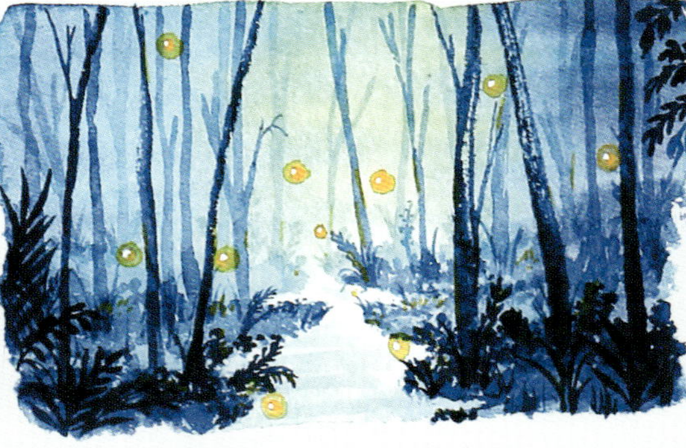

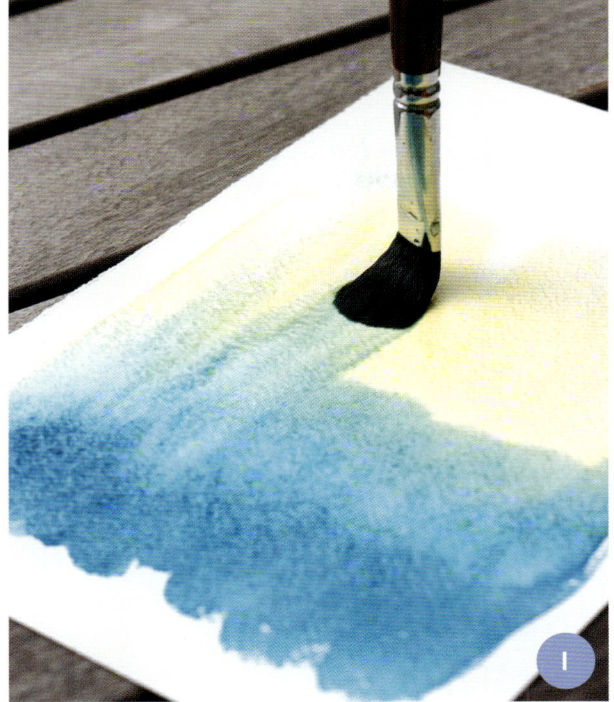

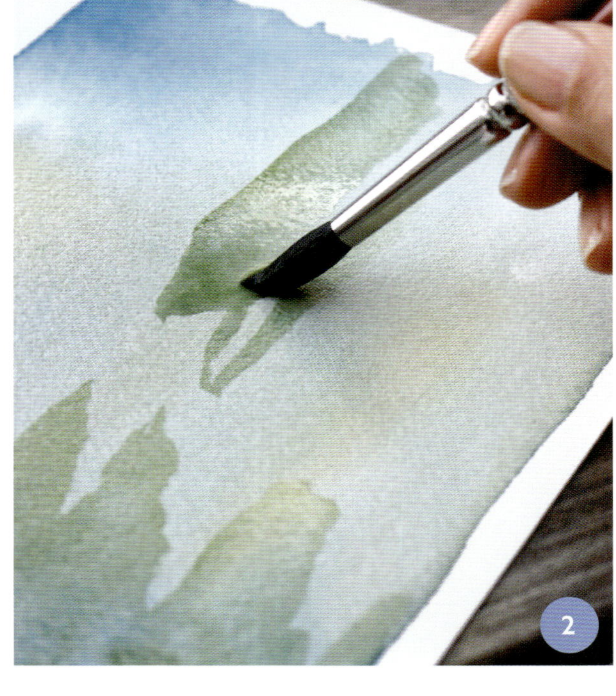

STEP 1. Start with the background layer painted with light value hues/colors to give it a sense of mistiness and depth.

Starting with your paper completely dry and using the large soft brush No. 16 loaded up with a light value of Cadmium Yellow, softly paint the middle section of the paper in soft horizontal brushstrokes not quite reaching the edges of the paper. Clean your brush and now load it up with a light value of indigo. With the yellow still wet on the paper, paint the left and the right sections of the paper using horizontal brushstrokes blending toward the middle section but not overlapping it.

Blend it slightly with only a few brushstrokes and let it dry.

STEP 2. Paint the ground level using a slight difference in value and color.

While the background layer completely dries, mix the soft green that you will use for the floor layer. Mix a two-part light value of Cadmium Yellow and a one-part light value of indigo to get a soft green. Now that the background layer is completely dry, load up your medium soft brush No. 8 with the medium value green you just mixed and start painting a horizontal line at about the middle of the paper, leaving a small gap in the middle of your line. Start dragging the paint downward but leave a zig-zag space in the middle of the paper to eventually create the illusion of a path or a small stream of water that disappears into the horizon.

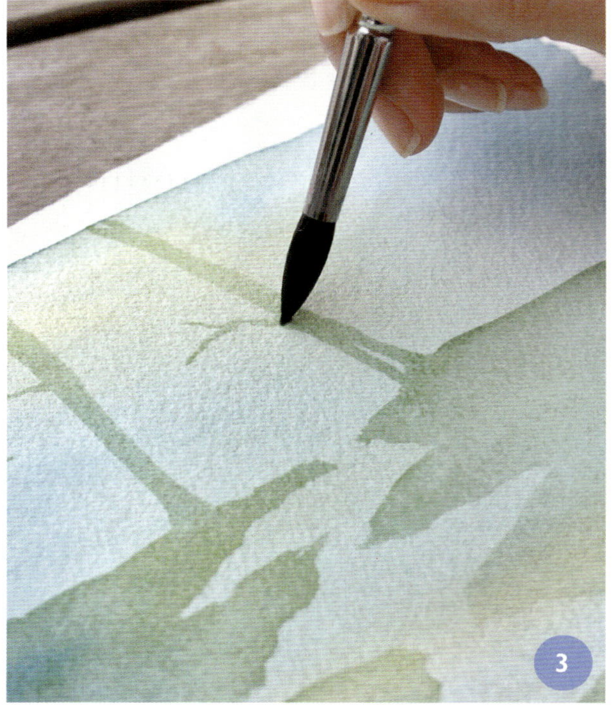

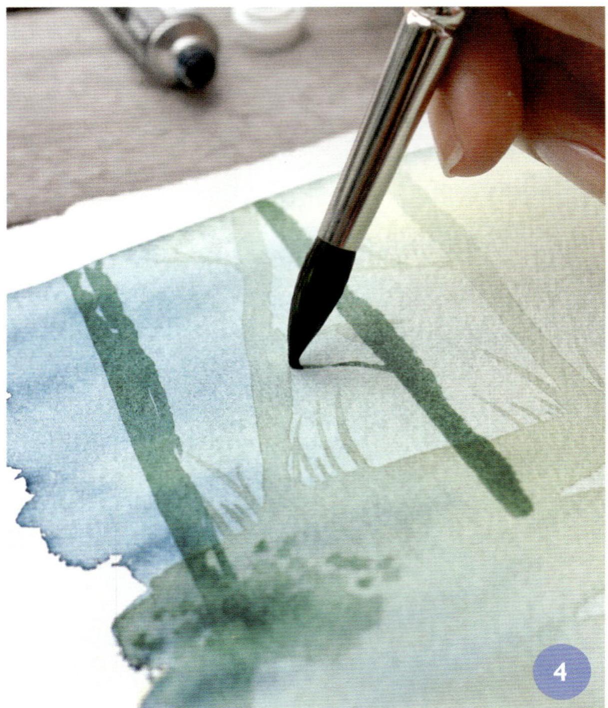

STEP 3. Paint the trees that are farthest in the background.

While the ground layer is still wet, using the same brush and the same light value green, paint a few tree trunks with branches that grow from the top edge of the ground surface you just painted.

Note: Please note that more often than not, trees do not grow in a straight line, so feel free to add a little angle to your tree trunks.

STEP 4. Paint as many trees as you like, staggering them and layering them to practice your value stages.

Using the same brush, go ahead and paint three or four layers of trees using the same method explained in step 3, but each time add a bit more indigo to the pigment mixture to increase its value.

Painting these long trunks with branches in an almost repetitive manner is almost like painting long, soft leaves. Please go ahead and start practicing the synchronization of your brushstrokes with your breath for a moment of mindfulness and relaxation.

Each time you create a new layer of trees, you can add texture to the ground by lightly stippling the tip of the medium soft brush on the paper. You can also add vegetation by softly painting grass with light, vertical, curved brushstrokes using your small synthetic brush No. 1. A few dabs of paint will appear as wild vegetation.

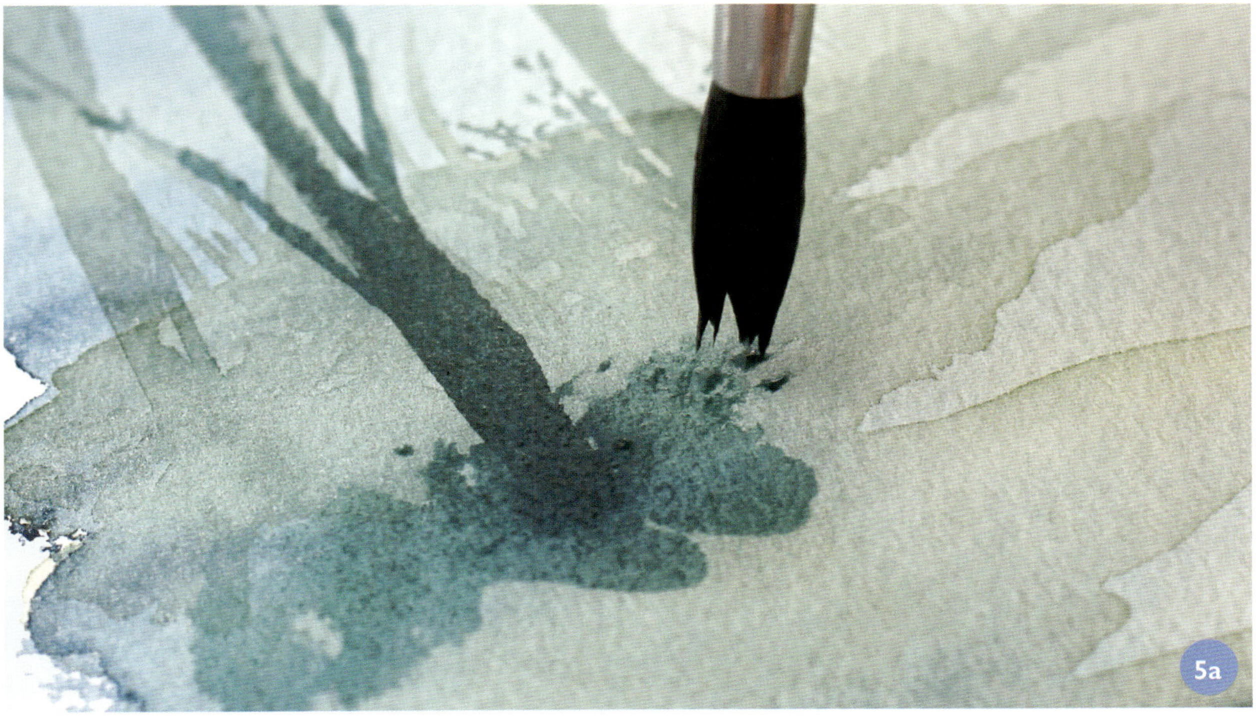

STEP 5. Add a very important layer of depth to your painting to make you feel like you are truly immersed in this magical forest.

After your trees and ground are completely dry, using your synthetic brush No. 1 loaded with a dark value indigo, start painting wild vegetation and flowers around the edges of the painting. Go ahead and practice the leaves and loose abstract flowers you learned in the Loose Autumn Wreath project (page 49) or the Soft and Flowing Leaves from the first project (page 19). Remember that this vegetation is larger in size as to appear in the foreground.

The soft brushstrokes and repetitive nature of painting this wild vegetation will help you finish this painting, leaving you relaxed but ready to go on an adventure! Although hopefully not an eight-hour hike.

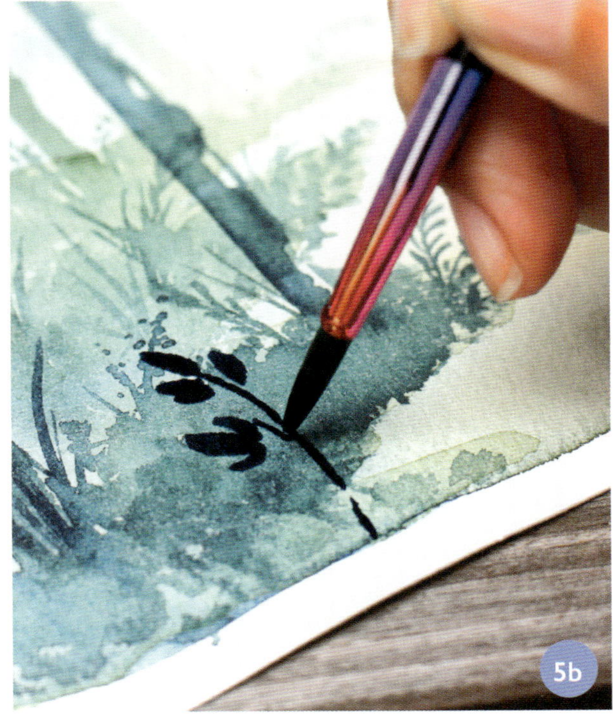

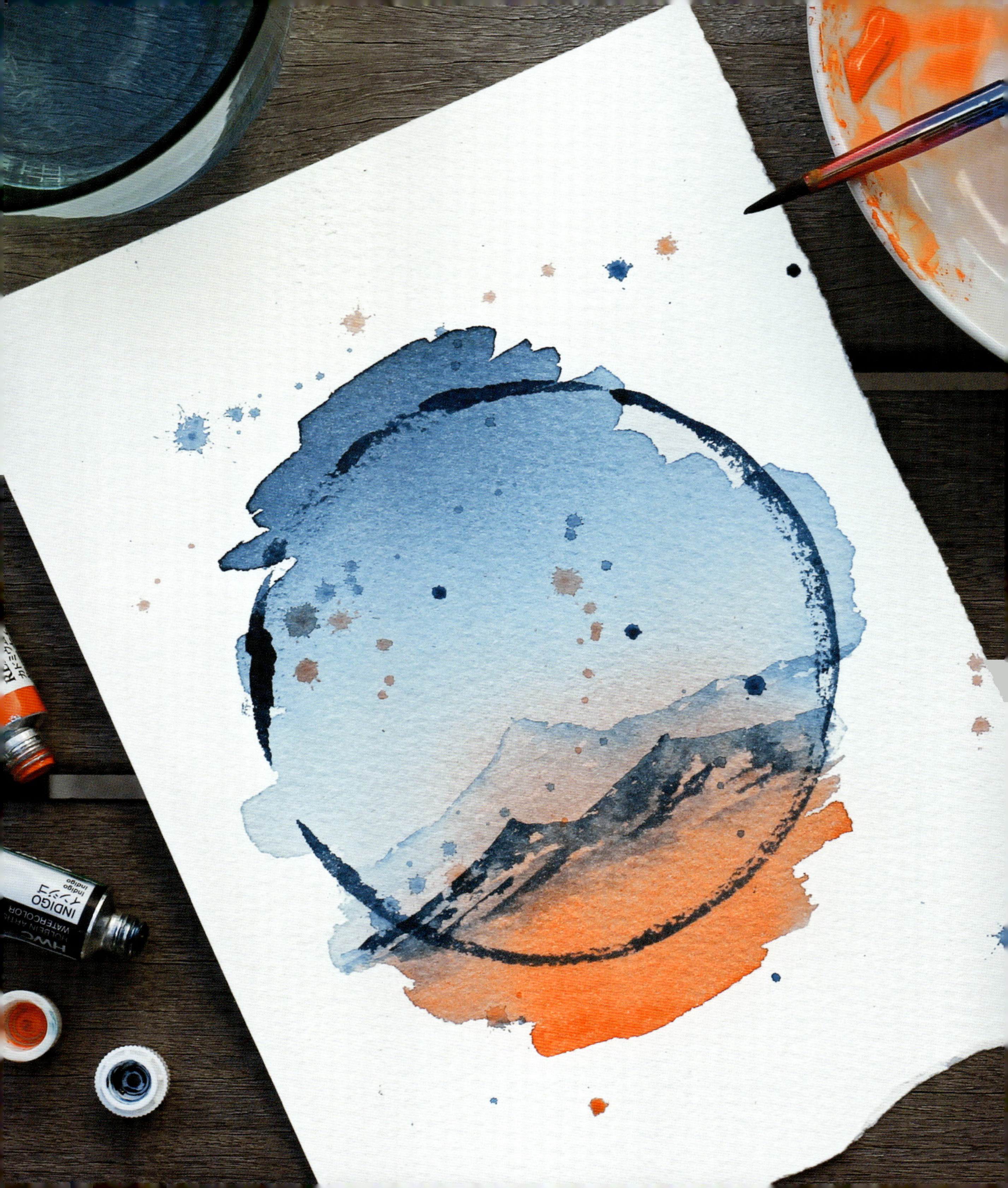
HWC
WATERCOLOR
INDIGO
インジゴ
Indigo
indigo

Desert Mountains

The closest I have been to a desert is when I did a cross-country road trip with my parents and we stopped at the Painted Desert in Arizona. The vastness of the landscape makes you feel so small, yet the small hills in the foreground make you feel welcomed. You could just walk into this landscape and feel like you were part of this grandiose and vast environment. Another very surreal part of this landscape was the deep contrast of the vivid orange hills and the intense blue sky.

In this project I would like to introduce a fascinating form called the Enso. Although there is a deep Zen meaning in this shape, I like to simplify it in terms of creating a simple shape in a free and uninhibited motion, which allows the natural movement of my body to simply create.

This project will allow you to immerse yourself in this wonderful color contrast and subtle mountain shapes, and you will frame it all with an Enso to emphasize the unity of the landscape with yourself.

Materials

- Indigo
- Cadmium Red-Orange
- Synthetic round brush No. 6
- Synthetic round brush No. 2

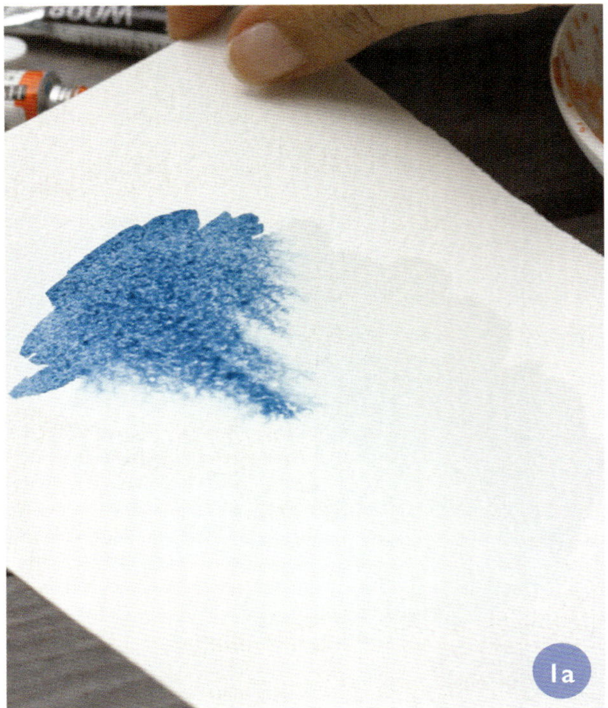

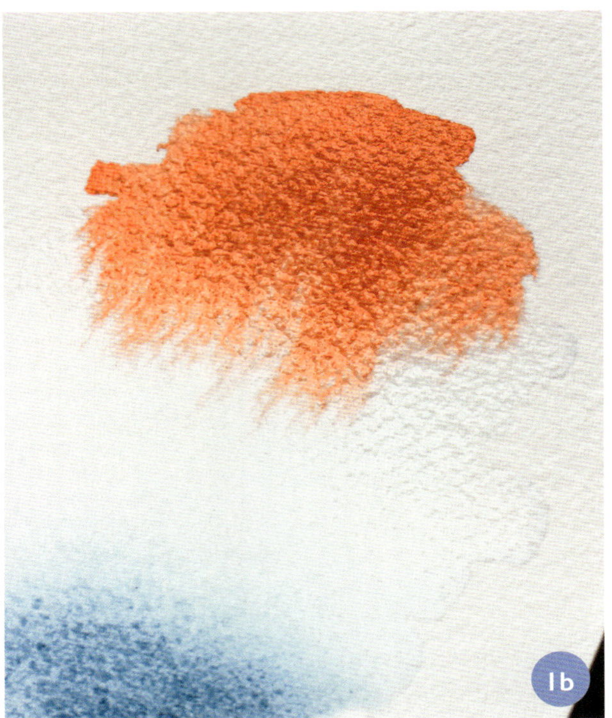

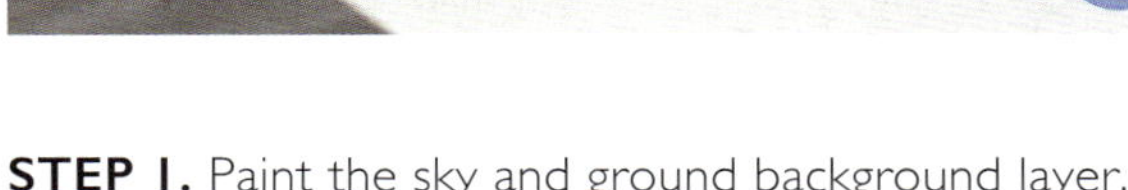

STEP 1. Paint the sky and ground background layer.

Starting with a dry piece of watercolor paper, using your medium synthetic brush No. 6 and only clean water, "paint" a circle with very rough edges, filling up the entire page without quite reaching the edges. I really like to emphasize and encourage the idea of imperfection here; it is actually better for the composition to not emphasize the edges of the circle perfectly. Think of painting a circular-looking blob if you will. Once you have your wet/glossy surface in a somewhat circular shape, load up the same brush with a dark value of indigo and dab it only on the top edge of the wet circle. Move the paper vertically a little to allow the pigment to flow downward no farther than the midpoint of the circle. Take a moment to appreciate the movement of the pigment as it mixes with the water and slowly flows like little streams making their own paths, much like you are with your art journey, slowly and steadily making your own path.

While the surface is still wet, repeat the same steps but with the Cadmium Red-Orange, starting at the bottom of the wet circle and moving the paper again to make the paint flow toward the indigo.

Allow the two pigments to blend only a little bit in the middle of the circle. You will want to maintain a lightness where the two colors meet. Lay flat to dry.

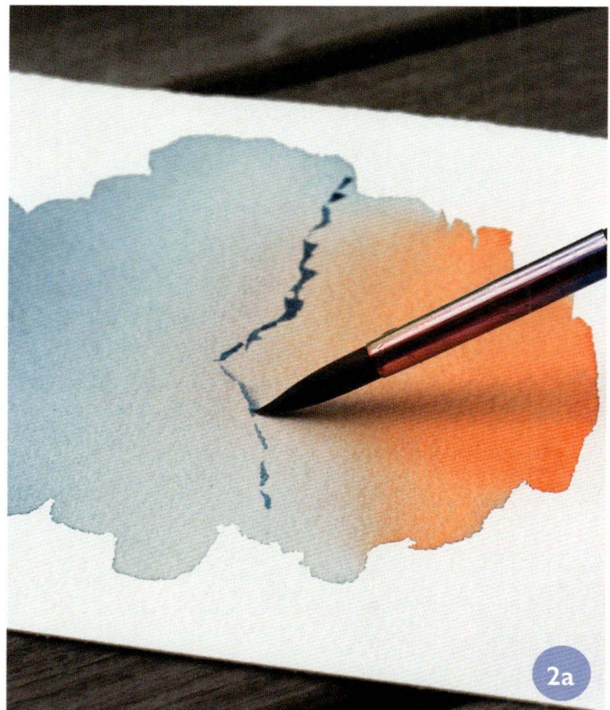

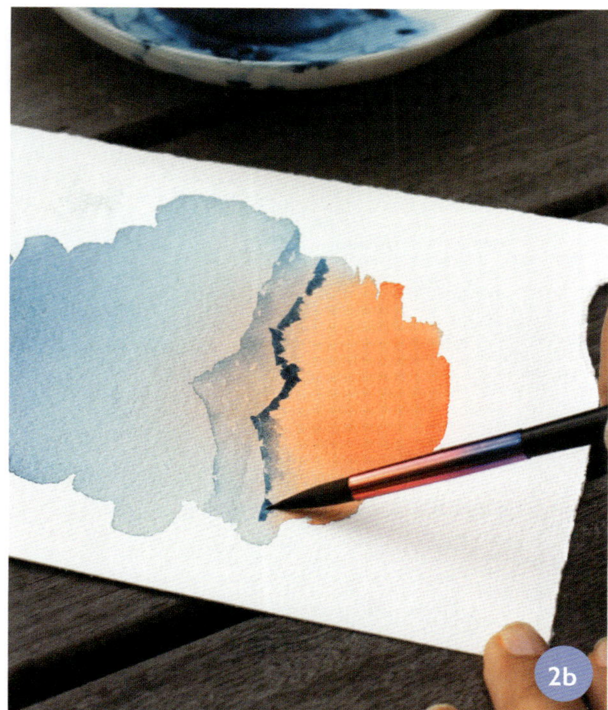

STEP 2. I find this step very relaxing because it allows you to clear your mind as you let your brush paint wiggly lines. Your mind doesn't have to focus on anything in particular. You just let the brush do all the work for you.

Once the surface is completely dry, use the medium synthetic brush No. 6 to lightly paint the top edge of the background mountain with a light value of indigo. Next, clean your brush and use it damp to push the indigo of the wiggly line downward to diffuse it and make it disappear with the orange background. Wait a few minutes for this first mountain to dry.

Repeat this same step for the foreground mountain using a medium value of indigo. With very light brushstrokes at a downward angle, you can add texture to the mountain.

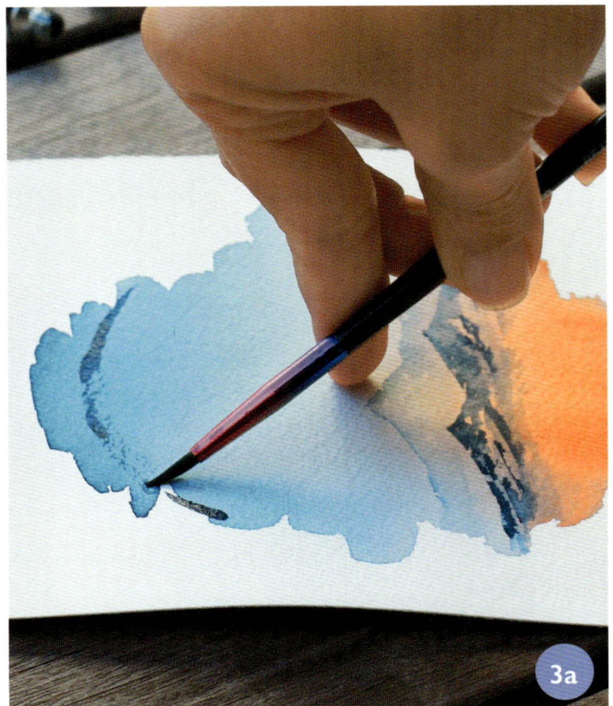

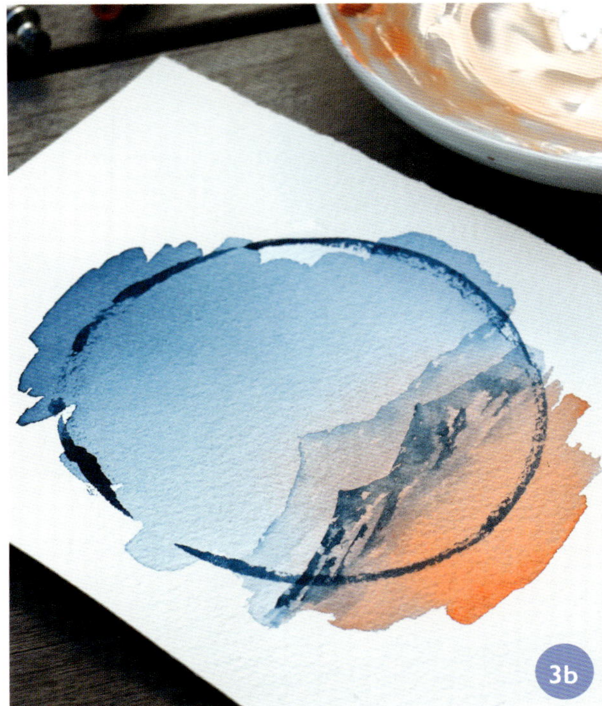

STEP 3. Frame your composition with an Enso.

Make sure your small synthetic brush No. 2 is fully loaded with a dark value of indigo for the Enso to flow smoothly with one brushstroke. Using your index finger as an anchor point and holding your small brush in a horizontal position, place your index finger in the center of your painting. Bring your brush at an angle for the tip of the brush to touch the paper and rotate the paper to create the circle. This is the moment where you fully let go of any preconceptions of what this painting should be and simply let your hand create something imperfectly beautiful. Allow yourself the freedom of not wanting to "fix" it. It came out how it came out and that is enough.

I hope that you were able to find a few peaceful moments while painting your desert mountains and found joy in the color blending of the sky and the ground as well as framing it with a beautiful Enso.

Magical Christmas Night

Don't we all love snowfall on Christmas Eve? It just feels so magical and exciting. One of the best parts of Christmas is going out with your family to find the best, tallest and fluffiest Christmas tree. For this project I wanted to re-create the feeling of the snow falling in a forest of trees while you look for and find the perfect Christmas tree. This magical tree will glow among the forest of wonderful pine trees.

In this project you will be practicing the wet-on-dry technique to create your sky as well as new techniques such as working with masking fluid and salt. The detail work involved in painting the trees will leave you feeling relaxed but with a clear and focused mind ready for the next task at hand.

Materials

- Indigo
- Soft round brush No. 12
- Masking fluid
- Fine grain salt

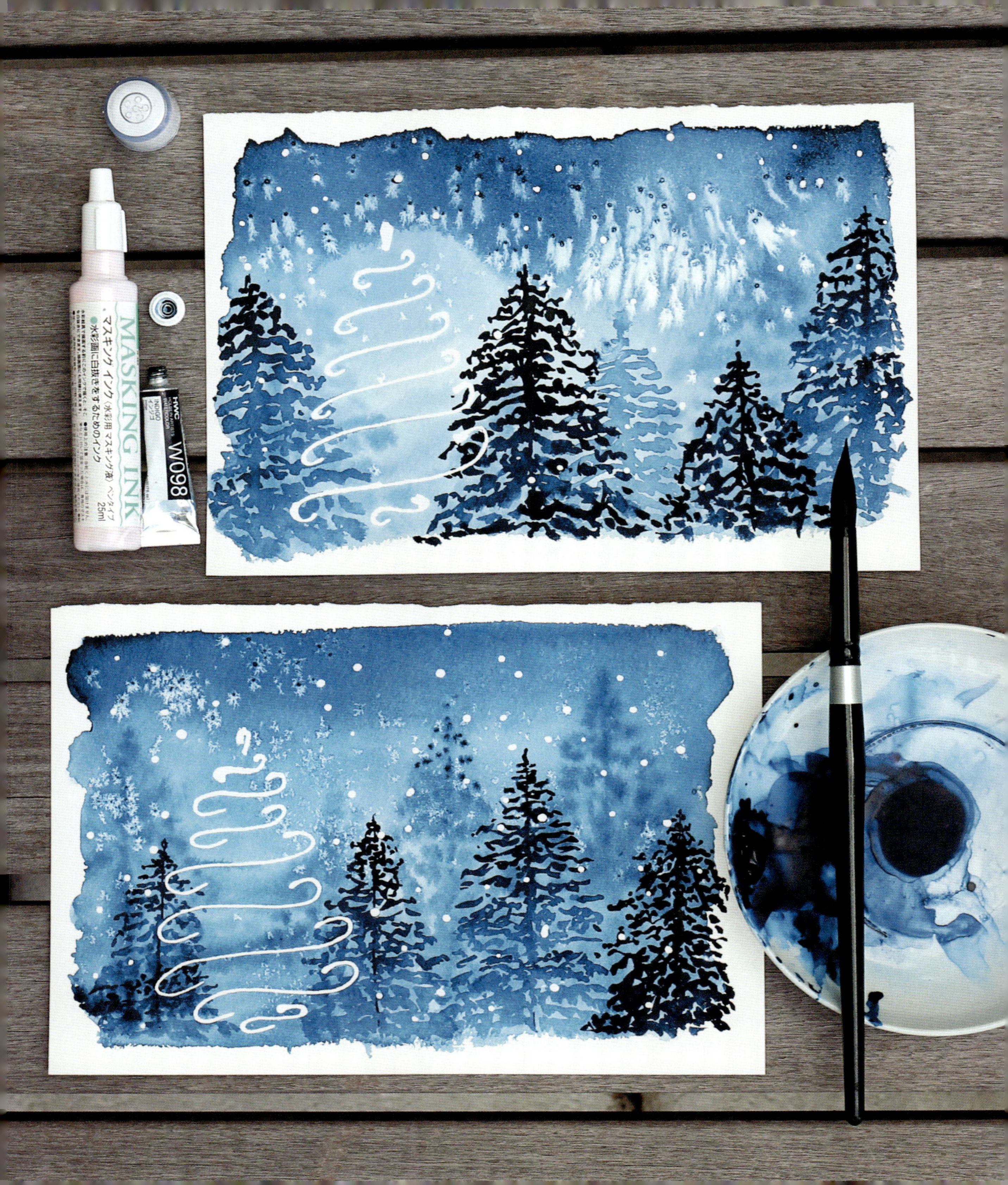

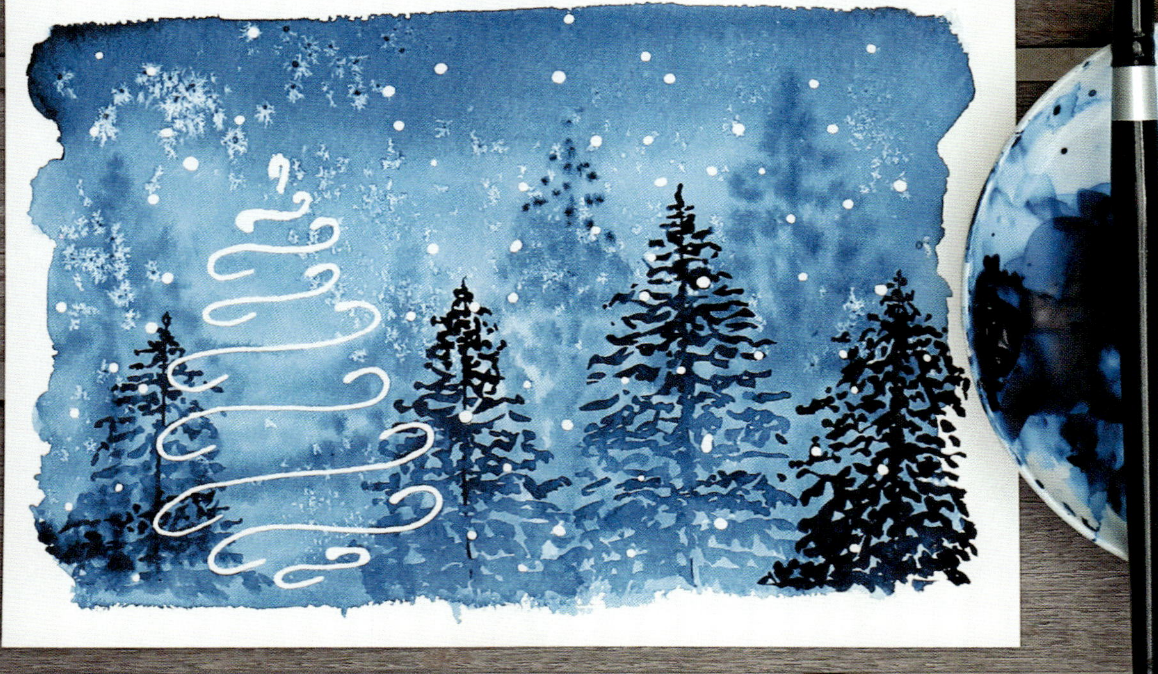

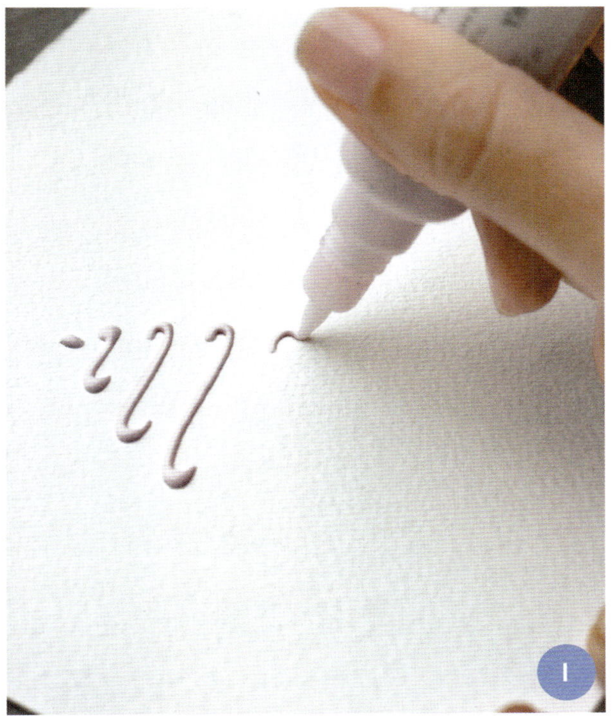

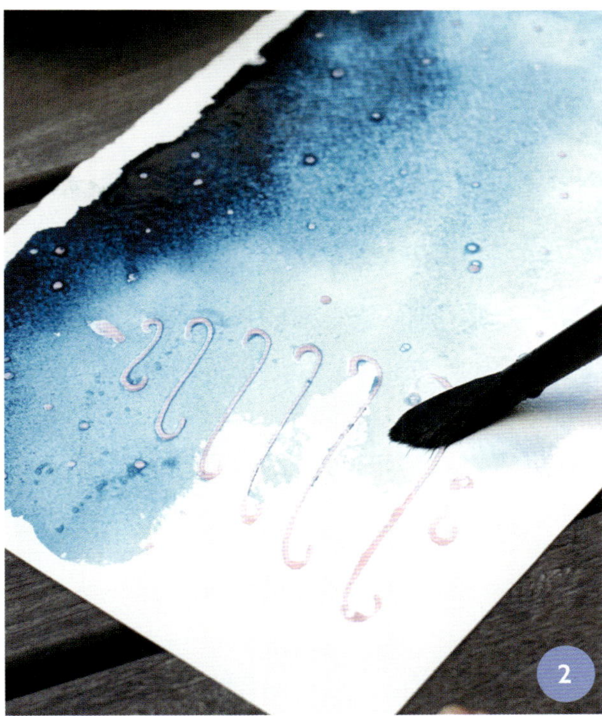

STEP 1. Paint your "glowing" tree with masking fluid.

Masking fluid usually comes in a container to be applied with a brush; it is kind of like glue but is water resistant. It is used for masking areas of a work that need protection when color is applied. You can use an old brush for this step, but I happen to have found a masking fluid in a pen at an art store in Japan. Because I would like to imagine my Christmas tree to be magical, I am going to "paint" a very abstract representation of a tree with the masking fluid.

In the middle of the left third of the paper start painting very small horizontal "S" shapes and with each "S" moving downward on the paper. These lines will gradually increase in size as you go down the paper. You can also dab small dots throughout the entire paper to make them look like stars. Let it dry.

Depending on the masking fluid you use, the drying time will vary. You will know when it is dry because it will look semitranslucent and will feel a bit tacky to the touch.

STEP 2. Focus on the background or sky layer using a wet-on-dry technique to maintain the intensity of the sky as dark and deep as possible. As with all the washes that I paint, I find this step one of the most satisfying to paint because I can seriously watch paint flow all day.

With your masking fluid and paper dry, load up your large soft brush No. 12 with a dark value of indigo and drag it across the top edge of the paper, leaving a small gap of white between the edge of the paper and the paint to retain a white frame in your composition. Gently drag the pigment all the way down and across the paper each time, adding a little bit of water to dilute the pigment and create a smooth gradient.

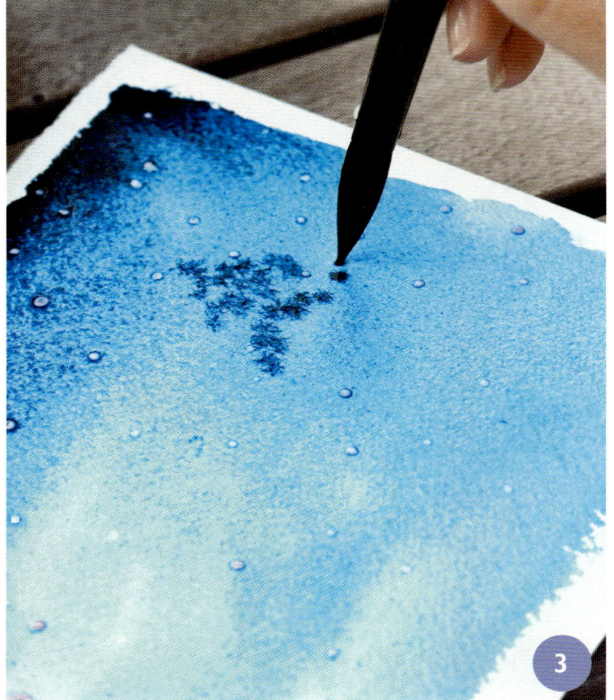

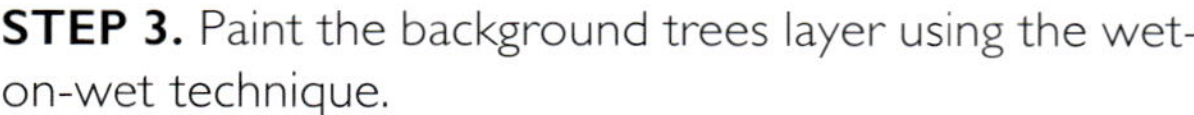

STEP 3. Paint the background trees layer using the wet-on-wet technique.

While the paper is still glossy, load up your brush again with the dark value indigo and start dabbing small dots in a triangular formation to create the farthest trees in the background.

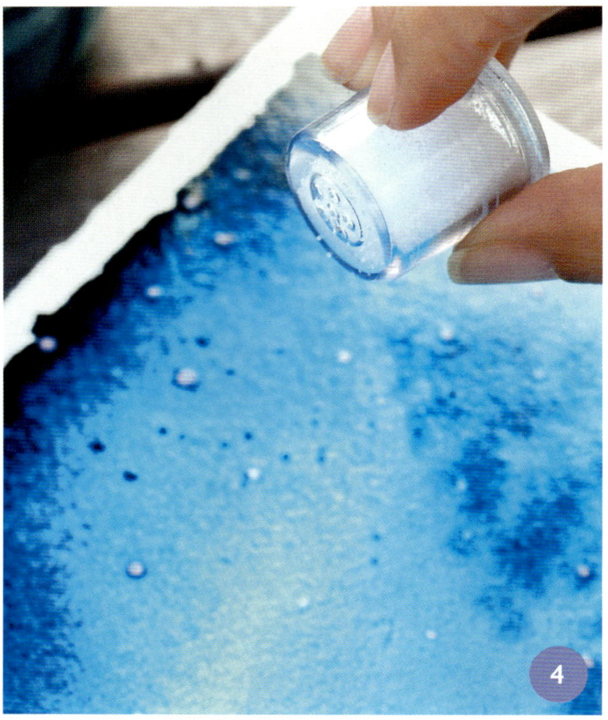

STEP 4. Use the salt technique to create the lovely and soft snowflakes. It is very important to use fine grain salt because the way it absorbs water is gentler than coarse salt.

While the paper is still a bit glossy, sprinkle some salt on the wet surface and watch it react to the pigment. This effect will create a magical texture resembling a soft snowfall. If you move the paper a tiny bit in a vertical way, the mineral of the salt will flow with the little molecules of water and create a "falling snow" texture on your painting. Should you decide to not move the paper at all, the salt minerals will simply create snow-like fragments suspended in midair. Both options are fantastic!

Note: It is important to not use a hair dryer to dry the painting because you might move the particles of salt and create a completely different texture that will not resemble snow.

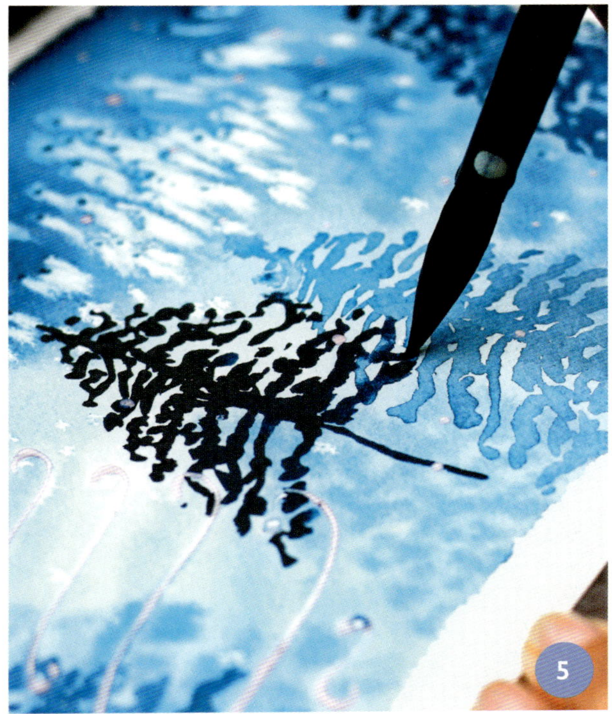

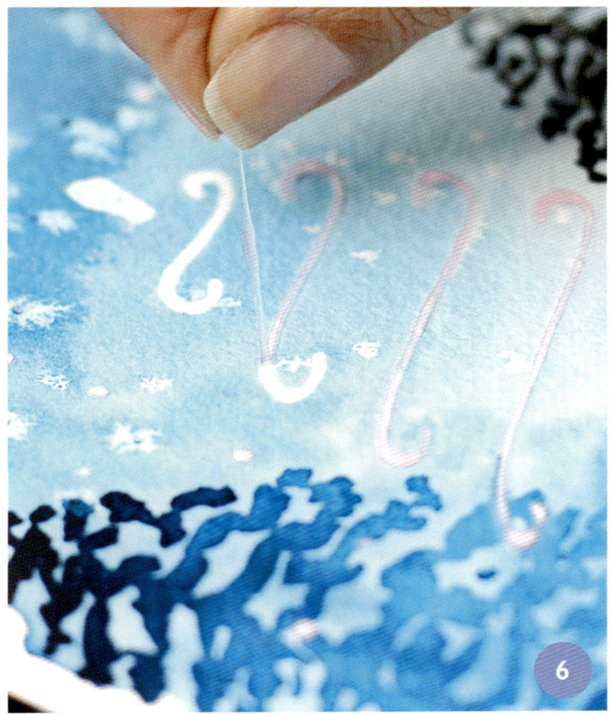

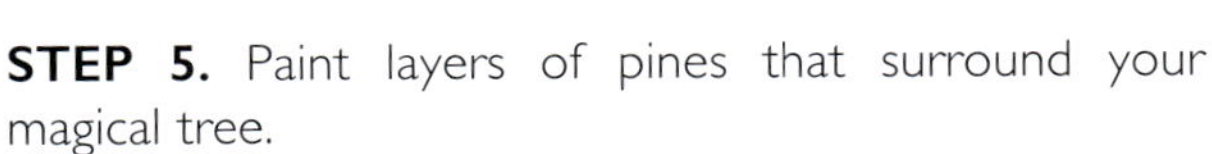

STEP 5. Paint layers of pines that surround your magical tree.

Once the paper is completely dry, you can start to add one or two layers of trees. To create the background trees, use a medium value of indigo and start painting the trunks of the trees with a few vertical lines that will grow up to about three-quarters of the paper height. It is better if you vary the heights slightly to add a bit of realism to your composition. Go ahead and start dabbing the branches in a triangular formation, getting wider toward the bottom. Let this first layer of trees dry.

Now, for the foreground trees, use a dark value of indigo and gently draw another set of vertical lines, but stagger them with the previously painted layer of trees. These trees can also be a bit shorter to give enough space to the background layer to be seen. Add branches to your trunks and dab wiggly lines increasing in size at the bottom of the tree. Depending on the quantity of trees you decide to paint, this can be a very relaxing exercise due to its repetitive nature and the freeing feeling of your body creating a beautifully imperfect set of trees.

STEP 6. Remove the salt and the masking fluid.

Once the painting is completely dry, start removing the dried salt by gently rubbing your fingers on the paper. As for the masking fluid, you can use the back of a brush if it has the angled end, but I usually just use my fingers. It is not only fun to feel like you are back in elementary school removing glue from your notebooks—I hope I wasn't the only one who did that—but pulling the strings of elastic off the paper gently and slowly is incredibly satisfying.

Now that the masking fluid and the salt are removed, you can look at the composition as a whole and feel that sense of magic, snow and sparkles that every Christmas should have.

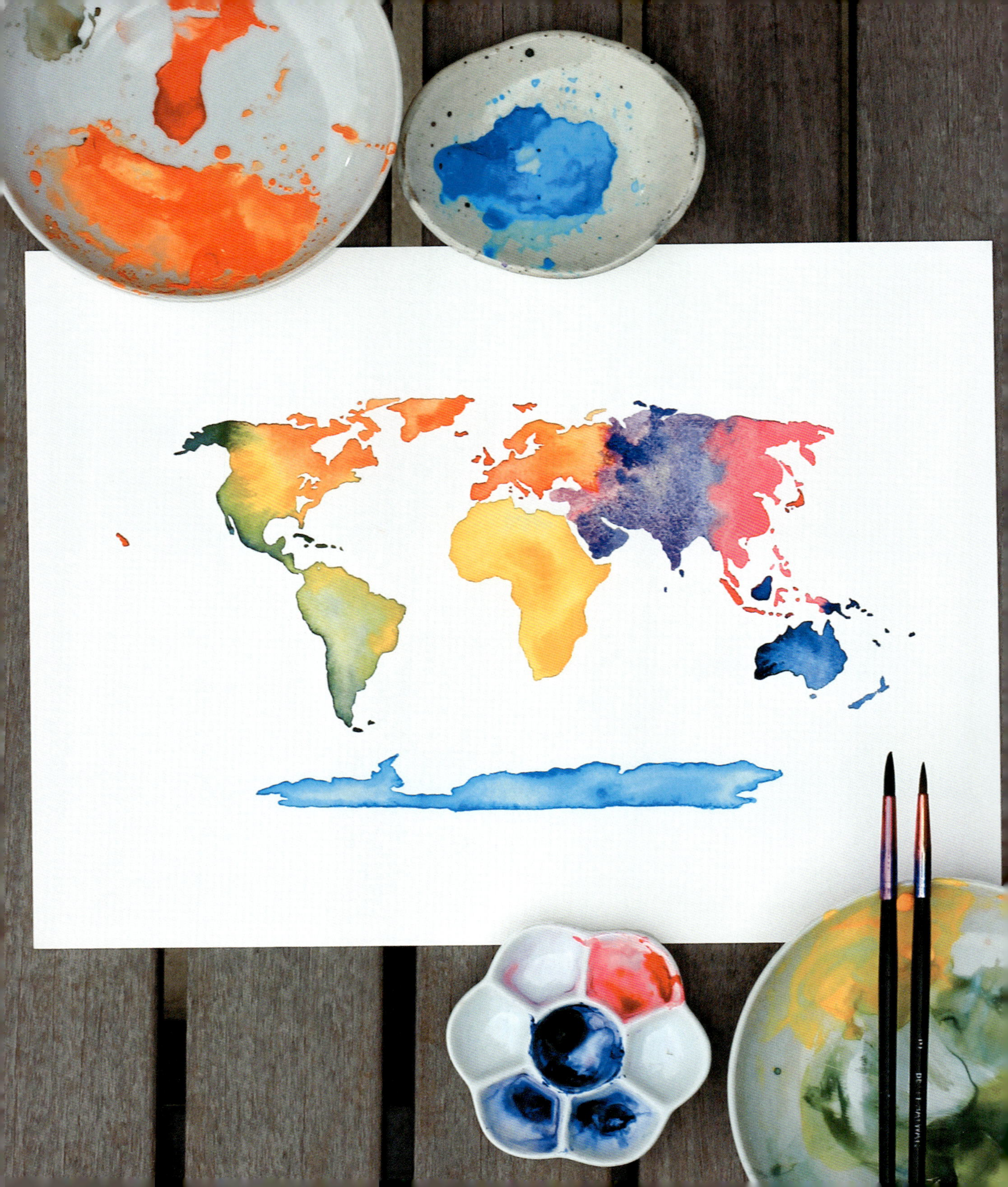

Wishlist Traveling Map

I'm obsessed with traveling; hence, this next project is one of my favorites, as it allows me to daydream and remember all the places I have visited, lived in and wish to visit in the near future. I hope you do the same as you blend your colors and travel around the world!

I understand that drawing and painting the entire world map can be scary and intimidating, but it doesn't have to be. All you need to do is trace a map from an image found on the Internet. Due to its simplicity in technique, please take a moment to appreciate the color blends that the pigment does on its own with the help of the fluidity of the water. Softly blending colors can be a very relaxing exercise as you allow your mind to get lost as the colors mix with one another seamlessly.

In this project you will start with a simple tracing exercise and move on to wet-on-dry as well as wet-on-wet techniques. It is a super simple and very relaxing project.

Materials

- Indigo
- Cadmium Yellow
- Cadmium Red-Orange
- Opera Pink
- Purple
- Turquoise
- Synthetic round brush No. 2
- Soft lead pencil
- Kneading eraser

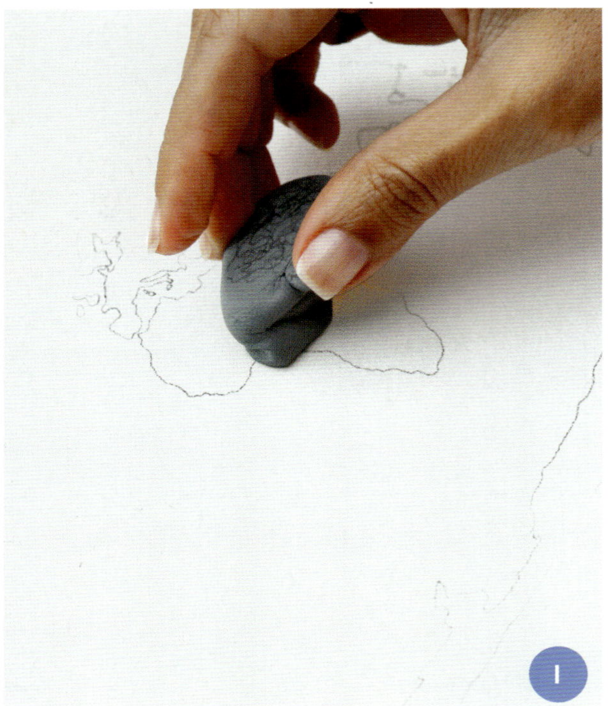

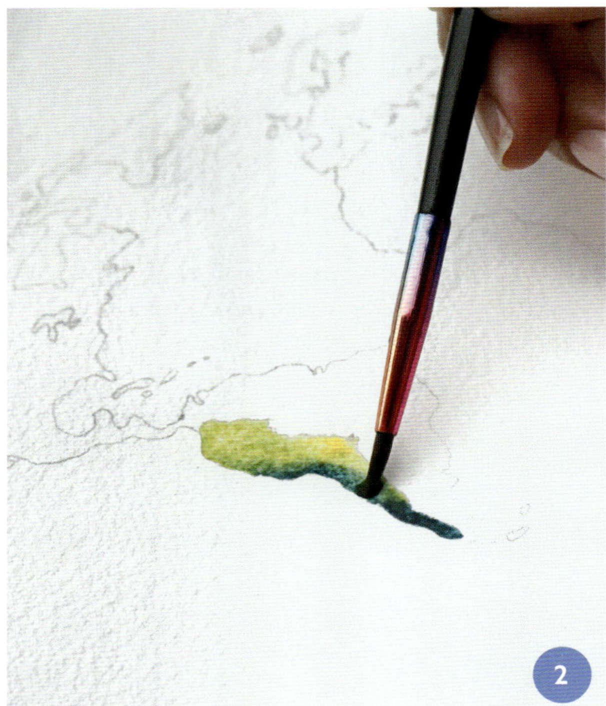

STEP 1. Get the outline of the map ready.

The technique that I use for tracing on watercolor paper is very straightforward. Print a world map from the Internet, tape it to a window or a light source, place your watercolor paper on top of it and lightly trace the outline with a soft lead pencil. Once you are done with the outline, bring your paper back to the horizontal surface or table and use a kneading eraser to lift a little of the pencil marks so they don't show through the pigment when you start painting.

STEP 2. In the next couple of steps you will be using a variation of the wet-on-dry technique as you start to outline the continents gradually, as well as using a wet-on-wet technique as you start blending colors to create smooth transitions within the continents.

I like to start with South America as it is home to me. The earthy color combination of a dark value indigo and a touch of medium value yellow makes this continent look grounded and tropical.

With your paper still dry, go ahead and start tracing the outline of South America with your synthetic small brush No. 2. Load up your small brush with a dark value of indigo and start painting the western edge of South America. Add a little water to the paper and start diffusing the indigo through the Andes. Clean your brush and load it up with a medium value of yellow and paint the opposite edge where Argentina is located. Drag the pigment inland and blend the colors as you go up through Brazil, Venezuela and Colombia. The colors will start to blend with very little effort. Do not try to blend them too much but rather allow the pigments to mix as they will.

As you move up through Panama and Central and North America, maintain the indigo edge to the west.

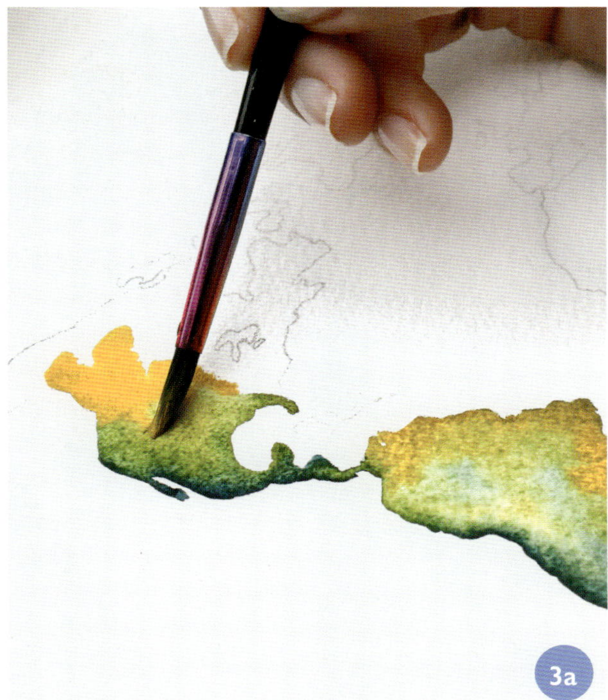

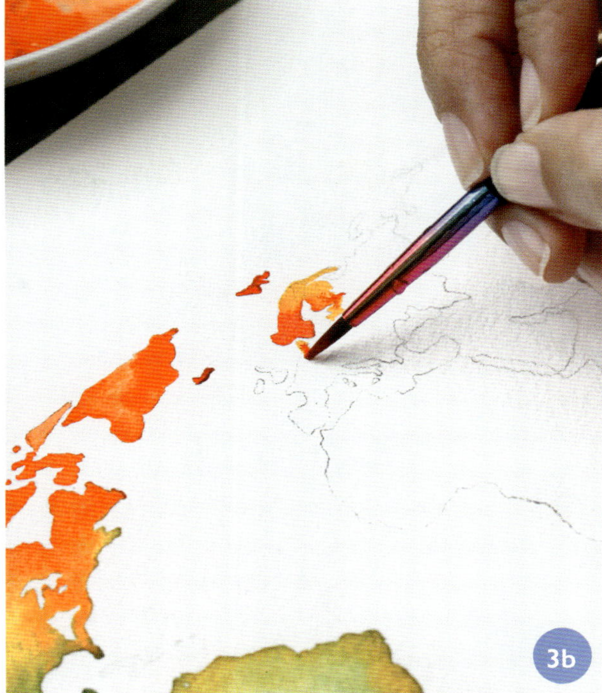

STEP 3. As you approach Canada, bring back the yellow and blend it slightly to keep the gradient mostly yellow toward the East Coast.

Note: Do not allow the paint to dry while you clean your brush and load it up with the next color; if needed, use more than one brush to facilitate changing the colors.

Move forward toward Greenland and Western Europe. With the yellow area still wet, start dabbing a little bit of a medium value of orange to blend smoothly with the yellow that covers the Midwest of North America. As you cross continents, imagine that transatlantic flight full of excitement for the adventures that await on the other side!

Moving to the continents on the other side of the Atlantic Ocean, keep working with the wet-on-dry technique, only using wet-on-wet when you feel the need to dab a few spots of a different color on a specific area.

Maintaining the consistency of the orange color through Europe with a few dabs of yellow through Sweden, push the color eastward with a bit of water to get a soft, light orange as you reach Russia.

I like to paint Africa as a solid yellow color with a light center because it feels happy, full of energy and life. Outline the entire continent with a medium value of yellow and softly blend it with water toward its center to give it a sense of lightness and transparency.

Asia gets a beautiful blend of Opera Pink and purple because in my very personal opinion, these vibrant colors represent the excitement and fascination I hold for this continent—Japan, you have my heart.

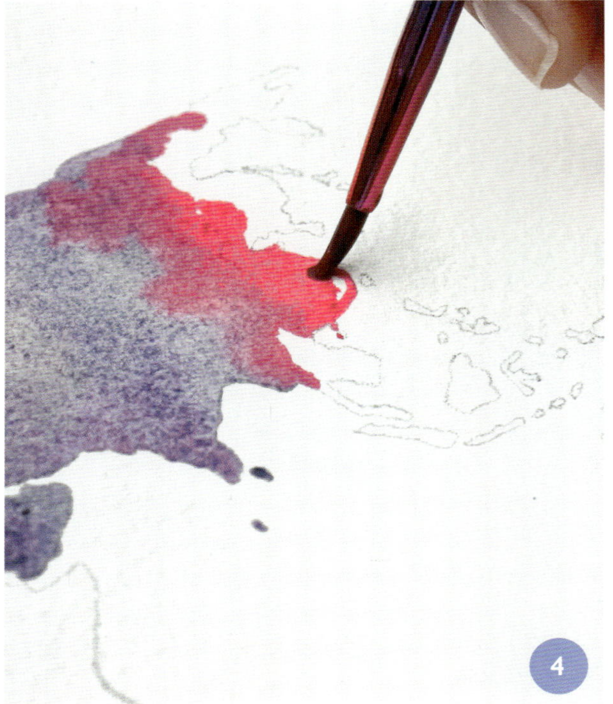

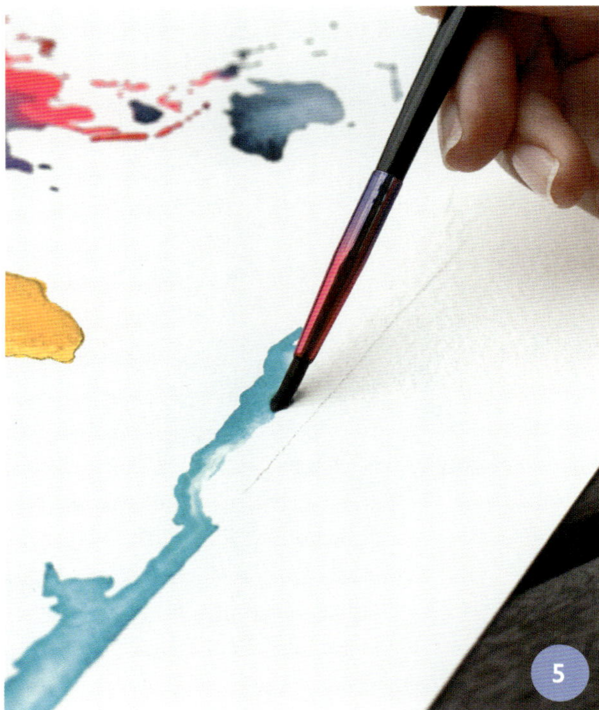

STEP 4. Transition south through Southeast Asia. You can blend back from Opera Pink to a single indigo color for Oceania. Please do not forget New Zealand. It is small but absolutely worth your while.

Go ahead and paint a few dots off the east coast of Australia to emphasize the small Pacific Islands, because who doesn't dream of the Pacific Islands?

STEP 5. Last, Antarctica gets the icy turquoise color because its ice-covered landmass and massive icebergs must be absolutely fascinating to visit. As with Africa, outline the continent with a medium value of turquoise and blend it with water toward the center to create a nice gradient.

I truly hope you got to lose yourself in this project and daydream a little. May your next adventure be as colorful, vibrant and exciting as this project made you feel.

Beautiful Moon Phases

The cyclical nature of the changing phases of the moon brings to mind the Japanese term *mono no aware*, or the awareness of the impermanence of things and the gentle sadness and wistfulness at their passing. Sounds so melancholy and beautiful at the same time, doesn't it? This is what the moon represents to me on a very personal level. The moon changes every day so subtly it is almost imperceptible, but so do we. We must be mindful that every day we change a tiny little bit, just like the moon.

I hope this project brings you a sense of peace and mindfulness as you gently paint the ever-changing phases of the moon.

Materials

- Indigo
- Synthetic brush No. 8
- Small round object (approximately 3 inches [7.5 cm] in diameter) or compass
- Soft lead pencil
- Kneading eraser

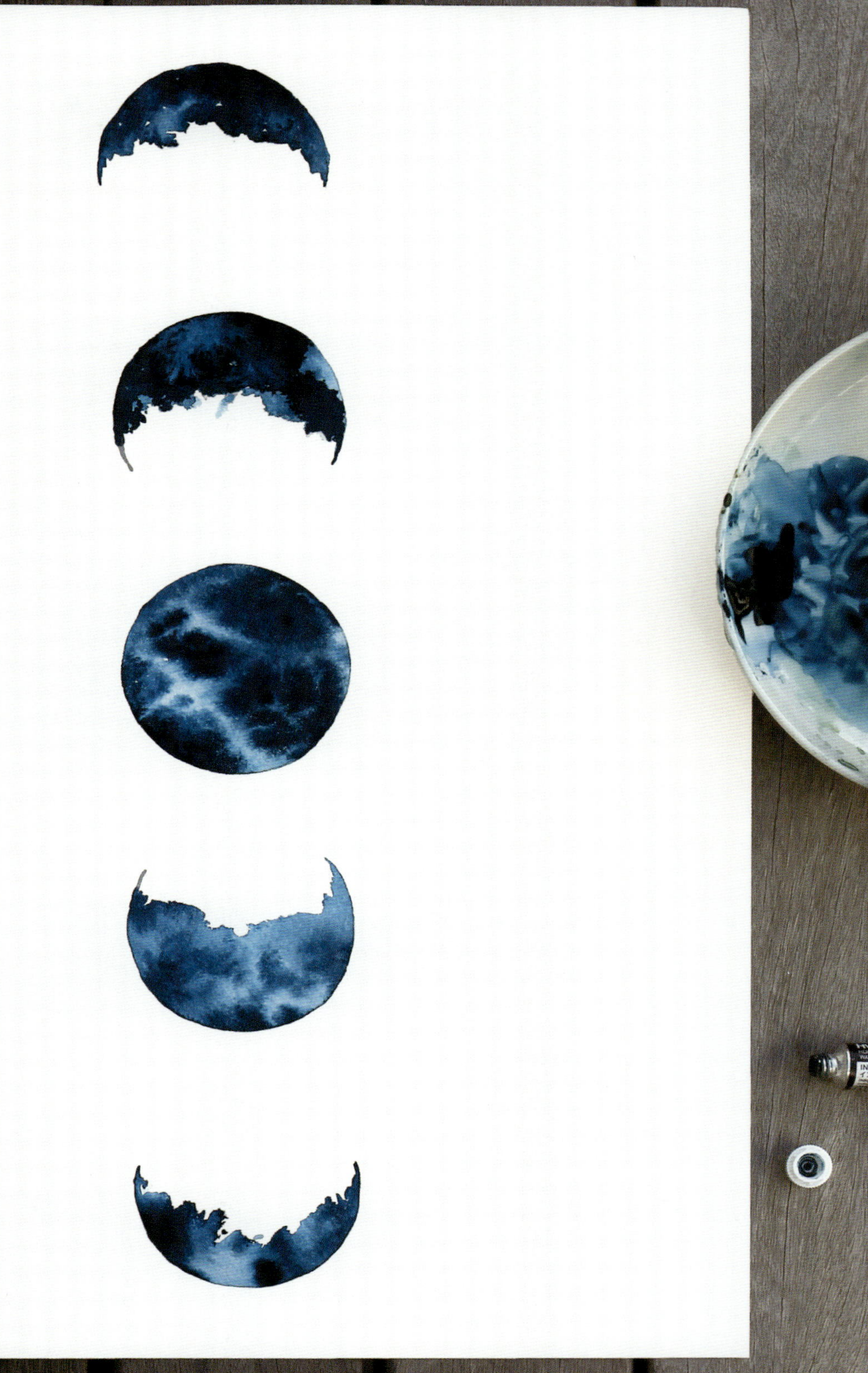
HWC
WATERCOLOR
INDIGO
インジゴ

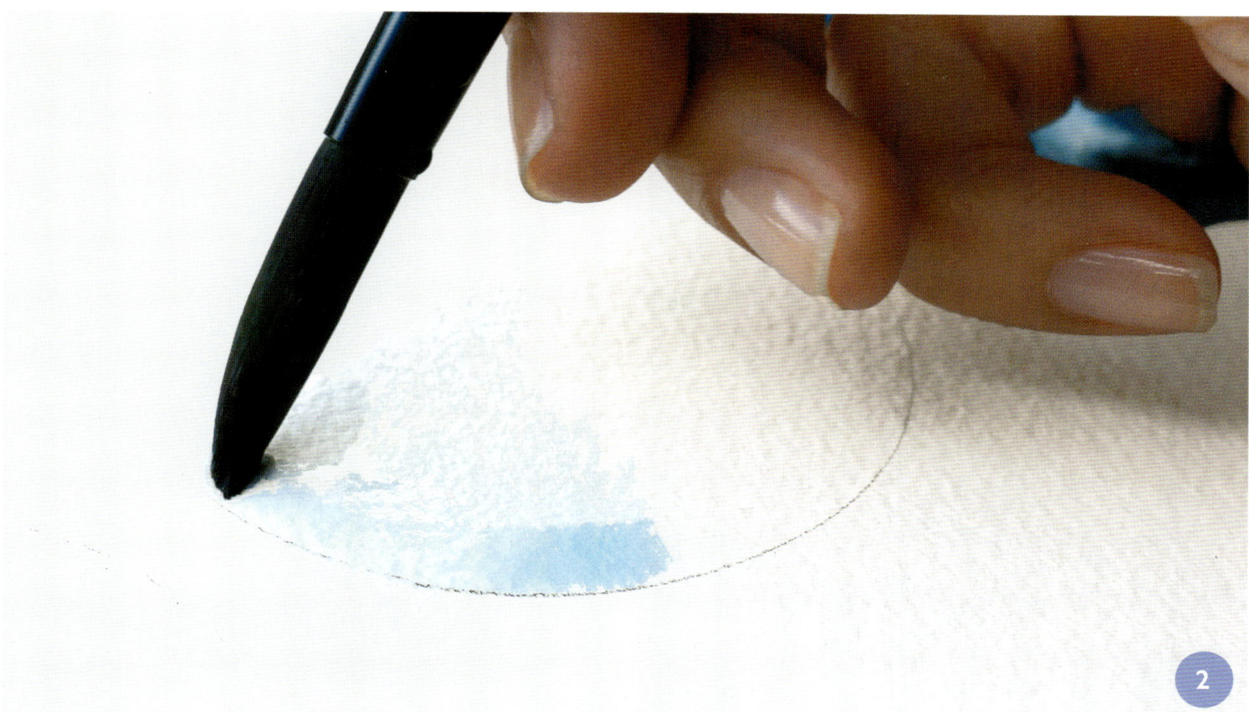

STEP 1. With the soft lead pencil, very lightly draw five identical circles in a row by tracing the small round object, ideally in the center of your paper. It doesn't have to be super precise—I mostly eyeballed it.

I will explain in great detail how to paint the waxing crescent moon, as it might be the trickiest one in regard to proportions and technique, but you can follow the same steps for the rest of the phases, each time filling in the circle a little bit more.

STEP 2. Now that you have your circles ready, leave your paper wet, and load up your synthetic brush No. 8 with a light value of indigo and with the tip of the brush, gently trace only half of the outline of the circle.

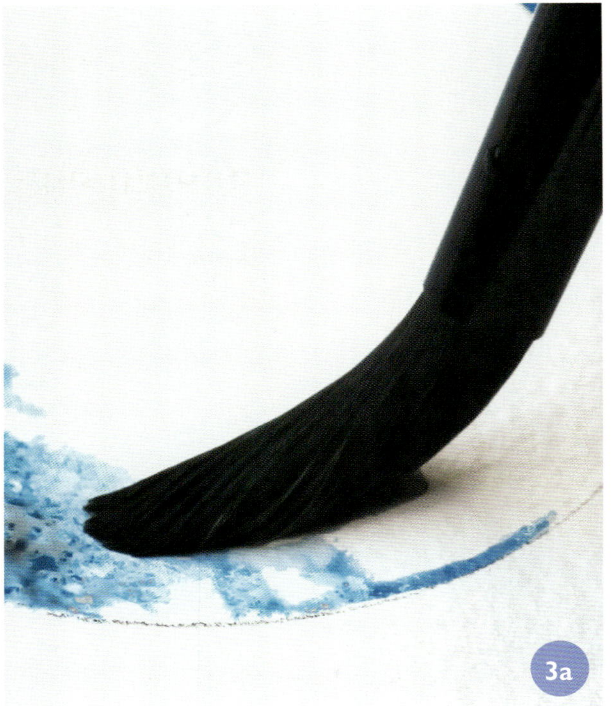

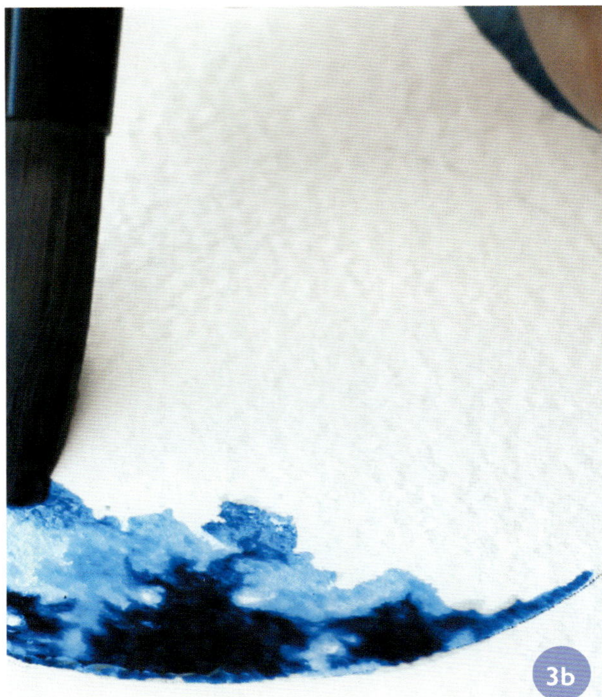

STEP 3. Next, add a bit more pigment to your brush and gently start dabbing the paint toward the center of the circle but not quite reaching the center. Use the belly of the brush in a push and lift technique to make uneven patches of pigment and an uneven inner edge.

Before the pigment dries, add a few dots of dark value indigo to create contrast.

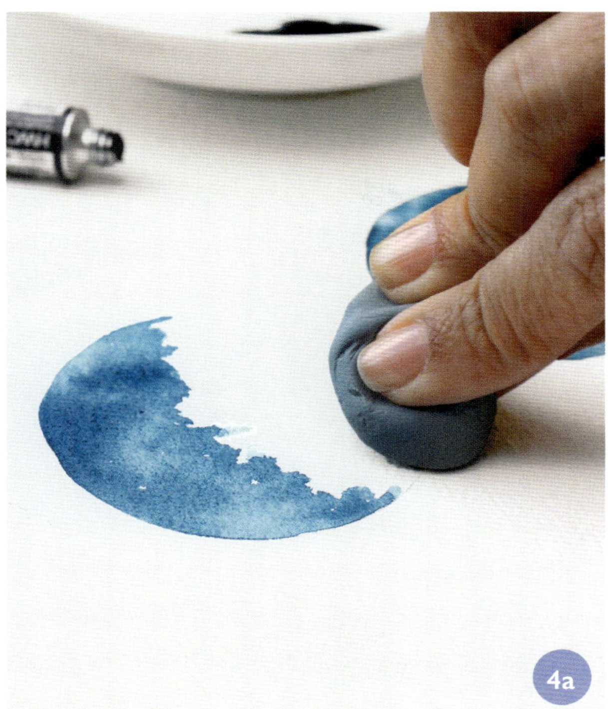
4a

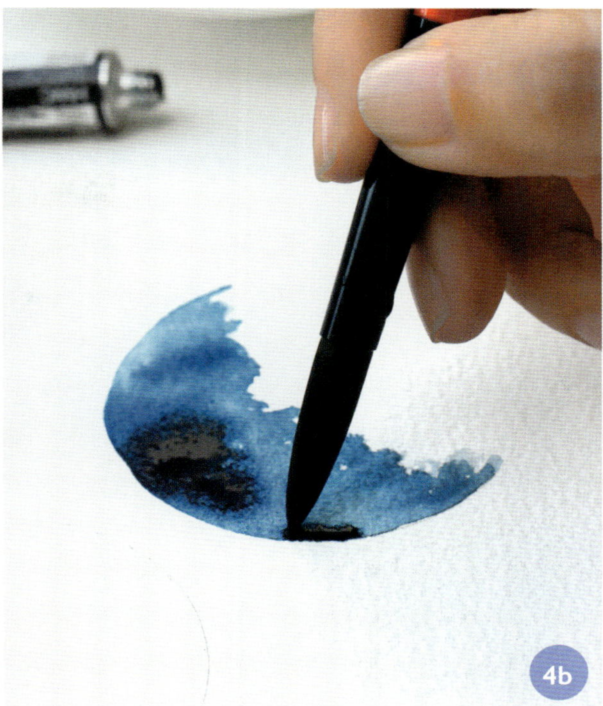
4b

STEP 4. When the pigment is dry, erase the pencil marks with the kneading eraser.

Should you want to add more contrast and uneven patches, add a second or third layer of indigo if necessary.

STEP 5. Follow the same steps for the other moon phases, but each time fill in the circle just a little more until you have a full moon. Once you have your waxing phases complete with your full moon, go ahead and use the same technique to paint in the waning phases until you have the complete set of all the moon phases. Remember to use the belly of the brush in a push and lift technique to create texture on the dry paper. The imperfection of the inner edge is what really brings the unique quality of the moon to the surface.

The natural imperfections of the moon and the gentle dabbing of pigment on paper can be very soothing and relaxing as you do not need to worry about making a perfectly shaped crescent moon.

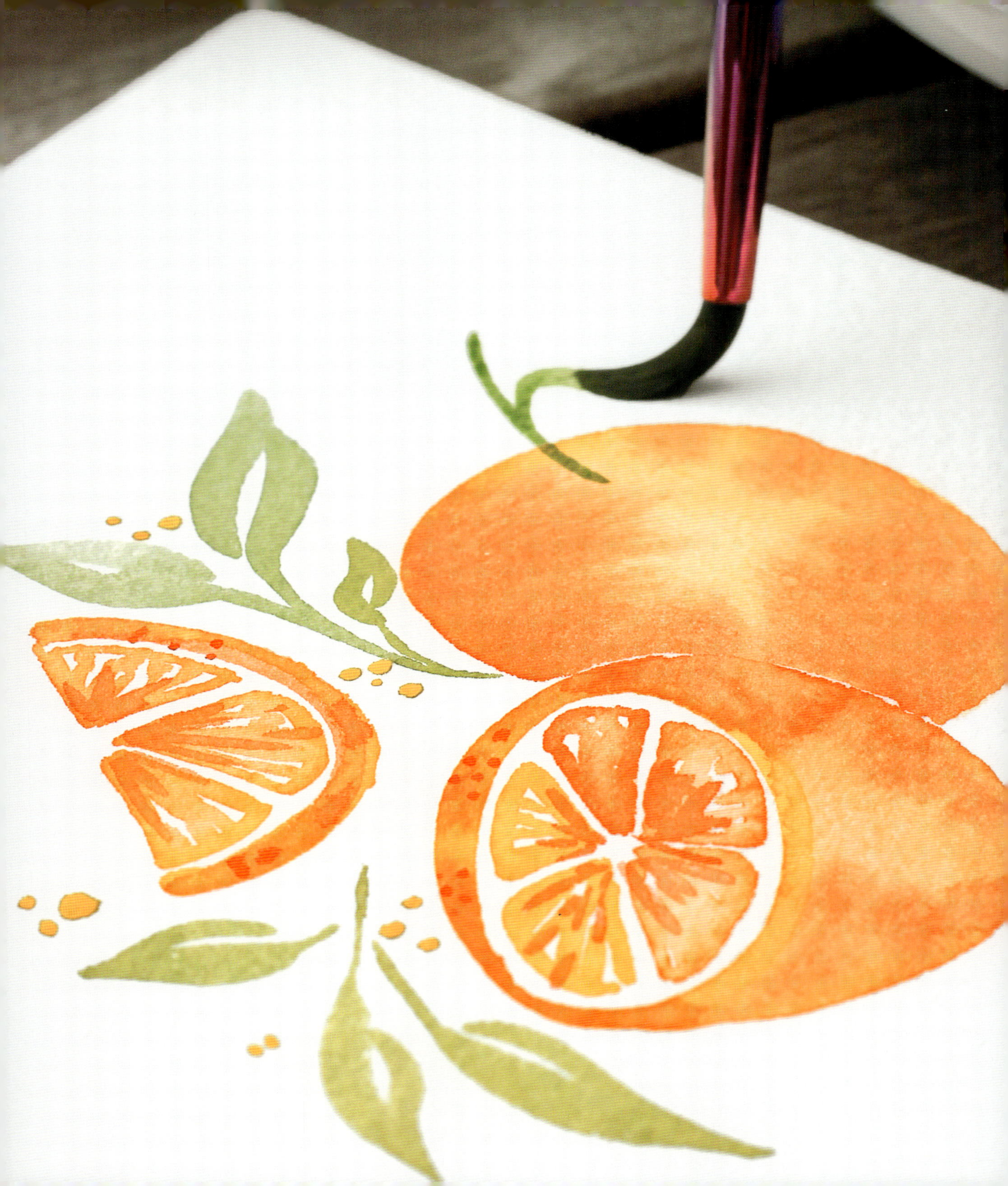

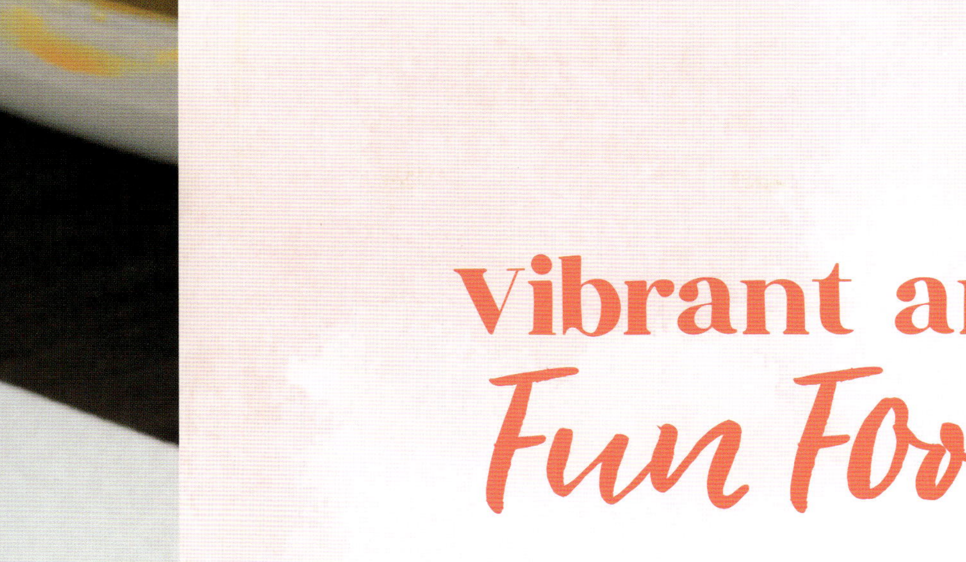

Vibrant and Fun Food

Fruits and vegetables are always so much fun to paint! The natural, vibrant colors are an artist's dream to replicate. Simplifying their shapes will make it very easy for you to create fun patterns or even start making invitation cards for a summer party or a fun fall get together.

I have chosen this particular set of fruits because painting them is incredibly relaxing. Their shapes are simple and their colors are so vibrant. Getting lost in the repetitive nature of the Plump and Juicy Blackberries (page 103) or taking a few moments to appreciate the blooms and blends of the Cozy Pumpkin Patch (page 117) are great ways to find a peaceful moment in your daily practice.

Please always keep in mind that anything that comes from nature is perfect in its own way. No orange is perfectly round nor is a pumpkin perfectly oval shaped. In the next projects, do not focus too much on the perfection of your shapes but rather allow yourself to explore longer, shorter and wider shapes and have fun!

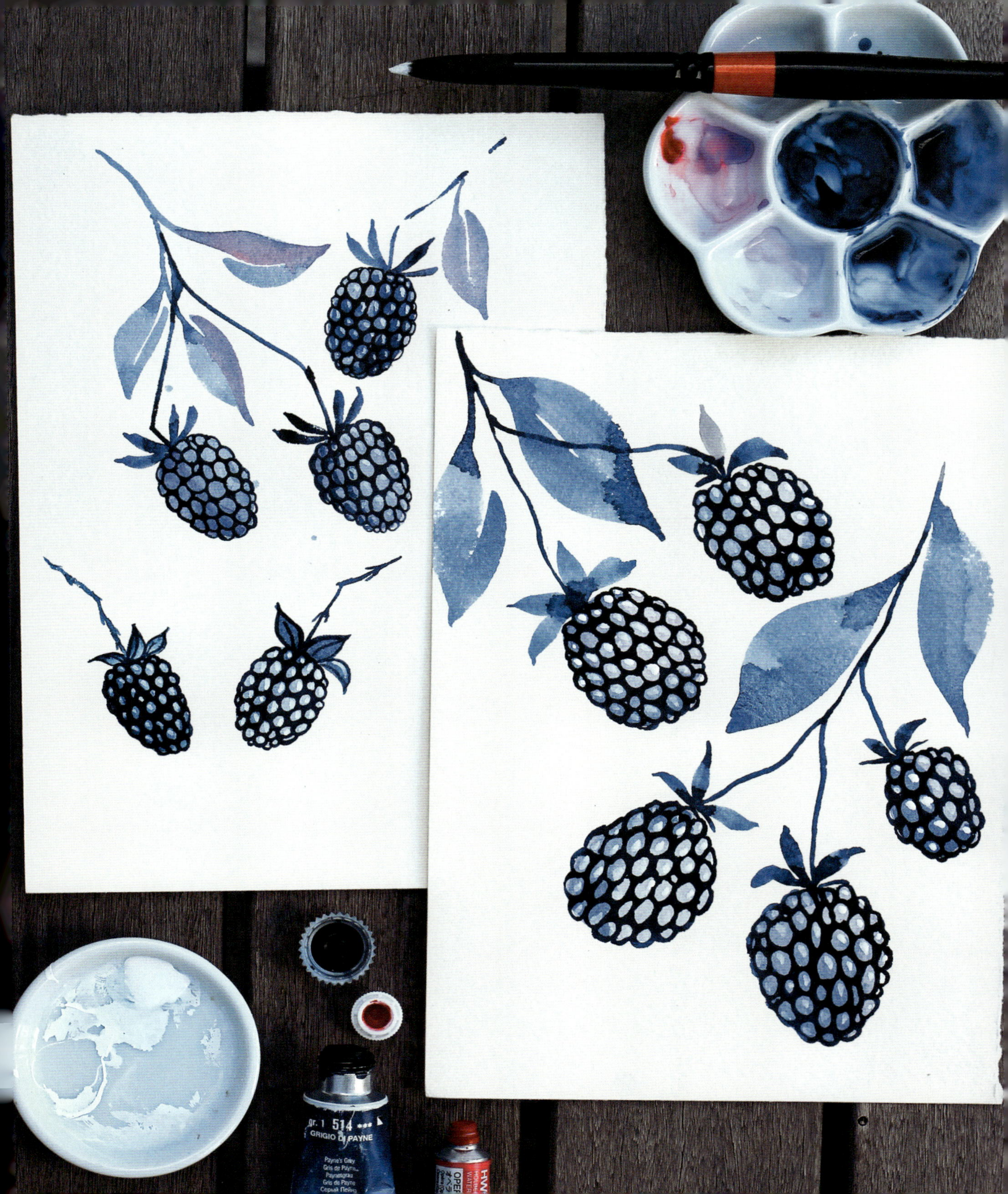
gr. 1 514
GRIGIO DI PAYNE

Plump and Juicy Blackberries

The tartness and earthy undertones of blackberries make them one of my favorite fruits to complement any dessert. The main focus of this project is to simplify the shapes, create layers using the wet-on-dry technique and find a few moments of stillness in your mind as you practice the repetitive movement of the blackberry's signature little spheres.

Materials

- Payne's Gray
- Opera Pink
- Acrylic White Titanium (1:2 water ratio)
- Synthetic round brush No. 8

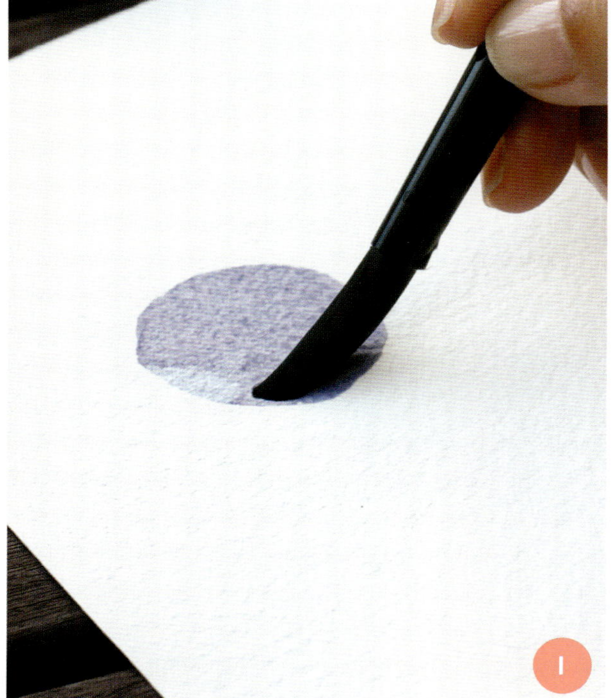

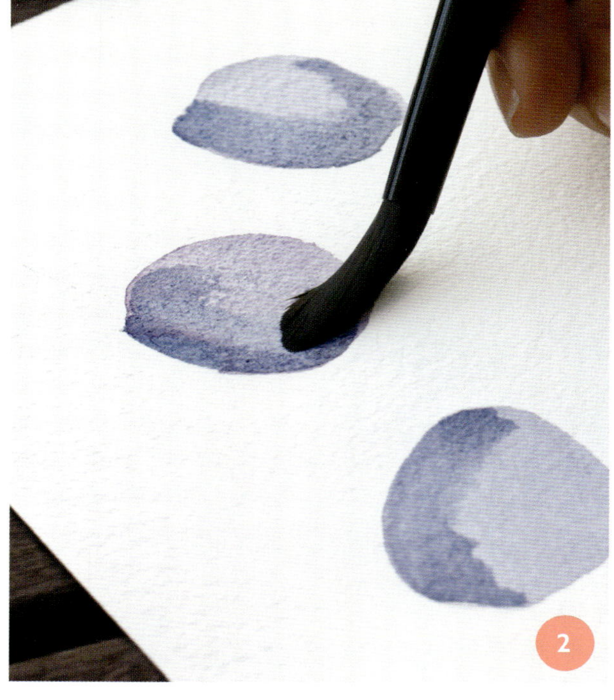

STEP 1. Paint the basic shapes of the fruit. Remember to make some of the shapes a bit more elongated or shorter or smaller than others. The more variation, the better.

On your mixing plate, mix a little bit of a medium value Payne's Gray and a light value of Opera Pink to get a medium value purple. Load up your synthetic medium brush No. 8 with the pigment and start painting the circles that will become the base of your blackberries.

STEP 2. Shade the shapes to add a bit of dimensionality. You do not want your blackberries to look flat.

While you wait for the first layer to dry, add a little more Payne's Gray to the mixture you previously created to get a medium value purple shade. Using the same brush, gently apply the paint on one side of the purple oval. Do not worry if it doesn't perfectly blend.

Let it dry completely.

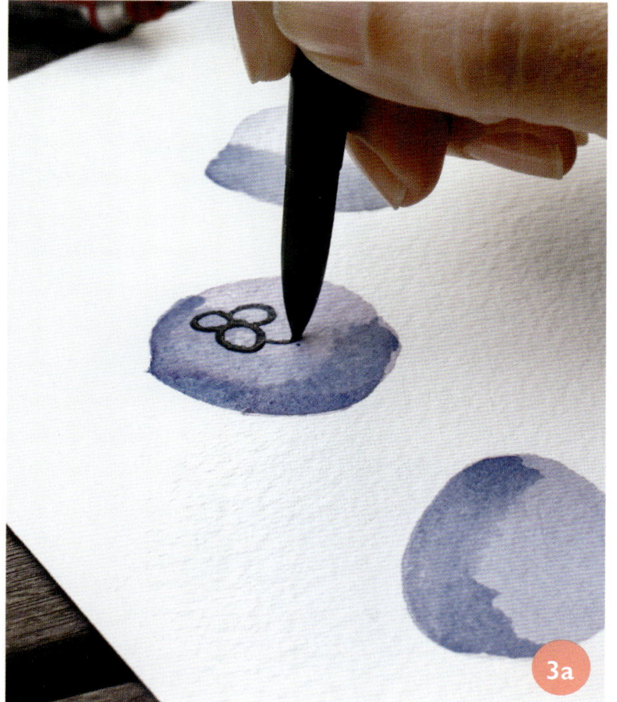

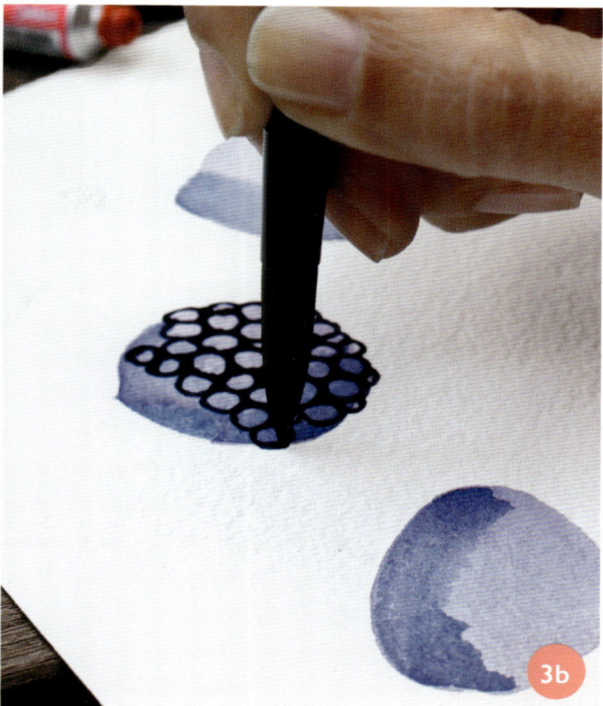

STEP 3. Add the lovely circular pattern that characterizes blackberries so well.

Using the very tip of the same brush loaded up with a dark value of Payne's Gray, start painting circles of different sizes inside the purple ovals that you painted in the previous two steps. Do this for all the previously painted purple oval shapes. By all means, paint outside the edge if you feel like it.

I particularly enjoy this part of the exercise because of its repetitive nature. With the painting of each circle you can become completely absorbed in the task and suddenly you are not thinking about anything else, not the unfinished tasks from work or that silly argument you had with your friend. Your mind can simply focus on these vibrant deep circles, utterly absorbed in the present moment.

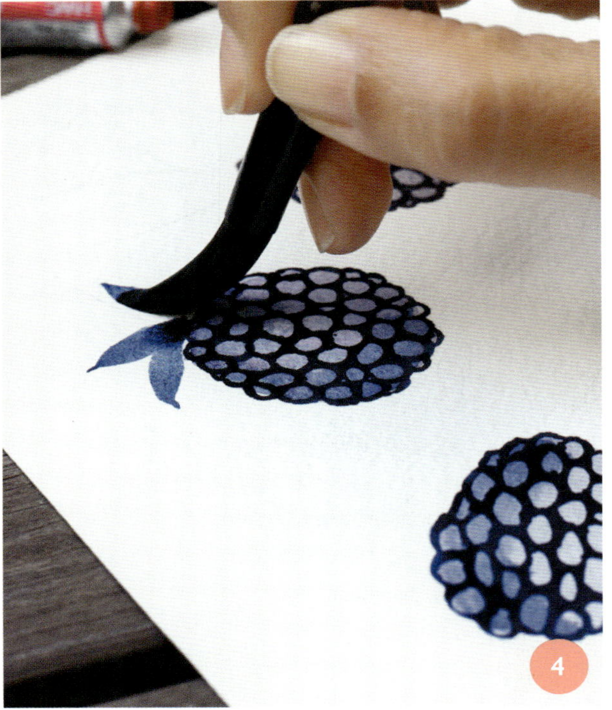

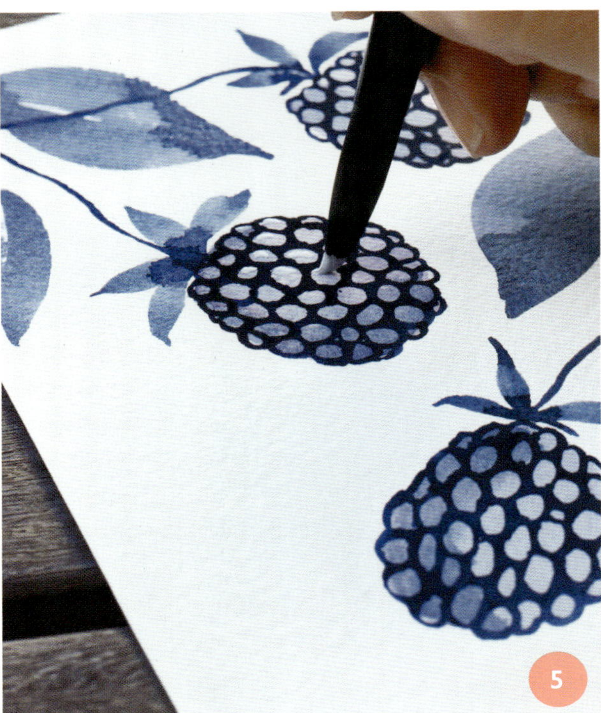

STEP 4. Paint the leaves of each blackberry. I chose to keep my composition very monochromatic, but you can go ahead and choose a different color for this step.

Load up the same brush No. 8 with the pigment of your choice at a medium value and drag it about for small leaves toward the top center of each blackberry. You may add variation to these leaves, making some shorter or longer than others. I personally like them when they look a little ruffled.

You may also add some branches to keep your fruits together or leave the blackberries alone and instead create a pattern. Should you decide to paint a few branches, using a dark value of Payne's Gray and the tip of your brush, paint an uneven line starting from the top of the paper toward the center top of the fruit. Try to connect a few of these lines at the top of the branch as to create small groups of fruit.

STEP 5. Add a bit of sparkle to your blackberries to make them look extra juicy.

Load up only the very tip of your brush with diluted Acrylic White Titanium and start dabbing small dots on every circle you created in step 3. Just like in step 3, dabbing these little dots can be very relaxing. Use this moment to take a few deep breaths as you dab away and clear your mind of anything that is not serving you at the moment.

Now that you have finished your pattern of juicy blackberries, take a moment to assess your mood. I truly hope that you were able to get into your flow state and are now focused and full of energy for the next project.

Refreshing Watermelon

Does anything say summer more than a refreshing slice of watermelon? Just imagine yourself relaxing by the pool with a few slices of watermelon on a plate and a good novel to read and you have yourself some much-needed me time!

In this project you will create a beautiful pattern of watermelon slices using the wet-on-dry technique to create the main shapes, as well as adding some details at the end.

Last, I would like to invite you to lose yourself in the relaxing flow of the pink as it flows to create the simple shapes of a few slices of watermelon, as well as to find a moment of stillness as you dab the details of the seeds.

Materials

- Rose Dore
- Indigo
- Cadmium Yellow
- Synthetic round brush No. 4
- Synthetic round brush No. 0

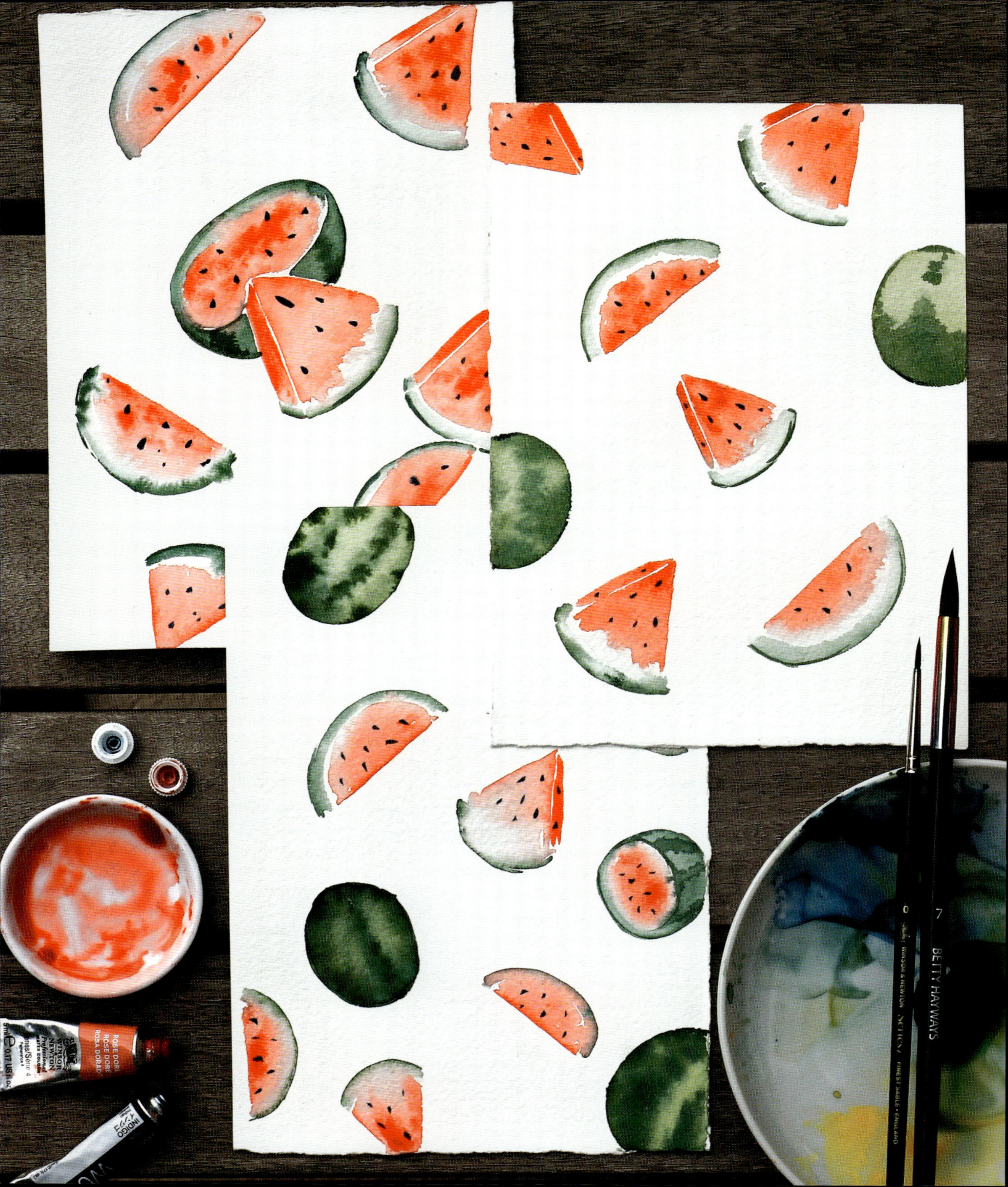
BETTY HAYWAYS

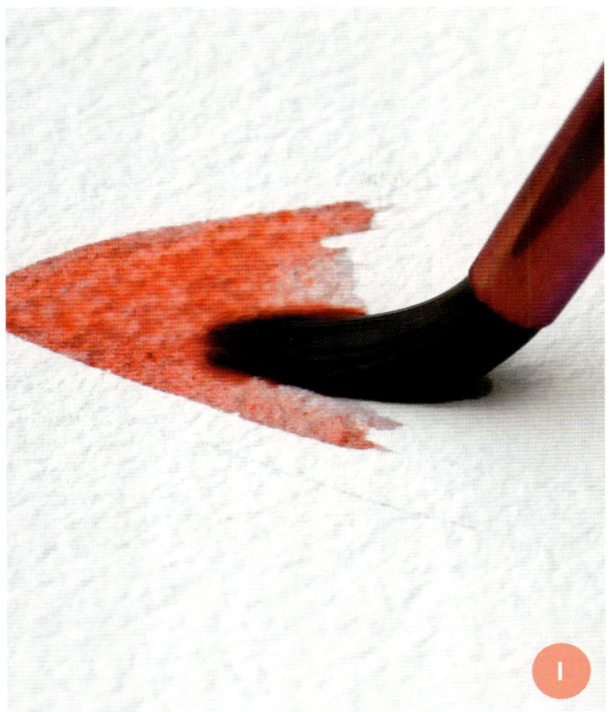

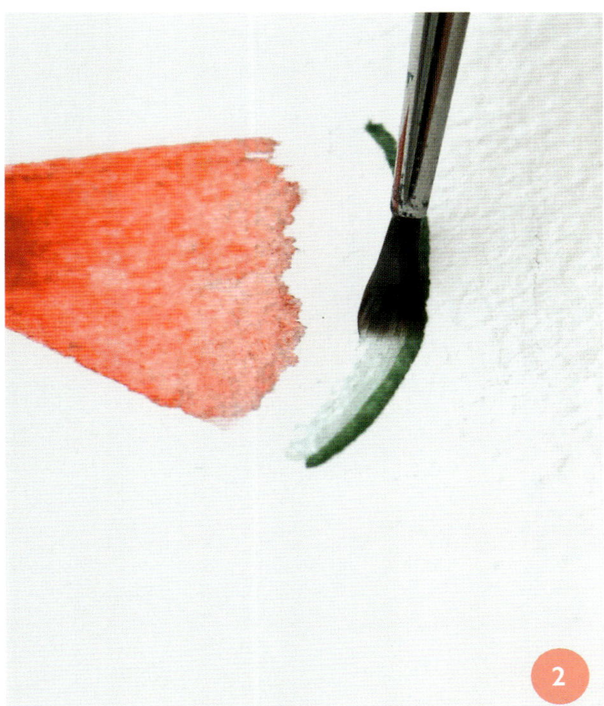

STEP 1. Paint the main triangular shape of the watermelon using the wet-on-dry technique.

Load your synthetic medium brush No. 4 with a medium value of Rose Dore pigment and start painting a triangle from the top down, leaving the bottom of the triangle with rough edges. You can achieve this by gently pressing and lifting the belly of the brush as you reach the widest part of the triangle.

STEP 2. Paint the skin of the watermelon using both a wet-on-dry technique for the edge and a wet-on-wet technique to blend.

While you wait for the triangular shape to dry, mix a two-part medium value of indigo with a one-part medium value of Cadmium Yellow to get a deep green that contrasts wonderfully with the pink shade of the main shape. Using the synthetic small brush No. 0 loaded up with the green you just mixed, paint a curved thin line at the bottom of the triangle, leaving some space to diffuse the rind with the skin. Clean your brush and load it up with just clean water. Gently drag the wet brush along the painted green line of the skin to soften and diffuse the edge on the inside.

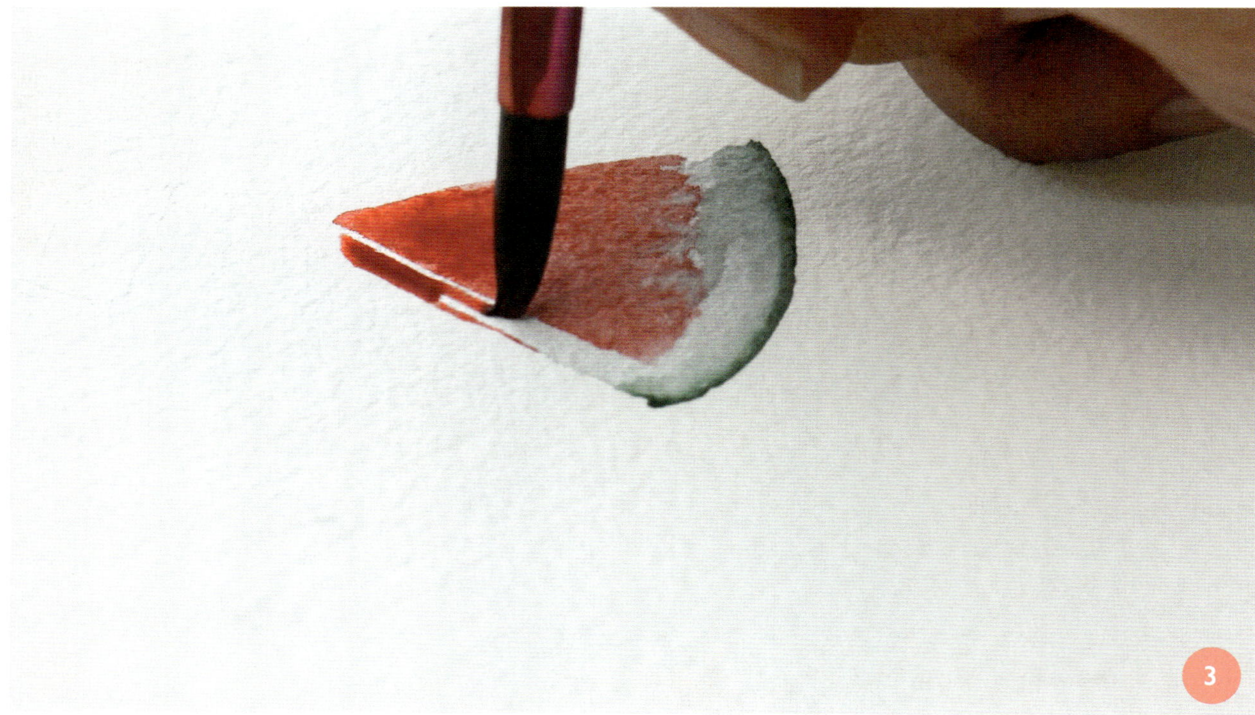

STEP 3. Adding a side to the triangular shape of your watermelon slice can help your composition become more dynamic and fun. Load up your synthetic medium brush No. 4 with a dark value of Rose Dore and paint a small line alongside the previously painted and dry triangle with a slight angle at the top. Please remember to leave a small white gap in between shapes to emphasize the edge of the main shape.

While the Rose Dore triangle dries, go ahead and paint different size slices all around the paper using the techniques described in steps 1 and 2. Please use this moment to focus solely on painting the pink triangles all over the paper. With this repetitive shape, find your flow and focus. With the gentle and soft movements of your brushstrokes, remember to also focus on your breath. Make it a point to take a deep breath in just before you put paint to paper, and as you paint the triangular shapes slowly let the breath go. After painting the basic shapes, let the paint flow and settle.

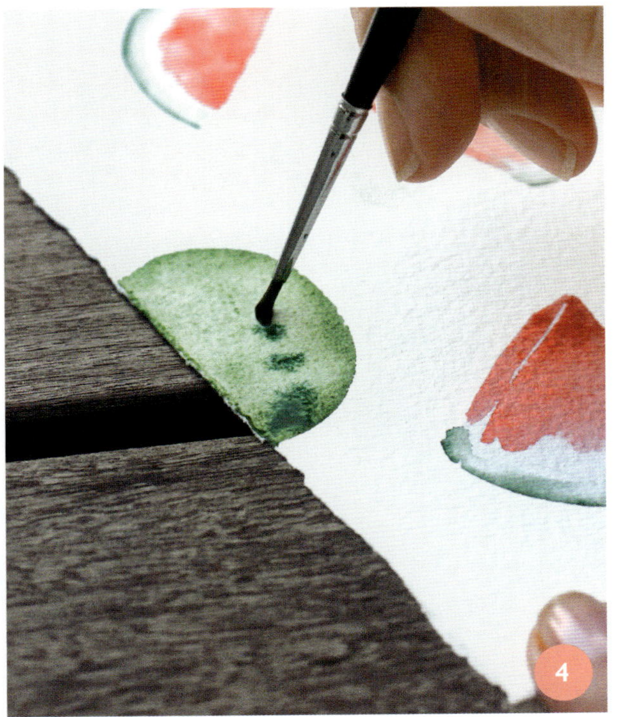

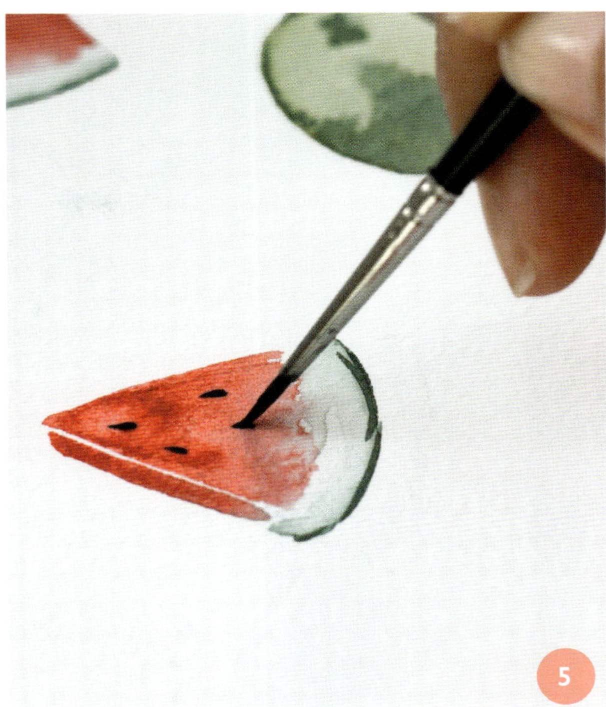

STEP 4. Add some whole watermelons starting with a wet-on-dry technique and later moving on to a wet-on-wet technique for details.

Wait until all triangle shapes are completely dry. Now, add some whole watermelons. Using the same color mix you used for the skin of the slices, paint green oval shapes behind a few of the slices or at the edges of the paper. While the green oval shapes are still a little wet, use a darker value green to dab a few curvy lines to emphasize the natural contrast and spottiness of the watermelon skin.

STEP 5. Paint the seeds.

Using your synthetic small brush No. 0, loaded up with a dark value of indigo, gently dab a few long dots within the triangles by using the push and lift movement of your brush. Being that you have to add these little dots to all of your slices, use these last few moments to lose yourself in the repetitiveness of the movements. Let all thoughts vanish from your mind if only for a few seconds.

I truly hope you found as much joy as I did in creating this fun pattern, and that you were able to clear your mind and find your flow.

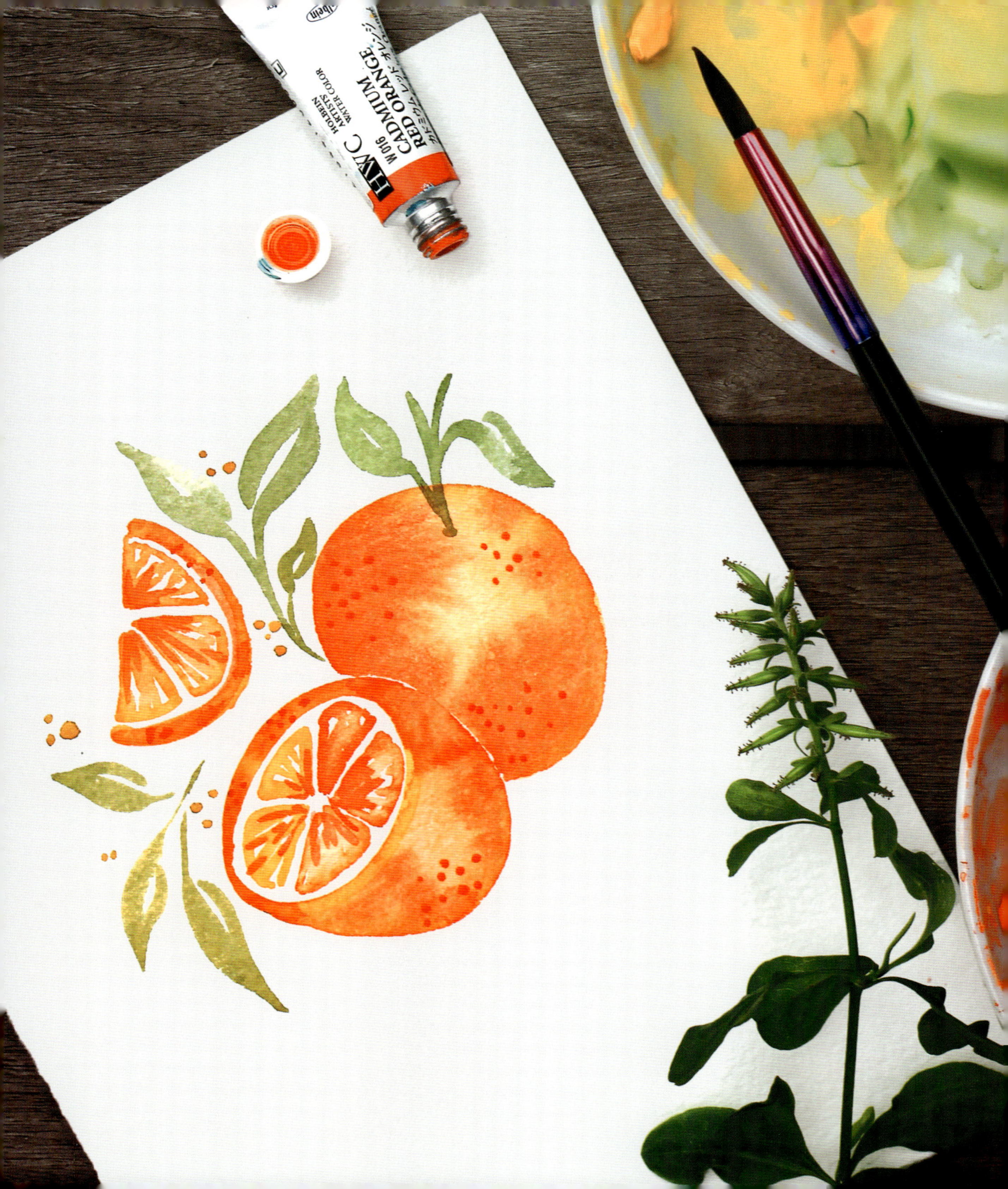
HWC
W016
RED ORANGE
HOLBEIN
ARTISTS'
WATER COLOR

Juicy Oranges

I distinctly remember the first time I tried a blood orange. I was about 30 years old hanging out at the studio of my grad school and a friend shared a slice of this weird-looking fruit. To this day, it is probably the best orange I have ever had. I didn't even know blood oranges existed, and now I obsessively look for them in fresh markets!

I often find myself creating patterns or orange slices because they are so easy to paint! The simple shapes of these oranges make this project very relaxing, and their vibrant colors leave you energized and in a great mood!

Materials

- Cadmium Yellow
- Cadmium Red-Orange
- Indigo
- Synthetic round brush No. 4

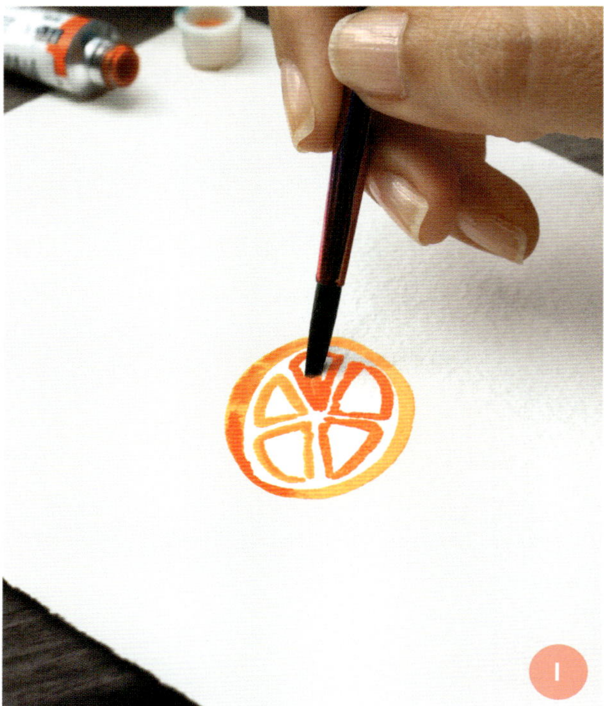

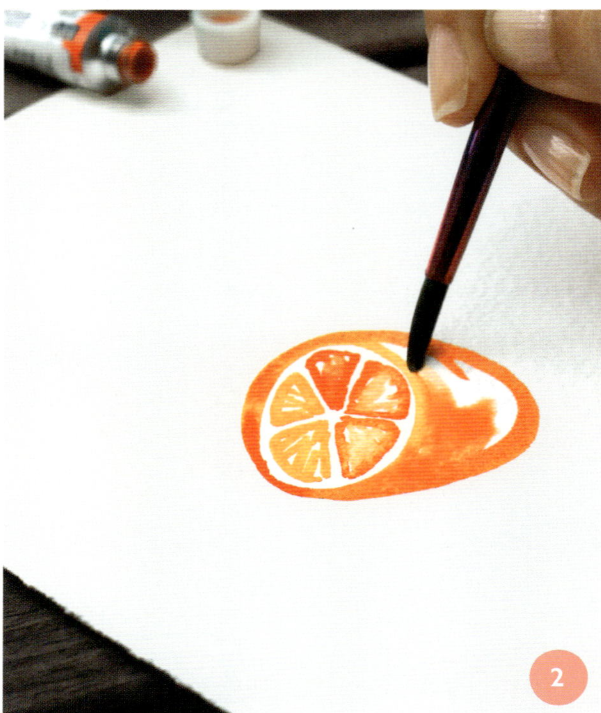

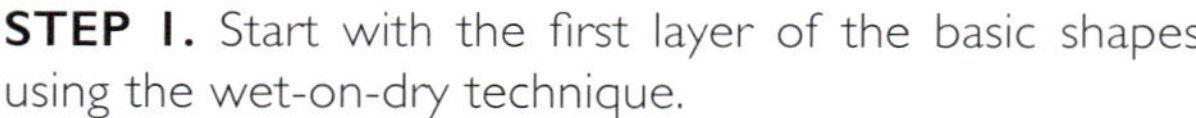

STEP 1. Start with the first layer of the basic shapes using the wet-on-dry technique.

Using your medium synthetic brush No. 4 loaded up with a medium value of Cadmium Yellow, paint a medium-sized circle of about 4 inches (10 cm) in diameter. While the circle is still wet, dab a few dots of medium value Cadmium Red-Orange around the edge to create contrast. Paint a few hollow triangles inside the circle and gently fill them in with small brushstrokes, leaving some white spaces in between each brushstroke at random.

STEP 2. Paint the back side of the orange.

To add the back side of the orange, paint a semicircle adjacent to the circle you just painted and fill it in with a solid layer of medium value Cadmium Red-Orange. Softly filling in shapes with color can have a very calming effect. It's like giving yourself a fifteen-second brain massage.

While you let this half orange dry, go ahead and repeat a variation of step 1 off to the side by maybe only doing half of a slice, or three-quarters. Or even both!

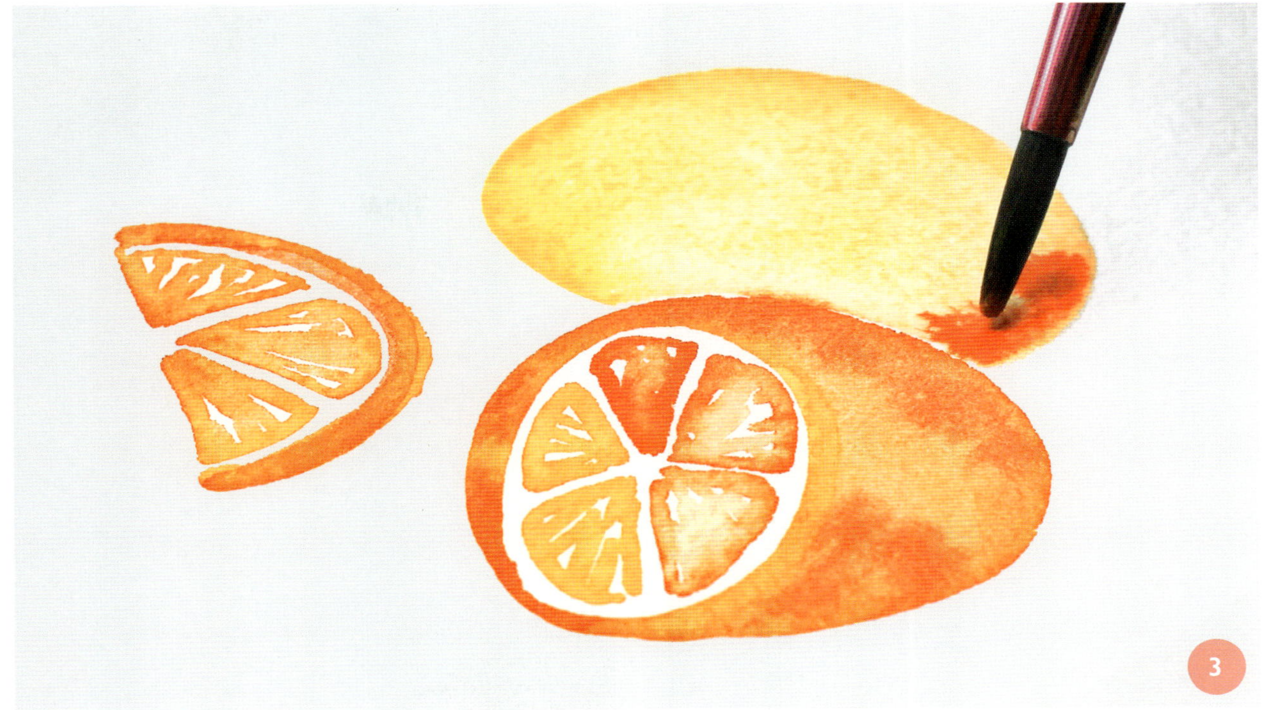

STEP 3. Complete your composition of oranges by adding a full-sized orange.

Once you make sure that the half orange you painted in the first step is completely dry, go ahead and paint a full orange in the background. Load up your brush with a medium value of Cadmium Yellow and paint a circle that seems to overlap the orange slice, but don't overlap the paint, just go around it.

Dabbing a few dots of Cadmium Red-Orange on the wet yellow surface can be very satisfying, and I encourage you to take a few seconds to marvel at how the two colors gently blend and settle. This technique adds texture and contrast as well as creates a bit of a shadow effect from the orange that is in the foreground.

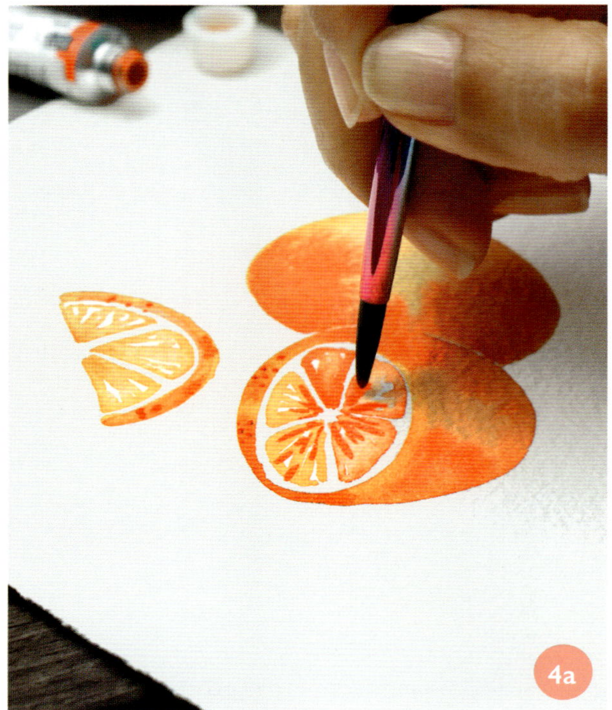

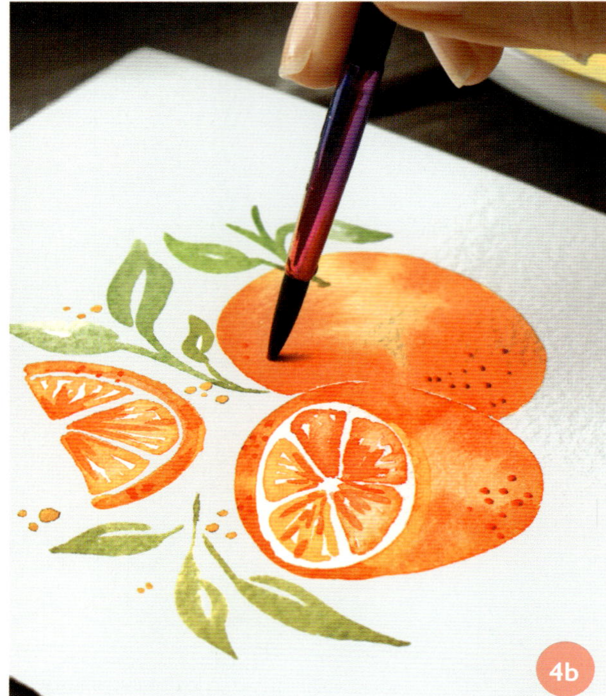

STEP 4. Add a second layer and a few details to your composition to add depth and texture.

Adding a second layer to your slices of orange can give them dimension and make them look juicier. With a dark value of Cadmium Red-Orange and the very tip of your brush, paint small dashes on top of the triangles that you painted in step 1.

With the same brush and pigment, add a few dots in groups to add texture to the skin of the orange.

Optional: Using a lime green (two parts medium value yellow and one part light value indigo), you can paint a few leaves like the ones you practiced in the first project of this book (page 19) to bring together all the elements in your composition.

Cozy Pumpkin Patch

For this project I would like to invite you to channel your favorite autumn childhood memories as you remember the first time you tasted the sweetness of pumpkin pie or had your first pumpkin spice latte. As the weather starts getting colder, we get more and more comfy in our blankets, spend a bit more time indoors and start feeling a bit more relaxed each day.

Should you choose to indulge yourself in the sweet aroma of a pumpkin spice latte or a delicious pumpkin soup, I hope you enjoy painting these colorful, misshapen and fabulous vegetables.

In this project you will be mainly practicing the wet-on-dry technique, delving slightly into wet-on-wet as we add a few details at the end.

Materials

- Cadmium Yellow
- Cadmium Red-Orange
- Indigo
- Green (a ratio of 1 part indigo and 2 parts Cadmium Yellow makes a beautiful green)
- Soft round brush No. 4

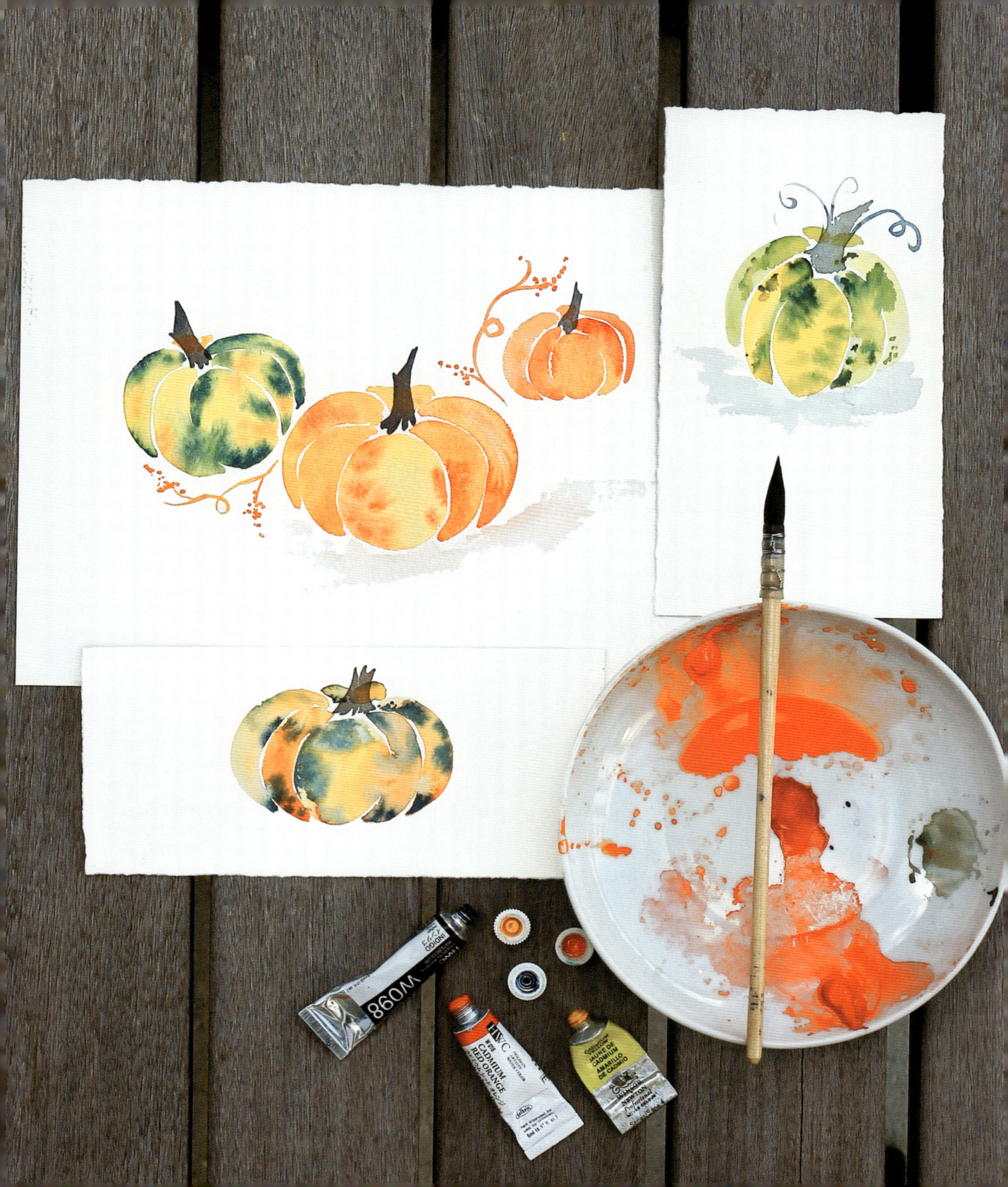
HWC
INDIGO
W098
HWC
W016
CADMIUM RED ORANGE
JAUNE DE CADMIUM
AMARILLO DE CADMIO
WINSOR NEWTON
Professional

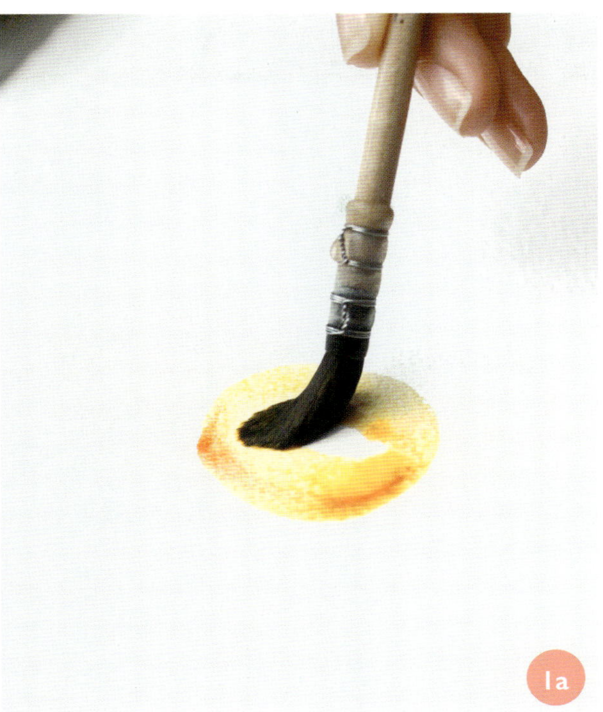

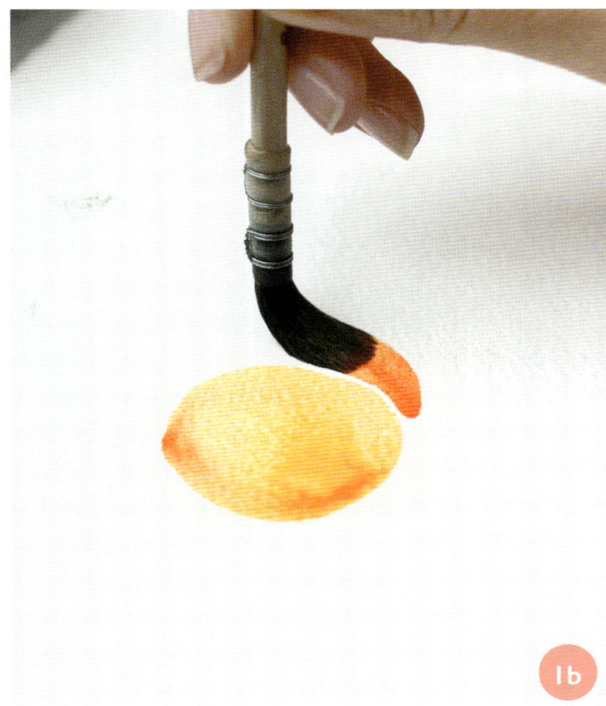

STEP 1. Break down the shape of the pumpkin to its simplest form.

A pumpkin in its simplest form is just an oval with a few "C" shapes adjacent to it.

Using your medium soft round brush No. 4 loaded up with a medium value of Cadmium Yellow, paint a small oval shape in the middle of your paper.

Adding a little bit of medium value Cadmium Red-Orange to the tip of the brush, in a single movement, paint a small "C" shape adjacent to the previously painted yellow oval. Remember to leave a small white line in between the oval and "C" to delineate the difference in shapes.

As with the very first leaves that you painted from the first project in this book, remember to take slow, deep breaths as you drag the brush mindfully to create your basic shapes.

You will be painting two "C" shapes on each side of the main oval shape and two very small ones at the top, leaving a white space in the middle for the stem.

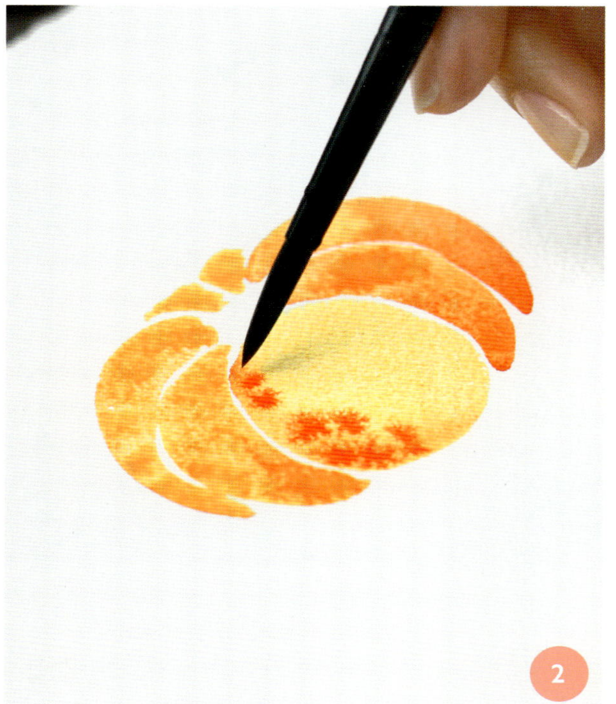

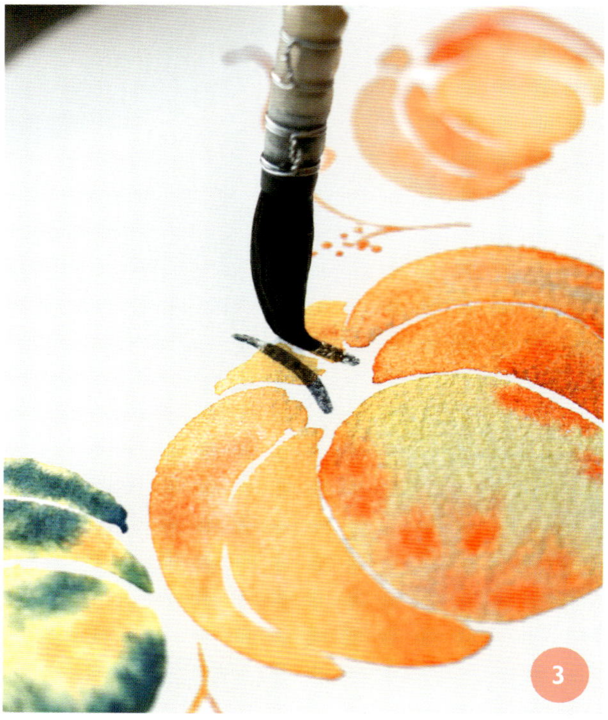

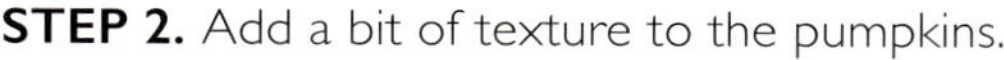

STEP 2. Add a bit of texture to the pumpkins.

Before your shapes dry, dab a few dots of medium value orange, indigo or green to give texture to the skin of the pumpkins and make them look even more natural. This is the point in this project where I absolutely love to stare at the little dabs of contrasting paint and watch them flow and expand on the wet surface. I invite you to take a few seconds to simply look at how the paint flows and moves. It is a very relaxing couple of seconds.

STEP 3. Add the stem of the pumpkin and it will no longer be just a shape but instead a real-looking pumpkin.

Once your basic shapes are completely dry, add the stem of the pumpkin with a medium value brown. On a separate plate mix a one-part medium orange and a one-part medium value indigo, which makes a deep brown.

In the white space left at the top of your "C" shapes, paint two opposing long "C"s and fill the space in between. You have yourself a pumpkin stem.

Go ahead and have fun with a color combination of a yellow-base pumpkin and a few indigo dots or an orange-base pumpkin and a green texture. Remember that a ratio of 1 part indigo and 2 parts Cadmium Yellow make a beautiful green. The possibilities are endless, and you can never go wrong with the color or shape of these fun pumpkin patches!

I hope you enjoyed this very simple yet very satisfying project and found yourself at times staring at the beautiful blooms as they traveled through the paper.

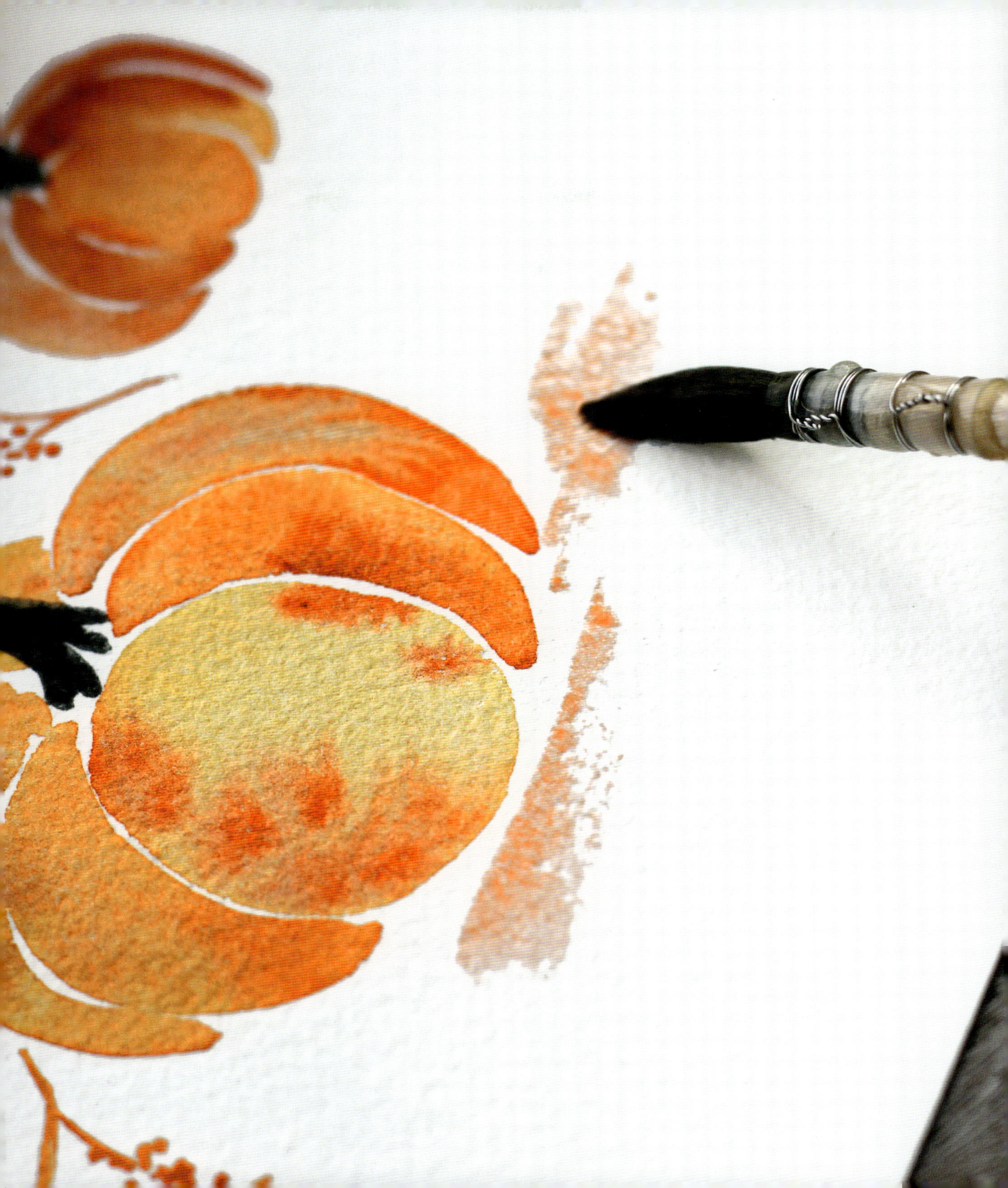

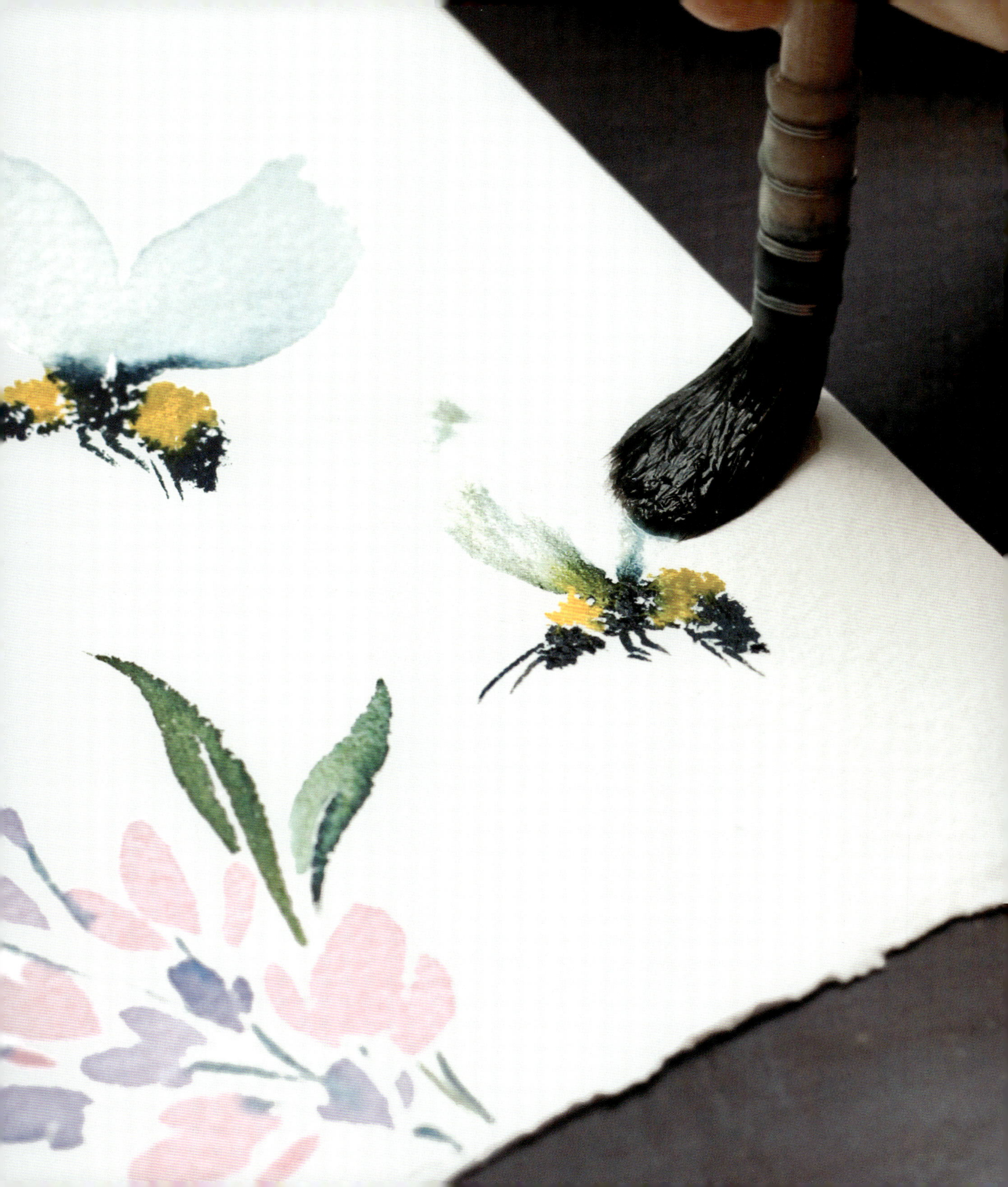

Cutest *Animals* in the World

The beauty and cuteness of animals! You just can't get enough of them! You might think that painting animals is so hard. How can you possibly capture something that is constantly moving?

Say no more! In this chapter I will share with you the simplest, most relaxing way to paint the cutest animals with the least amount of effort or stress possible. For example, some of my favorite animals to paint are small penguins because you really only need one color, one brush and some water; push the paint a bit and all of a sudden you have the cutest little playful penguins! And I might be biased to bees because of course we have to save them all, but they are also super simple to paint. I absolutely love the color contrast of a simple yellow with a simple indigo. How did nature create such perfect little things?

In this last chapter you will be putting to practice all the relaxing techniques learned throughout the book, ranging from the stippling technique learned in painting the Black-Eyed Susan (page 28) to the push and drag brush movements learned in the very first project as you painted the Soft and Flowing Leaves (page 19).

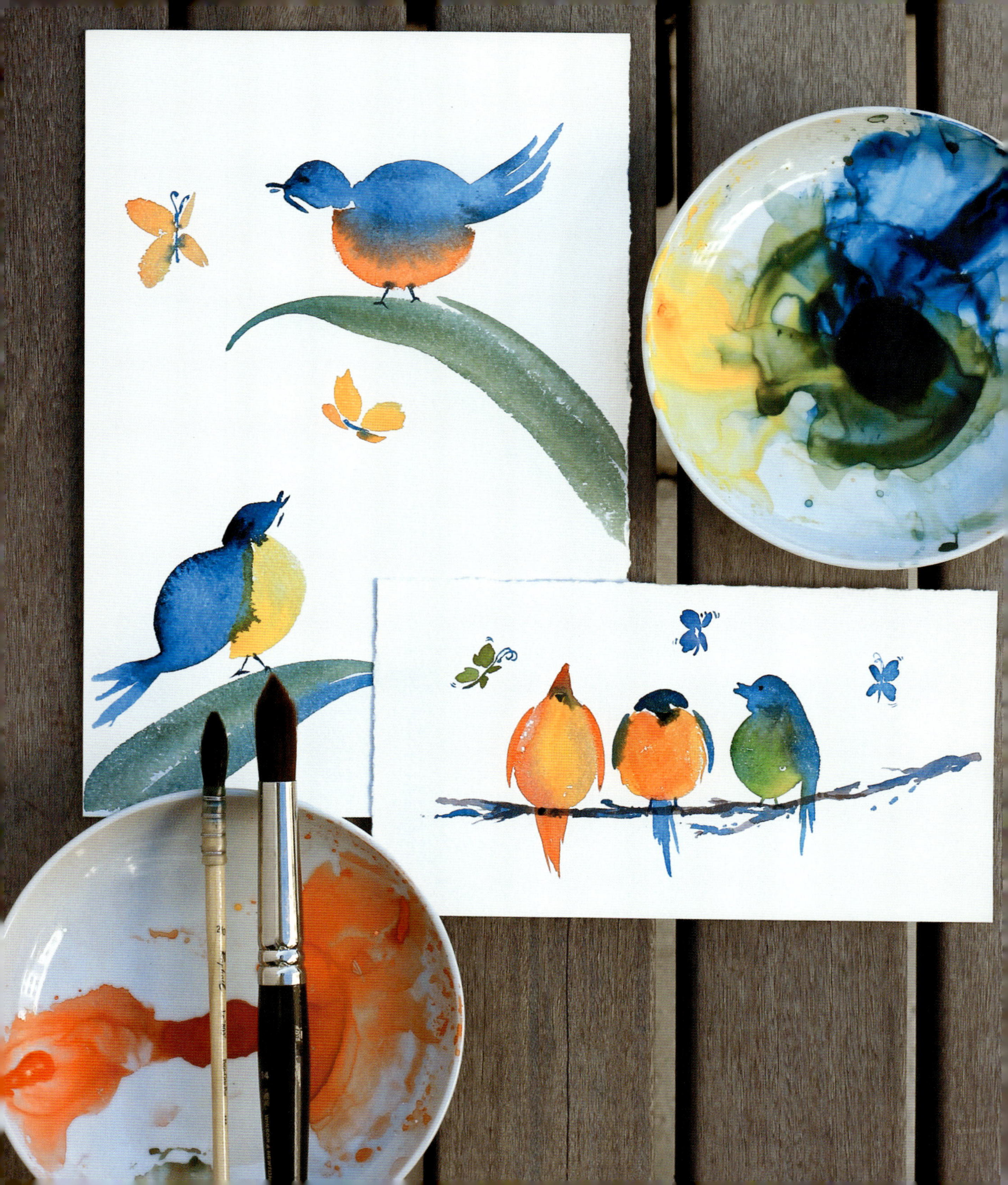

Chatty Little Birds

Fun fact: My alarm clock sound is the gradual increase in volume of chirping birds as the light of my alarm clock gradually gets brighter to mimic a calm and peaceful sunrise. Isn't that the best possible way to wake up every single morning? Worth every penny if you ask me.

Birds in their simplest form are three overlapping ovals with a few brushstrokes to make the tail and the beak. As you paint the body of the bird, I hope you find the singlular, very slow movement of the brush very relaxing and satisfying at the same time.

In this project you will be mostly working with a wet-on-dry technique as you paint the individual shapes that make up the body of the bird, but occasionally colors will blend within the shapes. Take a moment to appreciate these blends and let the watercolors flow where they want to flow.

Materials

- Cadmium Red-Orange
- Indigo
- Cadmium Yellow
- Synthetic round brush No. 14
- Soft round brush No. 4

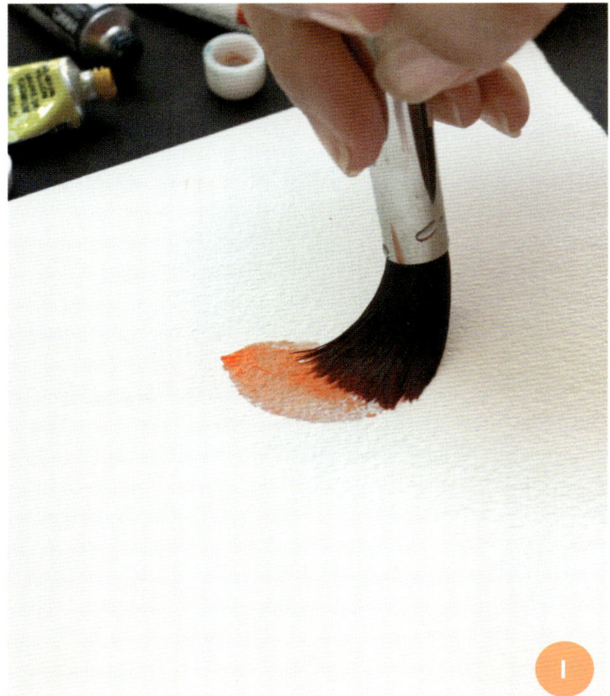

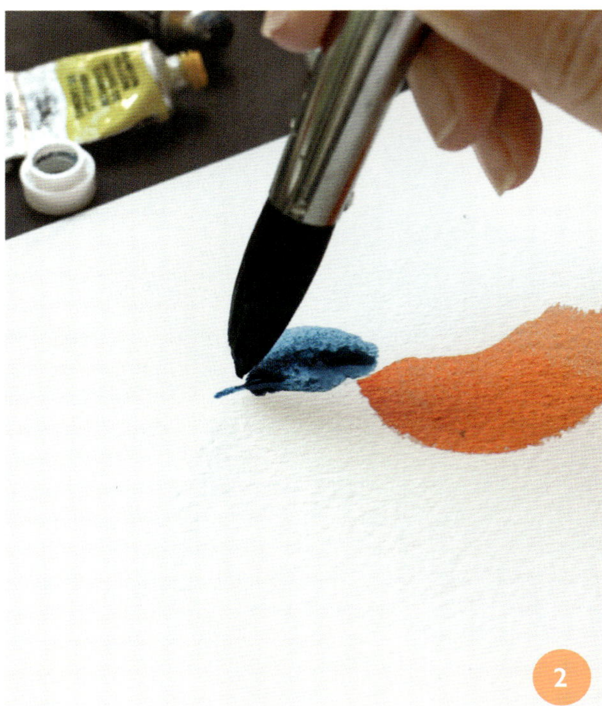

STEP 1. Paint the belly of the bird.

Load up your large synthetic brush No. 14 with a medium value of Cadmium Red-Orange and in one gentle and slow circular motion paint a half oval shape. Use the push and drag brush technique but be mindful to do it as slowly as possible to make sure that all the pigment in the brush stays in the paper.

STEP 2. Paint the head in a different color.

Clean your large synthetic brush No. 14 and load it up with a medium value of indigo. Paint a small half circle diagonally adjacent to the half oval to make the shape of the head and add a small beak with the tip of the brush.

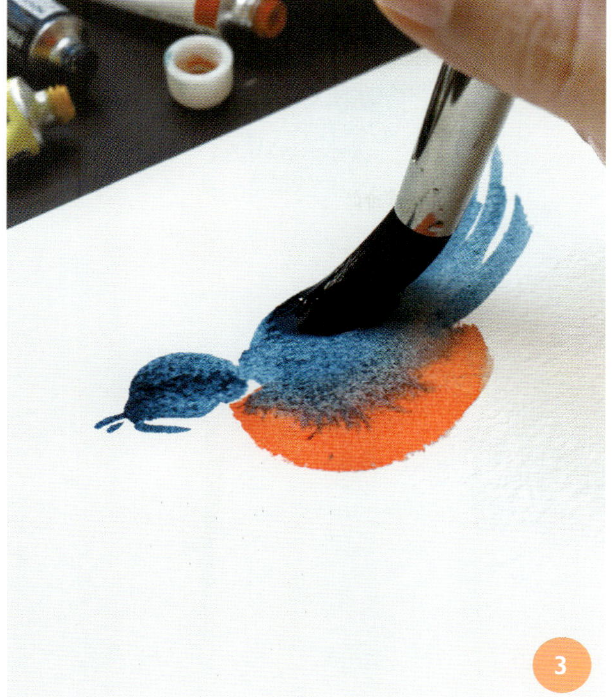

STEP 3. Complete the shape of the bird's body.

Using the same brush and pigment that you used to paint the head of the bird, complete the body of the bird with one or two brush strokes. Take a moment to appreciate the beautiful and natural blend of the orange and the indigo.

Please do not attempt to blend the colors yourself but let the pigment softly blend on the surface of the paper.

As you finish the upper body of the bird, using the same brush with the same pigment, gently drag the brush in a curved line upward to create the tail of the bird.

The smaller details such as the beak and the legs can be done with the very tip of the medium soft brush No. 4 and a little bit of dark indigo.

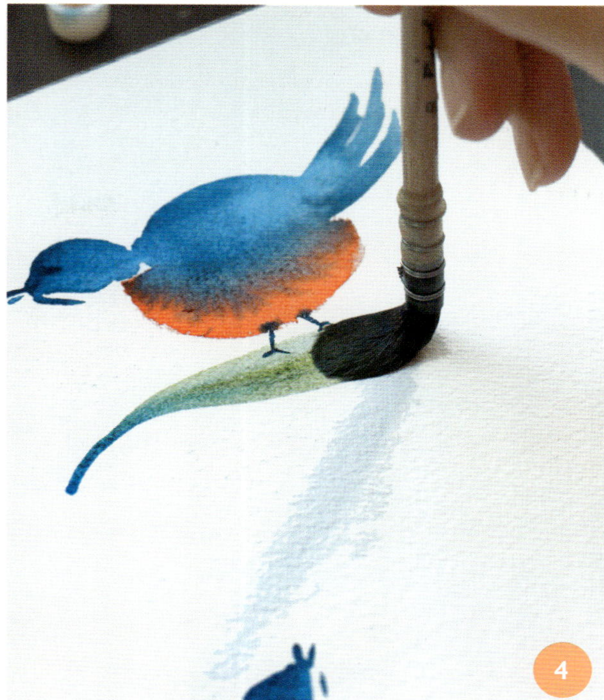

STEP 4. Give a little context to the birds by painting a leaf on which they can stand to make your composition look complete.

Use your medium soft brush No. 4 and load it with a soft green: mix one part medium value of Cadmium Yellow and one part light value of indigo. Start painting a long, curved leaf. Use the tip of the brush to start the leaf and then gently push and drag the belly of the brush onto the paper until you run out of paper.

Like in the second project in the book (page 23), painting long leaves can produce a very relaxing effect as you slowly drag your brush along the textured paper.

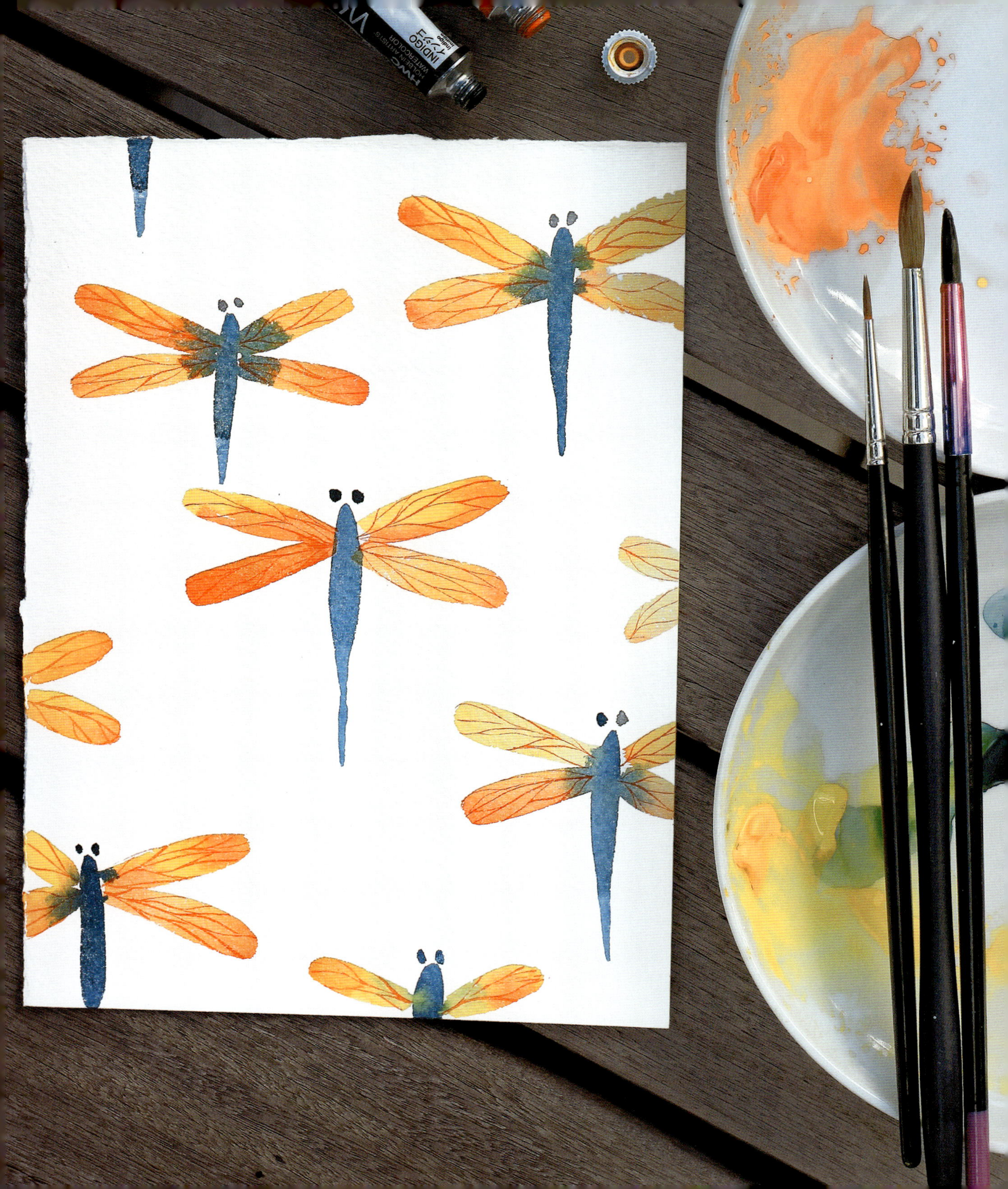
HWC
HOLBEIN ARTISTS'
WATERCOLOR
INDIGO
インジゴ
indigo
indigo

Delicate Dragonflies

When living in south Florida, you have to get used to coexisting with a variety of small insects. To be honest, small dragonflies are really the only ones I can handle. They are so delicate, fragile and translucent, it is almost impossible not to imagine them painted in watercolor!

I would like to use this project to once again emphasize the importance of synchronizing your breath to your brushstrokes as the wings of these delicate dragonflies are done in a single brushstroke. I hope you find painting this lovely pattern very relaxing and you can find a moment of peacefulness within your day.

Materials

- Cadmium Yellow
- Cadmium Red-Orange
- Indigo
- Soft round brush No. 4
- Synthetic round brush No. 4
- Soft round brush No. 0

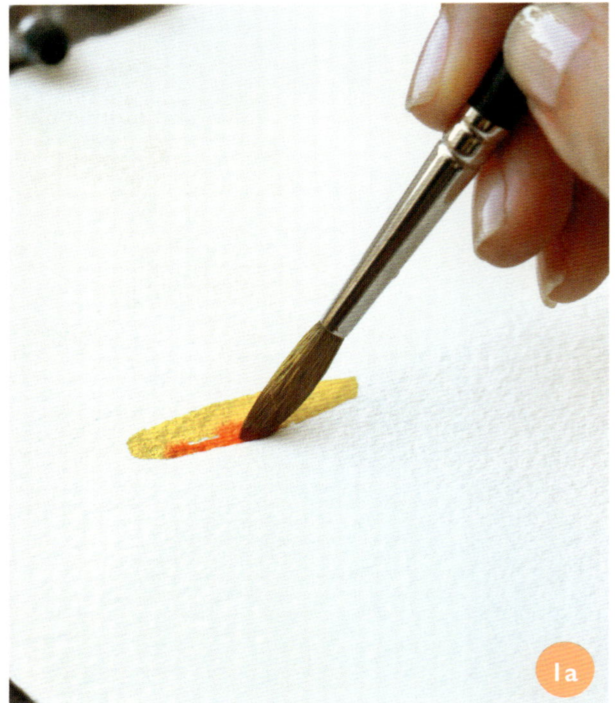

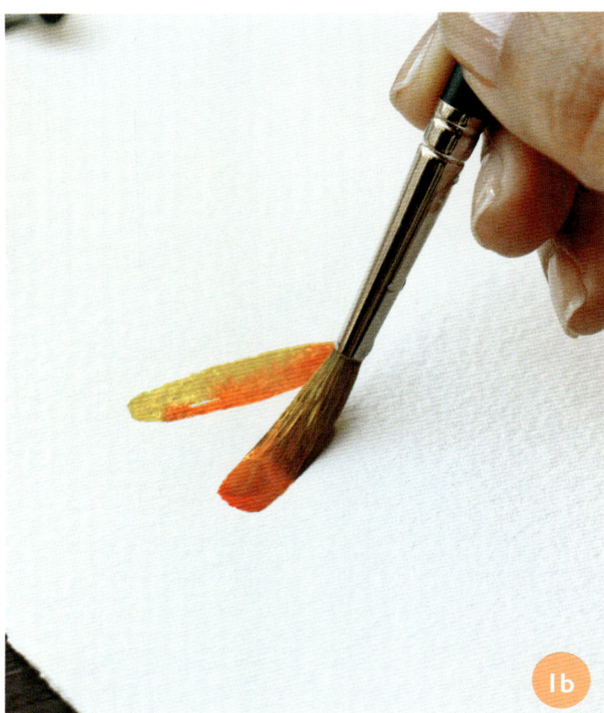

STEP 1. Paint the wings in a single brushstroke using the wet-on-dry technique.

Again, remember to be mindful of your breaths as you drag your brush gently on the paper. This will help your hand stay steady and your brushstrokes will flow easier.

With your medium soft round brush No. 4 loaded up with a medium value of Cadmium Yellow, gently paint a wide solid line about 3 inches (7.5 cm) long by dragging the brush downward at a slight angle. Dip the very tip of the soft round brush No. 4 in the Cadmium Red-Orange and gently paint the bottom edge of the yellow shape you previously painted.

With the same brush and pigment you just used, paint a second line with a swift single brushstroke of the same length, softly dragging the brush slightly upward.

Now, imagine the body of the dragonfly as a vertical line adjacent to the two shapes you just painted (we will paint the body a bit later). Leaving about a pencil's width empty, go ahead and repeat the previous step on the other side of said imaginary vertical line to create the other two wings and complete the dragonfly.

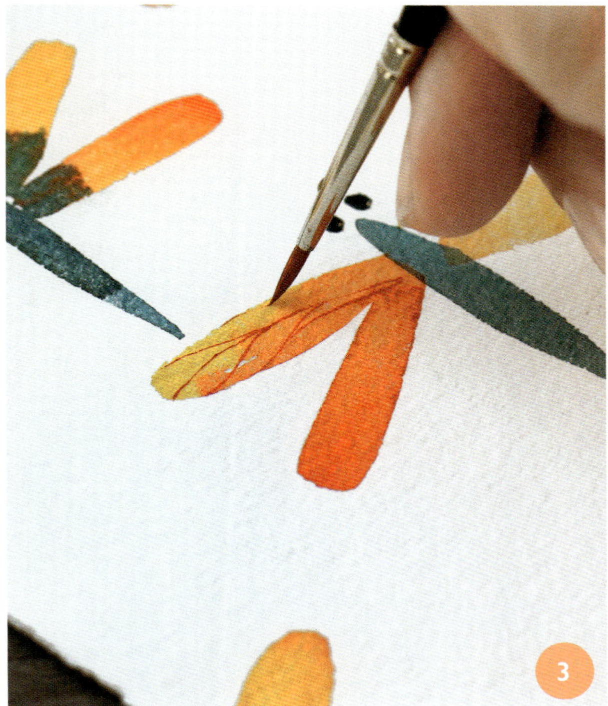

STEP 2. Paint the body of the dragonfly. This is a very minimal approach as simplicity is best when creating patterns.

With the medium synthetic round brush No. 4 loaded with a medium value of indigo, gently paint a vertical line in between the four wings. Make sure you start the line with the tip of your brush slightly lifted and as you paint your line downward, gently push the belly of the brush onto the paper. As you come to the end of the line, gradually lift up the brush. With the tip of the brush, paint two small dots at the top of the line to create the eyes of your dragonfly.

While you let this dragonfly completely dry, go ahead and paint a pattern of dragonflies all around the paper.

Once you can see that the first dragonfly is dry, move on to the third step and add some details to the wings.

STEP 3. With the small detail brush No. 0 loaded up with a dark value Cadmium Red-Orange, gently paint a line that crosses the middle of the wing in the long direction and add a few extra small, curved lines growing from the central line. Because you have to paint the same detail in all the wings and in all the dragonflies, this can be an exercise to help you find your flow and solely focus on these delicate lines. Let your mind slowly turn down the inner chatter and find a moment of calm peacefulness.

I hope that at the end of this project you can find yourself very relaxed and in a great mood looking at this lovely and delicate pattern of dragonflies.

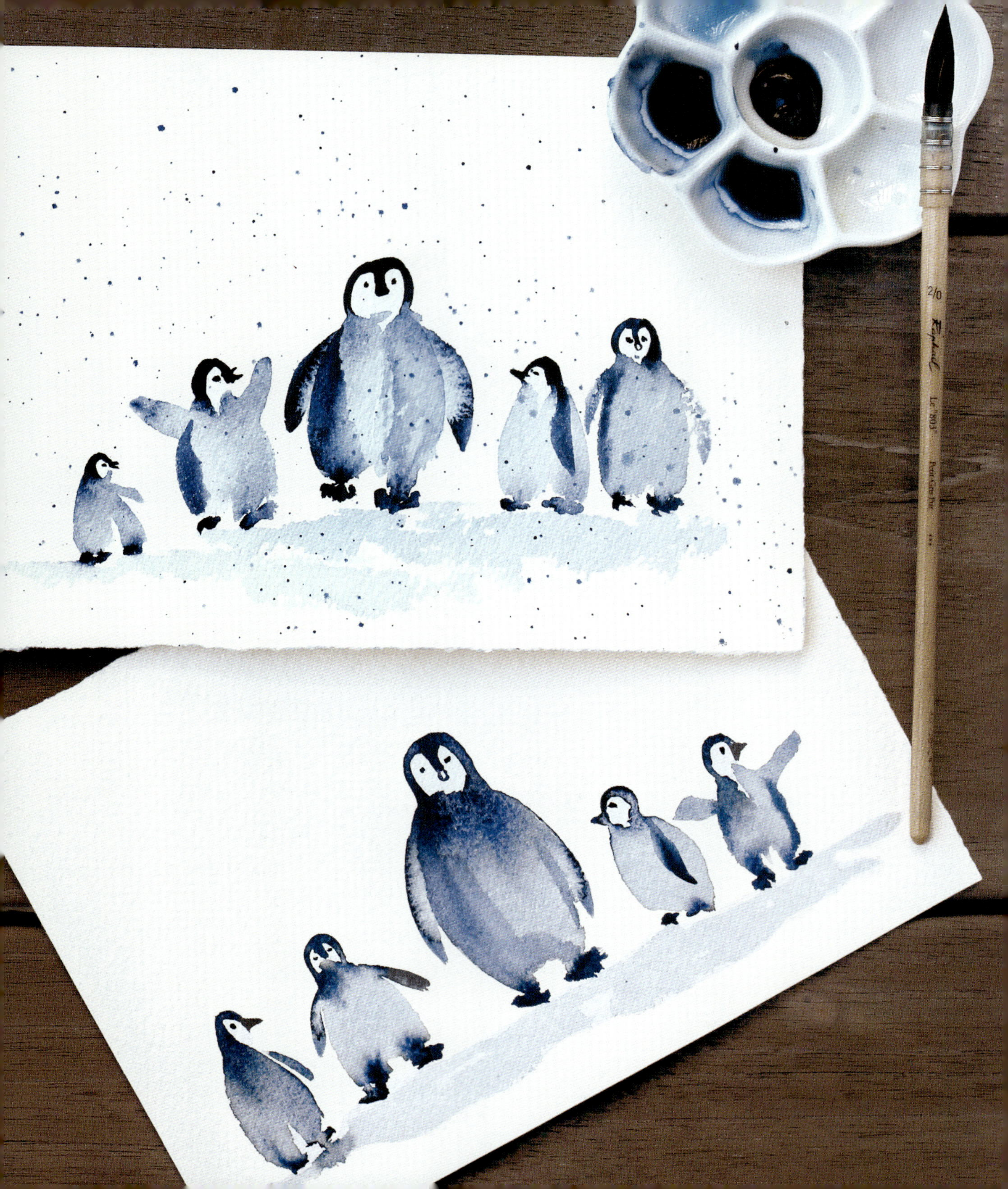

Friendly Penguins

"One can't be angry when one looks at a penguin."
—John Ruskin, November 4, 1860

This project is one of my favorites due to its simplicity, as well as because we get to play with the gentle movement of the pigment as it mixes with the water on the paper.

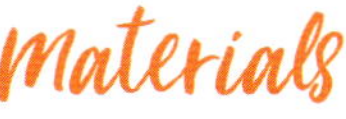

- Payne's Gray
- Soft round brush No. 2

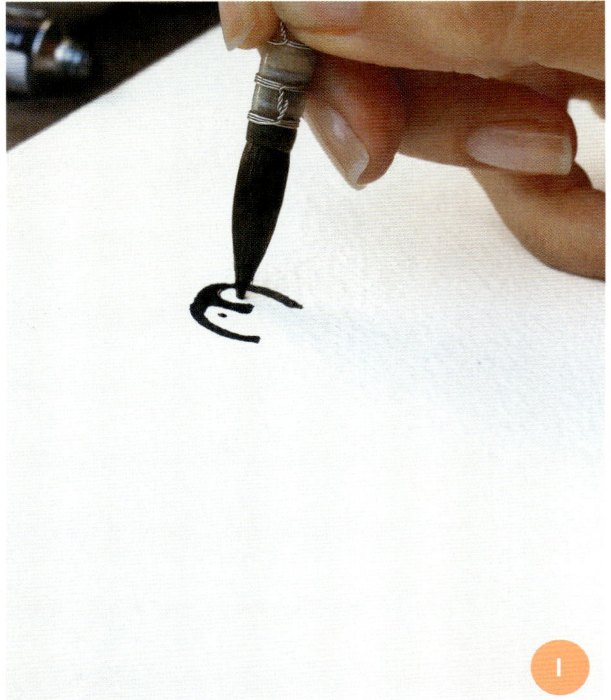

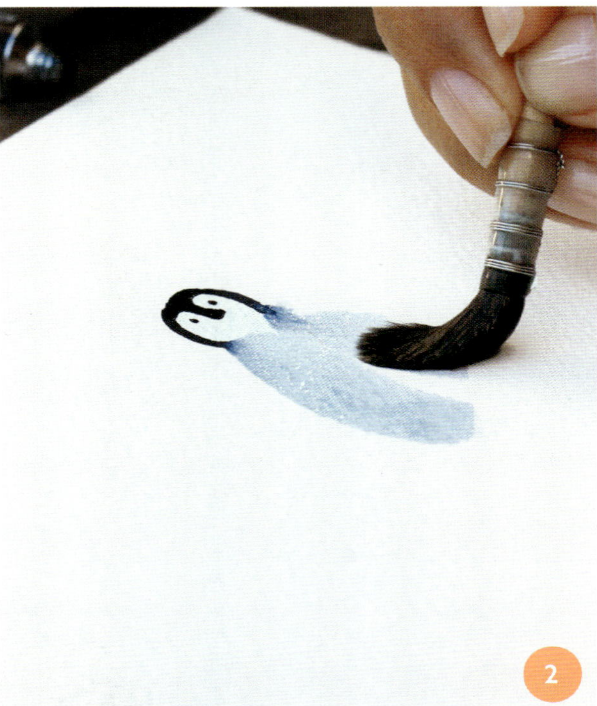

STEP 1. Paint the overall shape of the penguin's face using a wet-on-dry technique.

Using the very tip of your small soft brush No. 2 loaded with a dark value of Payne's Gray, paint an upside-down wide "U" shape with a line down the middle vertically. Add two small dots on each side of the line for the eyes.

STEP 2. Paint the body of the penguin. This is a particularly satisfying process as you watch the pigment flow effortlessly and create soft shapes.

Completely clean your brush with clean water, then start dragging the pigment from the bottom end of the "U" shape downward with a single push and drag brush motion to create the body of the penguin. Repeat from the other side of the penguin's face and you have the body of the penguin.

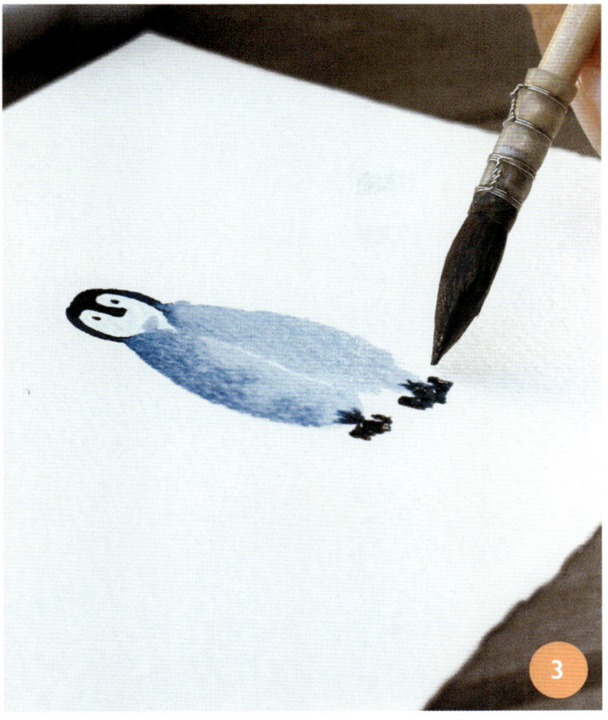

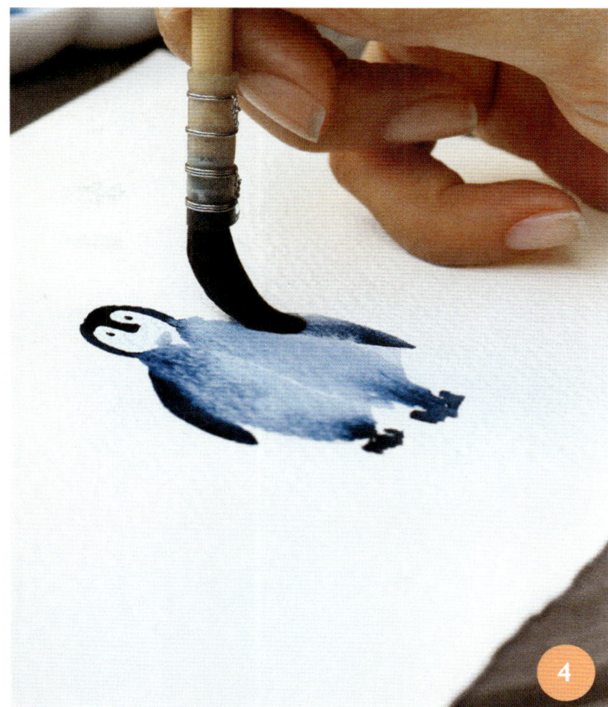

STEP 3. Paint the feet of the penguin.

Load up only the tip of your brush with the dark value of Payne's Gray and paint two wiggly spots at the bottom of the body of the penguin. Aren't these the cutest little penguin feet?

Tip: If you make one wiggly line slightly lower and smaller than the other, it will look as if the penguin is walking (lifting the foot to take a step).

STEP 4. Add the penguin's wings in a single brushstroke movement.

Using the same brush with only the tip loaded up with a medium value of Payne's Gray, move your brush from the bottom up. Placing the tip of your brush adjacent to the belly of the penguin, start painting the wing with the tip of the brush and gently push and drag the belly of the brush upward. End the dragging motion at the base of the head.

Take a moment to watch the dark value pigment blend softly with the water and let it do its magical dance.

Using the same technique of painting a dark value head and letting pigment flow into water to create the body, you can now paint penguins sideways or with wings up in the air. Make a family of penguins and have fun!

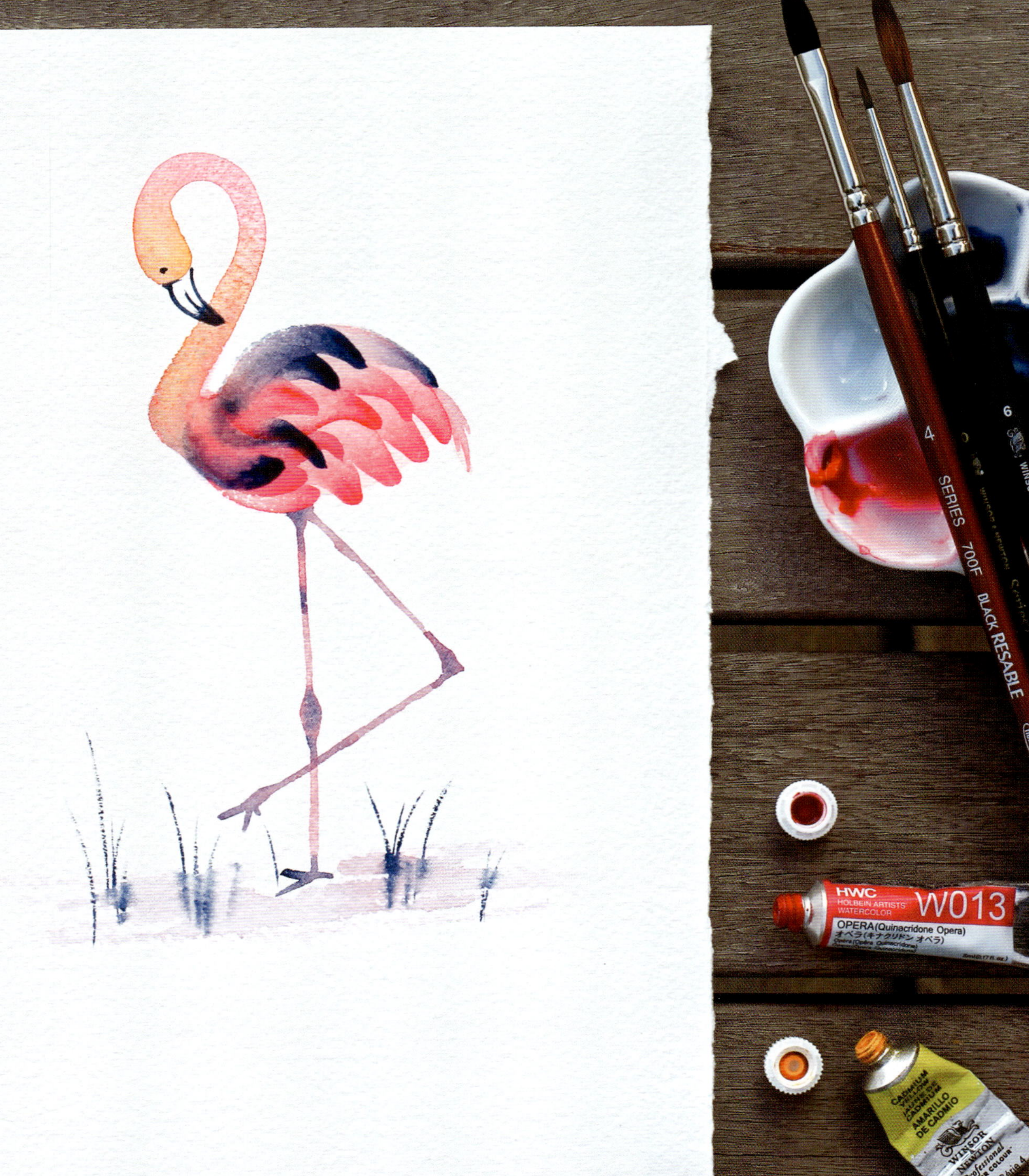

SERIES 700F BLACK RESABLE
HWC
HOLBEIN ARTISTS' WATERCOLOR
W013
OPERA(Quinacridone Opera)
AMARILLO DE CADMIO

Regal Flamingo

Aren't flamingos so regal, elegant and composed? They look fabulous with their long necks, skinny legs and pink fluffy feathers, minding their own business. And they are so easy to paint!

I will break down the main shapes of the flamingo into simple shapes that you can paint easily. You will also be practicing your soft and long brush movements that will make you feel calm and relaxed.

Remember that flamingos are soft and gentle, so keep this in mind with the movement of your long and short brushstrokes. Find mindfulness in the feathers and calmness in the soft movement of the long neck.

Materials

- Opera Pink
- Cadmium Yellow
- Payne's Gray
- Soft round brush No. 6
- Soft filbert brush No. 4
- Soft round brush No. 0

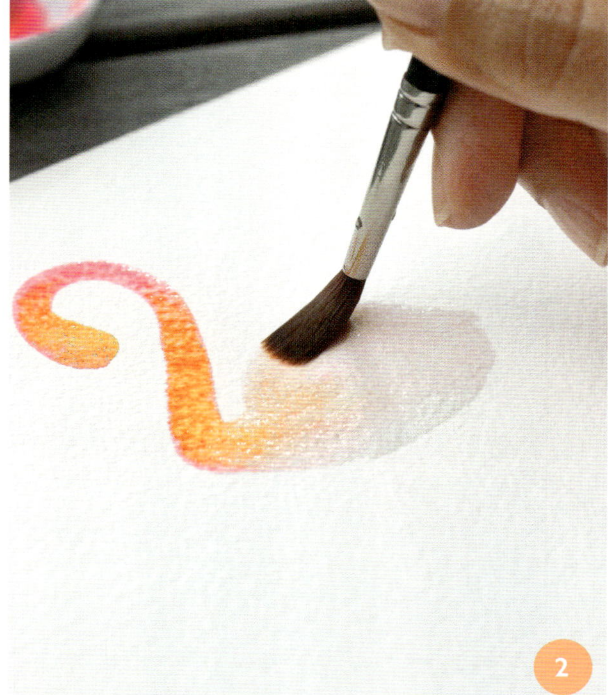

STEP 1. Paint the long, graceful neck using the wet-on-dry technique.

Using your medium soft round brush No. 6 loaded up with a light value of Opera Pink, paint a long and curvy "2" shape. Working with a wet-on-wet technique, add a bit of contrast to the neck shape by dabbing a few dots of a light value Cadmium Yellow onto the middle of the neck as well as the top. Allow the colors to blend naturally.

STEP 2. Paint the first layer of the body of the flamingo using the wet-on-dry technique.

Wiggle your brush in water just a little bit. Paint a medium-sized oval shape by dragging the pigment from the base of the neck to create a very soft, almost transparent body of the flamingo.

Let it dry completely.

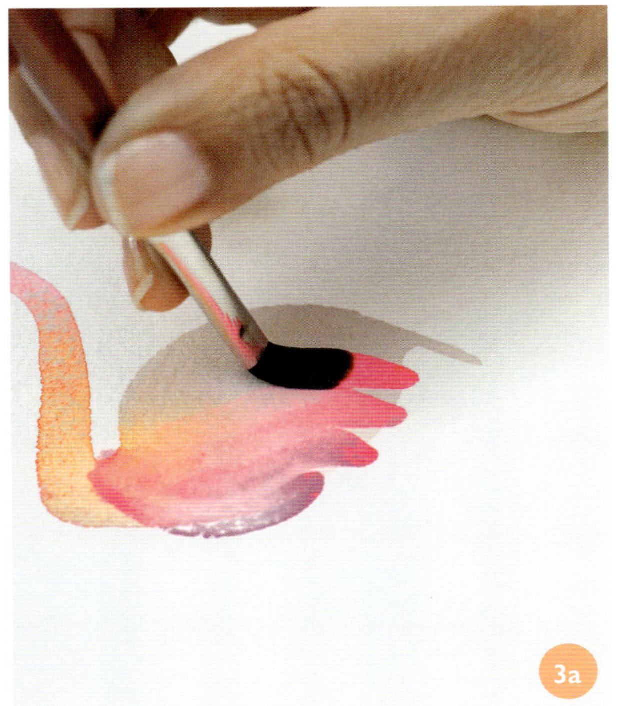

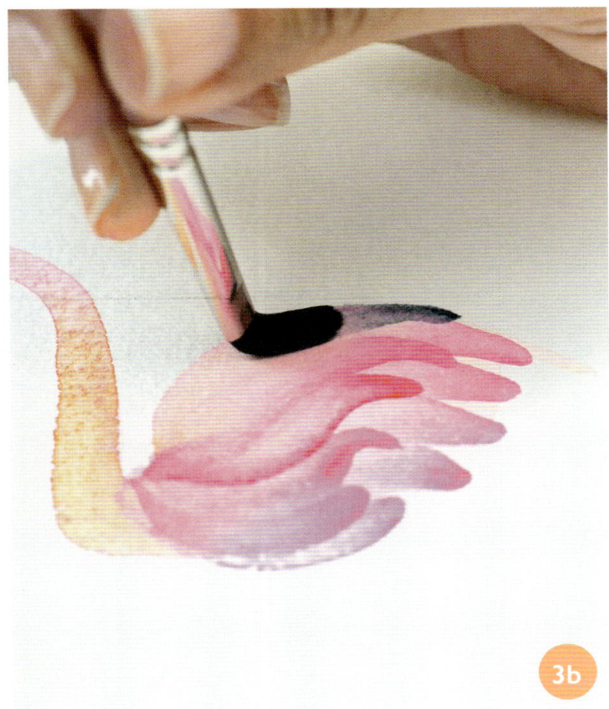

STEP 3. Paint the feathers that make the flamingos so characteristically regal.

Make sure your medium soft filbert brush No. 4 is dampened with clean water and only touch the tip of the brush with a medium value of Opera Pink. With a curved line in mind, slowly drag the belly of the brush from the bottom edge of the oval shape to where the base of the neck is located. Repeat this step four or five times, moving toward the tail of the body to create the first layer of the feathers.

Note: By loading only the tip of the brush with pigment, you create a gradient effect as you drag your brush. No need for further blending.

Repeat this step one or two more times depending on how fluffy you want to make your flamingo. Clean your brush after every layer to achieve a better gradient. Remember to let the paint dry between layers.

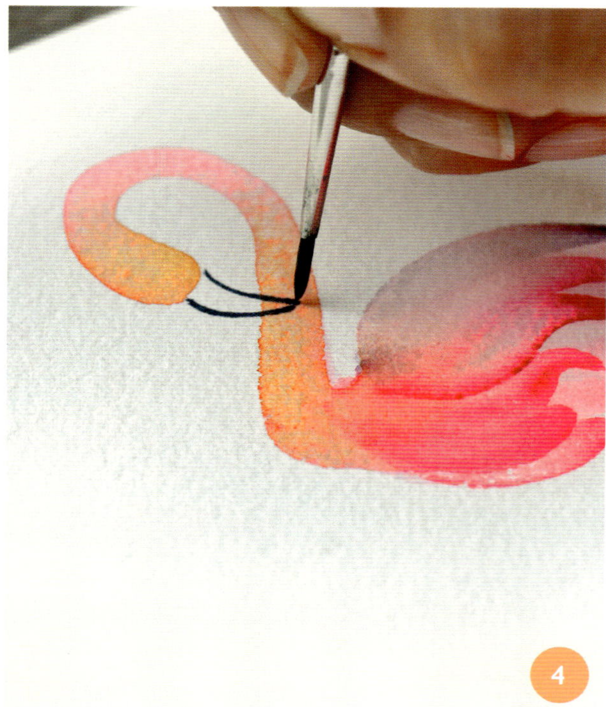

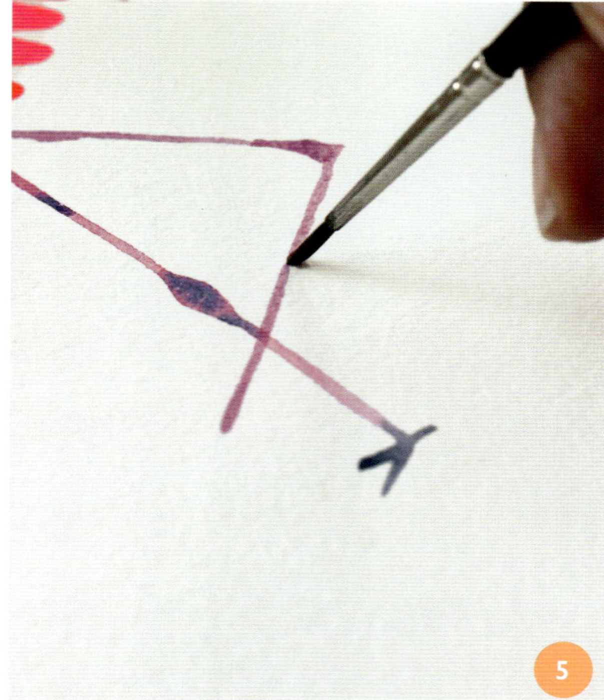

STEP 4. Paint the beak of the flamingo.

While the layers of the feathers dry, you can use the detail brush No. 0 loaded up with a little bit of dark value Payne's Gray to paint the beak of the flamingo. Starting from the top of the "2" shape, paint two curved lines that meet at a central point. Kind of like an ice cream cone, but a little curved. Paint a line down the middle meeting it back at the start of the head and fill in with Payne's Gray only a little bit of the tip of the beak.

STEP 5. Paint the long legs. Keep in mind that flamingos, like most walking animals, have knees, so add a little extra paint halfway through the leg to emphasize the knee joint.

Using the same detail brush with the same pigment, lightly add a little bit of medium value Opera Pink to the brush and, starting from the middle bottom edge of the flamingo's belly, paint a straight line down the paper as far down as you want, but make sure the legs are long, almost unproportionally long.

From the same base of the belly, paint a half triangle for the second leg. You can add the knees at the bend of the triangle or halfway through the straight leg with a few extra small brushstrokes. Add three small star-shaped brushstrokes to the end of each leg and you have the feet.

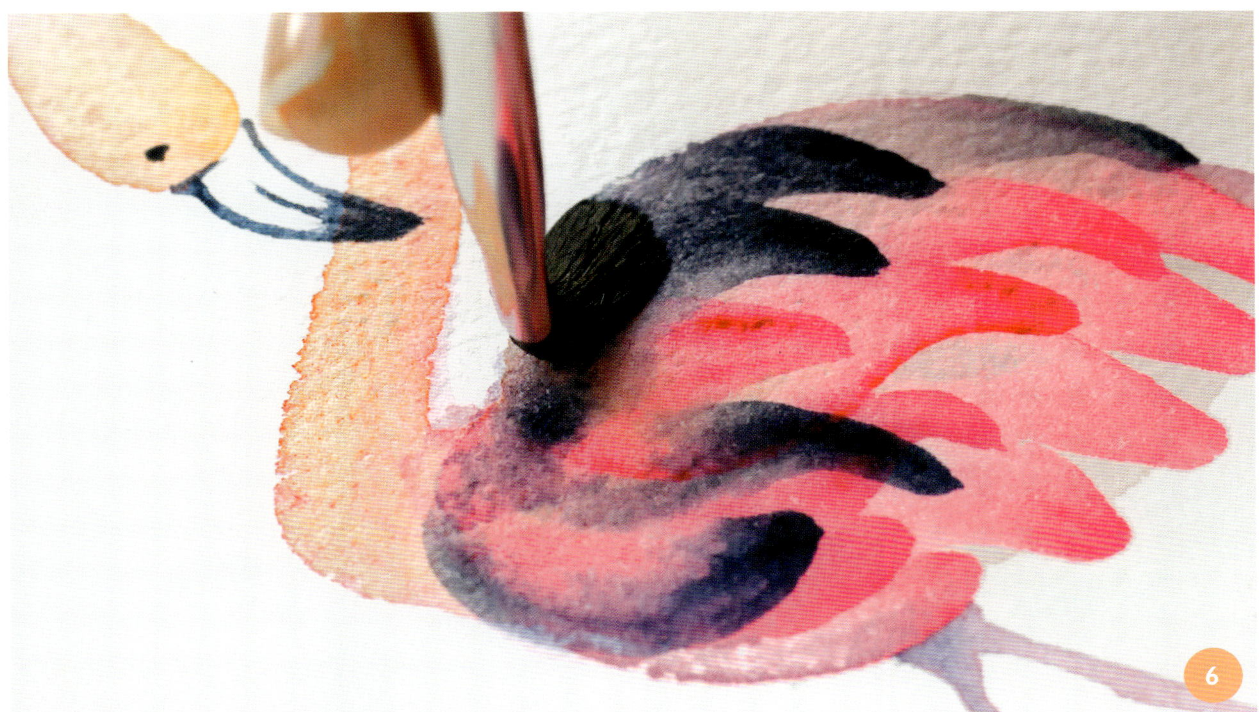

STEP 6. Paint the last layer of feathers to give your flamingo an extra layer of fluffiness.

For the last layer of the feathers, I like to introduce a darker color to create energy and contrast. Using a medium value of Payne's Gray, load only the tip of your filbert brush and paint your soft feathers at the very top of the previous feather layers you painted.

You may add some soft horizontal brushstrokes adjacent to the feet to resemble water or a few soft vertical brushstrokes for grass to complete your regal flamingo composition.

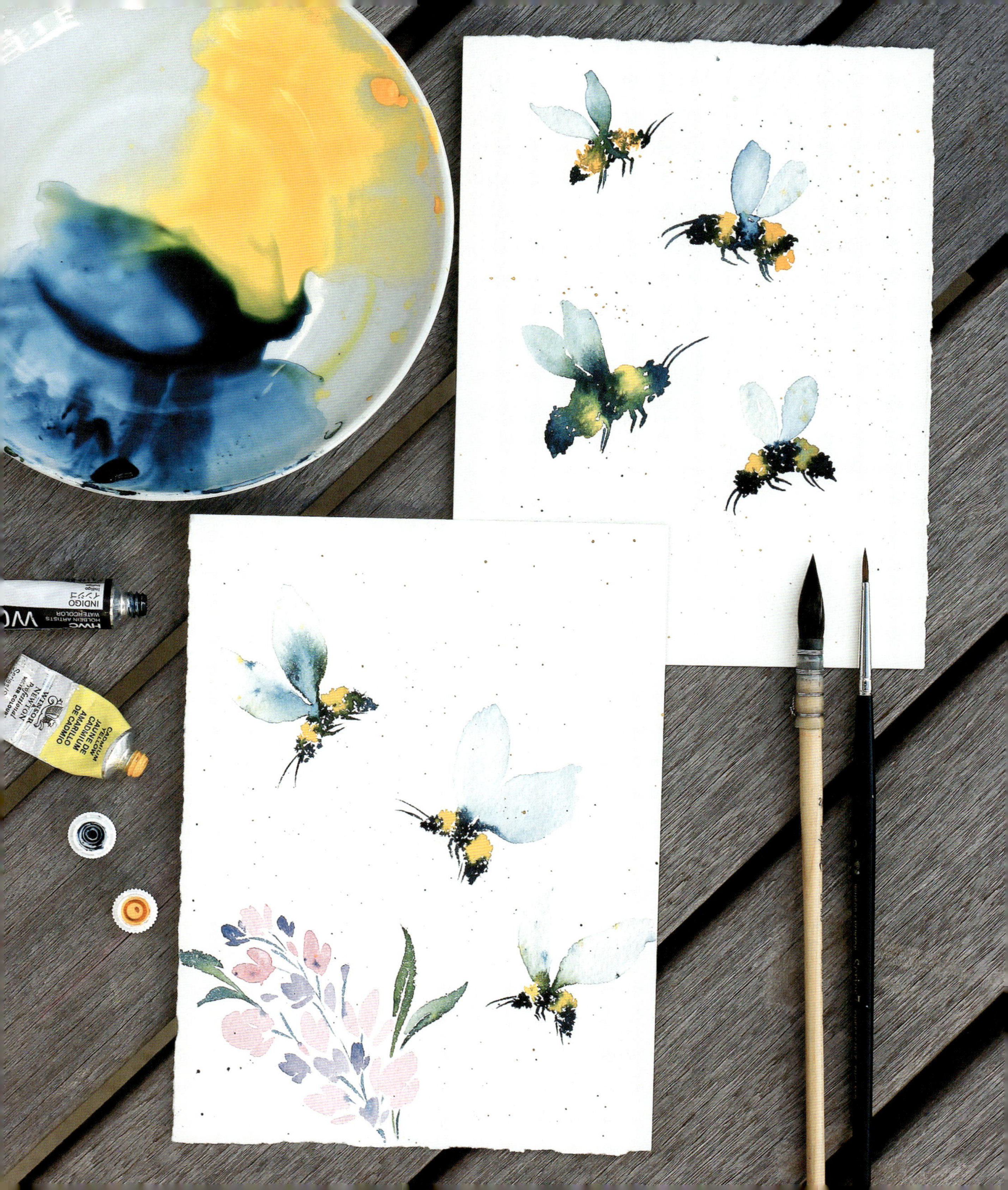
INDIGO
HOLBEIN ARTISTS WATERCOLOR
CADMIUM YELLOW
JAUNE DE CADMIUM
AMARILLO DE CADMIO

Whimsical Bees

I of course had to include bees because our beautiful planet Earth would not survive without their hard and diligent work. Their delicate wings and powerful sting represent the most amazing balance in life.

In this last project I like to emphasize one last time the importance of finding your flow as you build a strong relationship with your brush and your techniques. I hope you find a moment of serenity and peacefulness as you paint these lovely animals.

Materials

- Indigo
- Cadmium Yellow
- Soft round brush No. 0
- Soft round brush No. 4

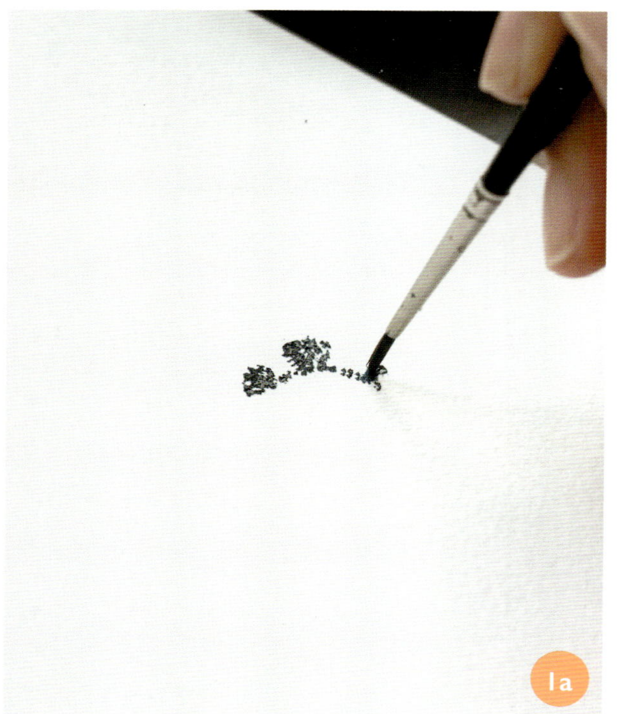

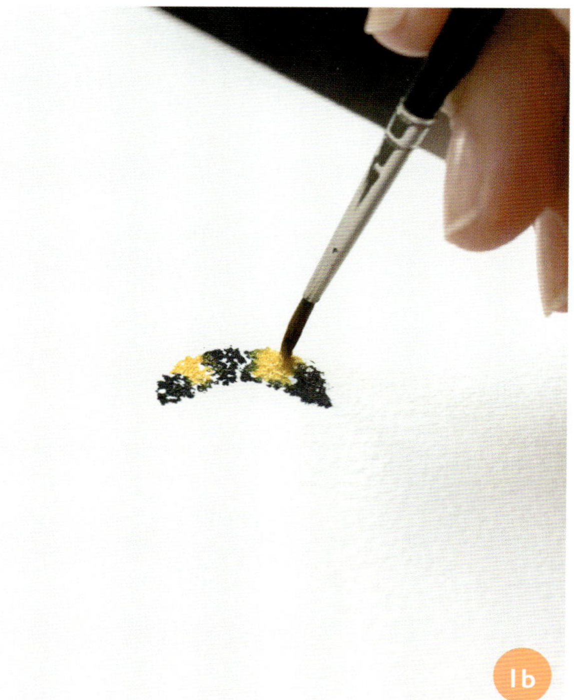

STEP 1. Paint the body of the bee.

Think of dividing the bee's body into two sections, the dark and the yellow. Start with your detail brush No. 0 fully loaded with a dark value of indigo and start dabbing a small, curved line. Paint three separate little groups of dabs adjacent to the line to create the first part of the body.

Completely clean your brush and load it up with a dark value of Cadmium Yellow and fill in the blank spots on the bee's body by also dabbing small dots to finish off the shape of the body.

STEP 2. Paint the details of the bee.

Load up the brush again with the indigo and paint small lines at the top of the bee's body to represent their antennae. You can also add the legs at the same time.

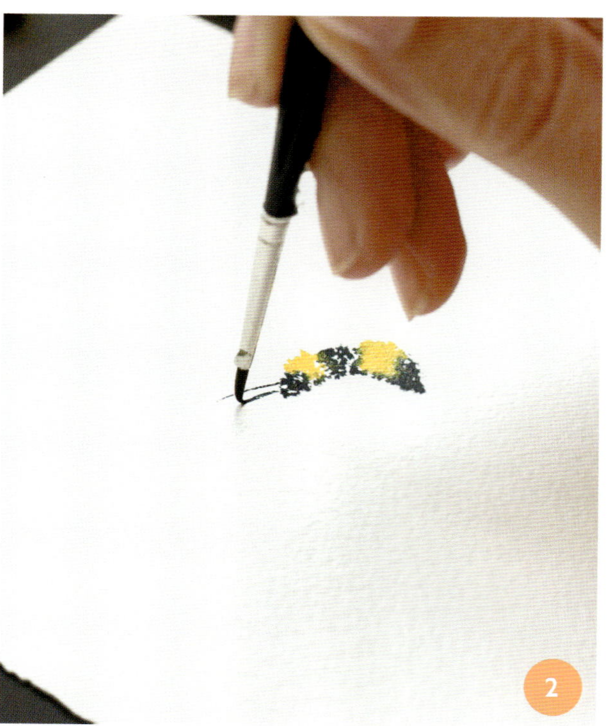

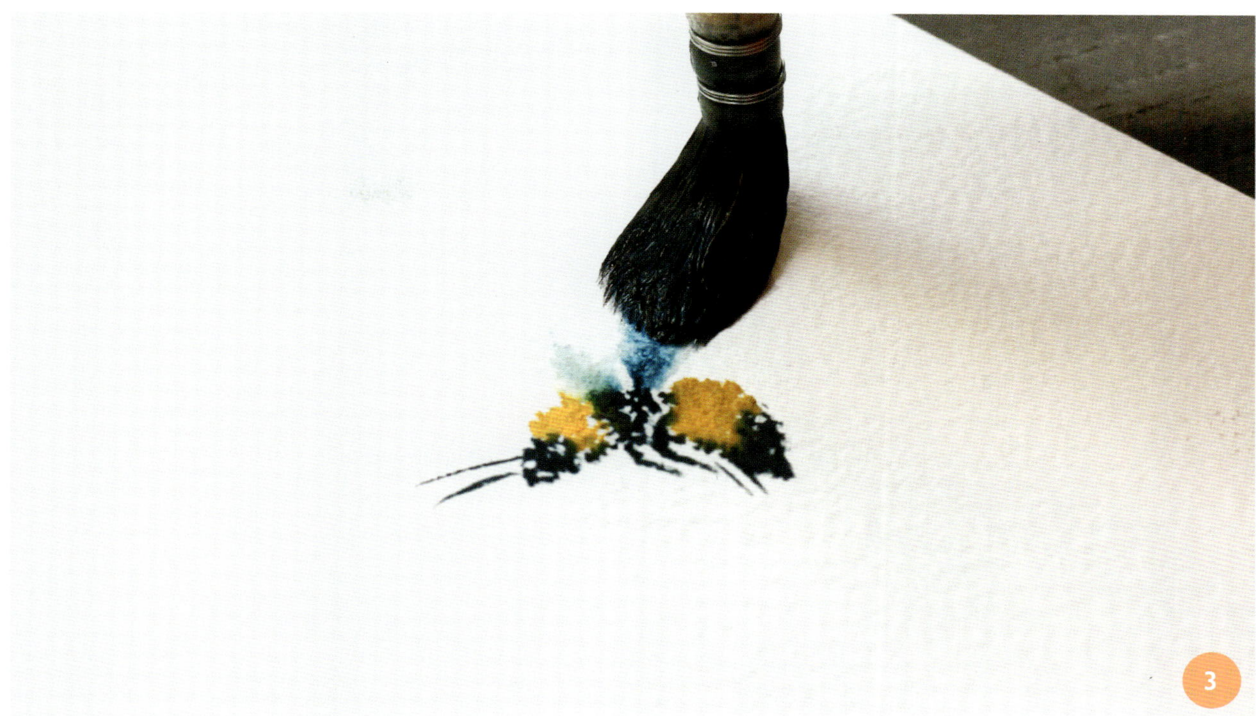

STEP 3. Paint the soft and transparent wings in a single brushstroke.

Use your medium soft round brush No. 4 loaded up with clean water to drag some of the indigo from the bee's body away and create the wing. Take a few seconds to appreciate how the pigment from the bee's body dissipates into the clean water and creates a very transparent surface that barely catches your eye. These magical watercolor moments are what captured me and made my watercolor journey very fascinating.

With these three easy steps you can create a beautiful composition of bees pollinating some of the flowers you painted at the beginning of this book.

Special Thanks

Special thanks to my sister Andrea for lending me her artistic eye through the development of this book, as well as her photography skills.

Also a very special thanks to Page Street Publishing for giving me the opportunity to write my first book.

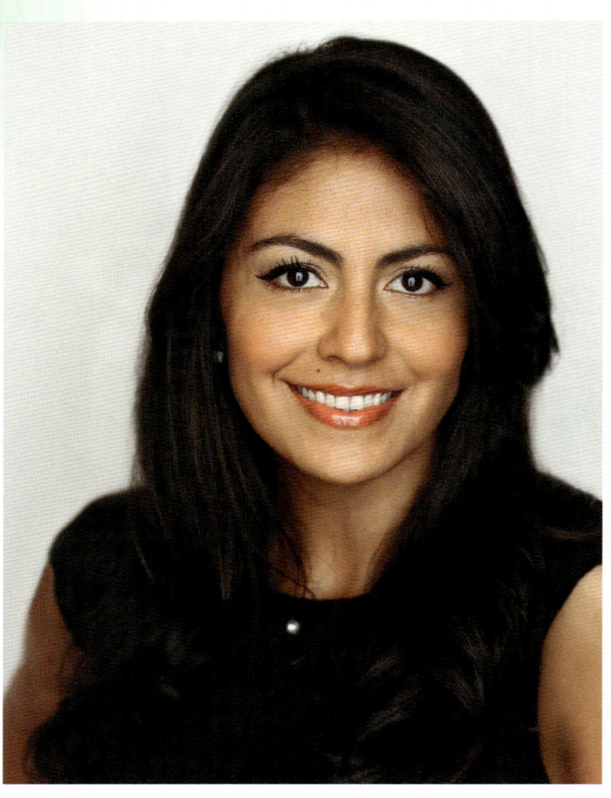

About the Author

Angelica Torres is a designer for themed environments. She went to undergraduate school for architecture and graduate school for theatrical design and is currently working in the field of building theme parks as her full-time job.

Angelica started practicing botanical watercolors in 2015 in search of a healing practice. She then created Love Letters to Milo in 2018 while living in Osaka to share with the world the meditative and healing aspects that she had found and practiced herself. Her practice grew from painting small five-minute doodles before going to work to learning and developing the skills to enjoy a fully meditative and mindful practice that comes with every brushstroke.

When she is not practicing and learning as much as she can about watercolors, she is often found daydreaming about her next travel destination, making YouTube videos or playing tennis.

Index

M

N

O

P

R

S

T

V

W